Values and the Search for Self

by

James A. Bellanca

National Education Association
Washington, D.C.

Previously published material used in this book may use the pronoun "he" to denote an abstract individual, e.g., "the student." We have not attempted to alter this material, although we currently use "she/he" in such instances.

—NEA Publishing

Library of Congress Cataloging in Publication Data

Bellanca, James A.   1937-
   Values and the search for self.

   1. Moral education.   I. Title.
LC268.B13   370.11'4   75-12724
ISBN 0-8106-1356-5

The publisher gratefully acknowledges permission to reprint from the following:

From "The Hollow Men" in *Collected Poems, 1909-1962* by T. S. Eliot. Reprinted by permission of Harcourt Brace Jovanovich, Inc.

From *I Seem To Be a Verb* by R. Buckminster Fuller with Jerome Agel and Quentin Fiore. By permission of Bantam Books.

From "Breath in My Nostrils" by Lance Jeffers from *When I Know the Power of My Black Hand*, © 1974 by Broadside Press. By permission of Broadside Press.

From *The Medium Is the Massage* by Marshall McLuhan and Quentin Fiore. © by Marshall McLuhan, Quentin Fiore, and Jerome Agel. By permission of Bantam Books.

From *Religion and Freedom of Thought* by Perry Miller, Robert L. Calhoun, Nathan M. Pusey, and Reinhold Niebuhr. Doubleday & Company, Inc., © 1954 by the Union Theological Seminary. By permission of Doubleday & Company, Inc.

From *On Becoming a Person: A Therapist's View of Psychotherapy* by Carl R. Rogers. © 1961. By permission of Houghton Mifflin Company.

From *Seven Arrows* by Hyemeyohsts Storm, Harper & Row Publishers, Inc., 1972. By permission of Harper & Row.

From *The Pursuit of Loneliness*. © 1970 by Philip E. Slater. Reprinted by permission of Beacon Press.

From *Learning for Tomorrow* by Alvin Toffler, editor. Reprinted by permission of Random House.

From *The Art of Loving* by Erich Fromm. © 1956 by Erich Fromm. By permission of Harper & Row, Publishers, Inc.

From *Death of a Salesman* by Arthur Miller. © 1949 by Arthur Miller. Reprinted by permission of The Viking Press, Inc.

From "Four Songs of Life" by Ray Young Bear. © 1971 by *South Dakota Review*. By permission of *South Dakota Review*.

Table of Contents

Preface

The purpose of this book is to help the reader — especially the classroom teacher — to become a more effective facilitator of learning. Based on the assumption that the most valuable learning is founded in self-knowledge and a resultant knowledge of others, the book presents a view of teaching as helping and caring within a supportive but flexible structure. In this view, the goal of each individual teacher or student is the ability to direct her/his own learning. Such an ability involves a five-step process of exercising personal control, assessing needs, setting up goals, using resources, and evaluating outcomes.

Being a good teacher-facilitator necessitates a knowledge of one's own attitudes, teaching style, and skills, and a willingness and ability to evaluate oneself. In fact, self-knowledge and self-evaluation are essential to the role of teacher-helper. For this reason, the ideas, suggestions, models, and strategy outlines contained in the text are designed to help the reader toward a self-knowledge that will enhance her/his knowledge of individual learners, in such a way that those learners may ultimately be made as independent and self-directing as possible.

Few of us would deny that valuing is one of the cornerstones of self-knowledge. Building on this major social belief, the author helps the reader explore the interrelationships of valuing, thinking, and feeling that make self-directed learning possible for both teacher and learner. In accepting the premise that what one values determines the choices that one makes, the author also accepts the corrolary belief that choices or decisions only have value if they are carried into action.

In developing the idea of *process,* the author leads the reader to realize that, in addition to helping the learner function independently, the teacher-facilitator also helps individuals function effectively in groups by guiding them to engage in synergetic effort — the cooperative use of their individual skills toward specific goals agreed on by the group. By building a support climate, the facilitator can lead students to an understanding of the difficult roles individuals play in a group and how to vary those roles for effective action. Related to this is the idea that exploratory thinking to help the mind generate alternatives enables an individual to "make something from nothing" I an ability that is in the truest sense creative. It is clear that this very ability is vitally needed at a time when our future — both immediate and distant — requires not only realistic prediction, but also ingenious problemsolving that may not have much in the way of tradition to support it.

The movement of the book, then, is from an initial examination of the reader's personal values and positions on key questions to suggestions and strategies that may help the reader lead others toward the self-knowledge and the development of effective relationships with others that together constitute the measure of relevance. Teacher and student become change agents with the ability to direct events, rather than submit to the unstructured chaos so many people fear may overtake our society.

Whether the reader wishes to read the book straight through, from cover-to-cover, or to dip into it at random wherever words or phrases seem particularly relevant or tempting, the activities — simulations, valuing-forms to be thought over and filled in, metaphors to be reflected on — will be invitations to a participation with the author in a creative quest. Such participation can lead to the satisfaction and pleasure that come from a sudden, increasing illumination — not only that of expanded personal knowledge but also that of a constantly deepening knowledge and appreciation of other human beings.

An Introduction

Writing this introduction highlights certain ambiguities I have had since I began writing the first pages of this book. On the one hand, I hesitate to dilute an experience, especially the experience I have wanted to create, by describing in the expository mode what that experience *should* be; on the other hand, I must realize that my personal involvement in the very humane learning environment which provides the daily space and time to teach experientially (as well as learn), which gives such clear priority to feelings and processes, to ideas and personal growth, and which challenges students and staff to share the creative act of learning, this involvement may place unfair expectations on the reader for whom content-centered learning is the familiar norm. To avoid being crowned King of Authority, a role assignment which contradicts the essential intent of this book; to preserve those values I place on *facilitated* self-definition; but to help those readers for whom this book is an introduction to process learning, I have elected to deal with my ambiguity by describing certain ground rules. Hopefully, these ground rules will explain where I am and how I feel about the self-directed learning process.

If I had decided to write in the expository mode, I would transcribe those absolute laws which you must accept as the final, irrevocable tablet of law — the *oughts*, the *musts*, the *shoulds*. But just as lectures do not work for me in the classroom — either as listener or speaker — expository theses do not work on the printed page.

Just as I will not *direct* my students along a path which says, "Listen and you will hear the gospel word," so I will not describe "the absolute word on self-direction" to you. When I make that statement, I am aware that you might interpret my stance as a hands-off "do your own thing" approach. I hope you will not. To me, a *laissez-faire* style is as equally valueless to learning as the dictatorial absolute. I find myself somewhere between those polar extremes. I see myself as a helper, a facilitator, a giver of support who has mastered certain skills and techniques which work for me in certain circumstances — but not always. I can no more direct you by providing magic formulas or absolute recipes than I can waste students' time with a moralizing lecture. In this spirit, I have used strategies and methods, adapted to print-form, which I feel will help you discover yourself, your values, and your stance on key issues. In this context, I know full well that you will react to concepts and define key words differently than I. I accept that. *In fact, I welcome any self-definition which this book helps you make.* I hope that you can learn to feel comfortable with this approach, even to the point in which you reuse the book a second or third time. My fantasy is that you will perceive yourself, more clearly after each reading, as the authority on your learning processes; the power who controls your learning and your life. That is self-direction.

If this book is your first exposure to inductively structured, experiential learning, you may find it more valuable to move slowly and reflectively. I find, even after many years of involvement in such experiences, that I benefit most if I support my journeys thru values, feelings, and beliefs by maintaining a daily journal. An early self-discovery was my need for the journal to control my focus. I have accepted this limit and disciplined myself to record for my own reflection the paths and discoveries uncovered by my search for self.

I could perceive of no result more disastrous than the use of this book as a repository of "games," "tricks," or "toys" for manipulating or entertaining students. I know that simulations, games, and values strategies can become humorous diversions, without the firm commitment that self-definition and self-direction result from an inherently supportive attitude toward life and learning, such strategies and games can become a farce, sometimes even a tragedy.

Conversely, if you can say to yourself, "Yes, I value self-definition and self-direction and I want to share my discovery with my students," you will have made the first clear step away from being the respository of truth, the fountainhead of knowledge, toward becoming a facilitator who shares expertise with those who freely choose your support. Undoubtedly, you will experience as much discomfort, confusion, and anxiety at that step, as you will when you attempt to use the first strategies in this book or when you "process" a chapter for the first time. As a partial remedy, you might recall your feelings the first time you learned to swim, or ski, or master any new skill.

Throughout the book, you will encounter the word *process*. In the basic sense, process is a noun which delineates the flow of ideas, feelings, values, and beliefs as the individual takes control of learning. As a verb, it takes on more significant meaning by defining those acts, both internal and interpersonal, which comprise that umbrella action which I have called self-direction: the taking of personal control — assessing needs, setting goals, using resources, and evaluating (not to mention the prerequisite affective processes). In the closure form at the conclusion of each chapter, process takes a third use, the formal exercise which asks you to reflect on the total learning you have gained in the chapter. In this sense, processing not only asks you to review the concepts you have garnered (WHAT), but also to recognize inductively the chapter's purpose (WHY), the chapter's processes and strategies (HOW), and to apply your learning to a situation which has meaning private to you. In a sense, the *what*, the *why*, and the *how* become your content; in the final processing, you discover that personal value which you can creatively apply to your self-definition. Static knowledge becomes your creative action, your self-direction.

"Know thyself."
Aristotle

"Within each of our
own Separate Lodges,
deep within ourselves,
there is also part of this
same Great Medicine
Fire of the People. The
questions wer are al-
ways asking is "who
am I", or "who is this
living spirit, this fire?"
The questioning of this
mystery is the begin-
ning ofour search for
Understanding or our
Fire of Self. . ."

Hyemeyohsts Storm,
Seven Arrows

"Charley, the man
didn't know who he was"
Arthur Miller, *Death
of A Salesman*

Searching For Identity

The search for self is not unique to our age. The questions "Who am I?," "How do I relate to the people and events around me?," and "Where am I going?" have echoed and re-echoed across every known boundary. History and literature record the names in fact and symbol —

Antigone
Ulysses
Job
Theresa of Avila
Galileo
Goethe
David Walker
Susan B. Anthony

Coltrane
Jane Addams
Malcolm X
Paul Tillich
Gwendolyn Brooks
Einstein
Simone de Beauvoir
Willy Loman

Add-A-List

INSTRUCTION. To the list given above, add the names of persons you know from direct experience, literature, history, science, or wherever, whose values and actions are focused on the quest for identity: the search for self, for personal meaning, for positive relationships with other persons, places, or events. Limit yourself to three minutes.

1._____
2._____
3._____
4._____
5._____
6._____
7._____
8._____
9._____
10._____
11._____
12._____
13._____
14._____
15._____
16._____

The names you listed may give you some inklings about yourself. Are you on your list? Is there anyone from your cultural or racial heritage? From your own sex? From your group of friends? From other ethnic or social groups? From the opposite sex? From your students? What conclusions do you draw about yourself from your list?

Reflecting

Spaceship Me

INSTRUCTION: This is a self-reflection exercise. You have many options for its use. (1) Read the reflection slowly. Stop and meditate between words and phrases. (2) Have someone read the images to you — slowly and softly giving you ample time to meditate on each word and phrase. (3) Use a tape recorder. Read the reflection aloud. Proceed softly and slowly. Allow *more than ample time* between each word group. Then play back the entire meditation.

As a first-go at the ideas and processes of this book, you may want to limit yourself to the first option. This will enable you to concentrate on the strategy's content. However, to appreciate *the process of reflecting,* you will want to *experience* the meditation. For this, as well as the practice you will receive if you choose to share this meditation or others with students, the tape recorder may make the most sense.

The content of this meditation, as with others throughout the book, is geared to the issues and ideas relevant to the interaction between you, the reader, and the purposes of the book. In use with students or other teachers, use the strategy, but adapt the content to the audience's needs.

A helping word: each reflection begins with a suggestion that you relax and get comfortable — without falling asleep. Be sure that you take the time to slow yourself down, clear your head, and concentrate on yourself and your external processes — how you feel, what images you see, the sensations that impinge from the outside. The more successfully you can control your feeling, thinking, imagining processes, the more you will enrich the reflection experience for yourself. If you are not used to meditation, don't be discouraged at the difficulties you first encounter.

Make yourself comfortable . . . settle into a position which allows you to relax . . . close your eyes . . . breathe softly . . . get into your rhythm . . . relax . . . recall the names on your add-a-list . . . let their faces float across your mind's eye . . . picture each person in her or his time . . . the civilization . . . the environment . . . the personal conflicts . . . become one of those persons . . . who are you? . . . how do you feel about yourself and your times? . . . what makes you most uneasy about yourself? . . . about those around you? . . . for whom or what are you searching? . . . return to yourself . . . who are you? . . . what do you value? . . . what attitudes and beliefs shape your actions? . . . how do you feel about yourself? . . . your relationships with other persons? . . . where are you going? . . . see yourself as a spaceship . . . get a sense of your size: your length . . . diameter . . . capacity . . . thrust . . . as you hurtle through space, chart a course . . . what is your heading? . . . your destination? . . . what obstacles are in your path? . . . your chances of survival? . . . how do you feel as you hurtle through the space-void? . . . arrive at your destination . . . how do you feel now? . . . savor your reactions . . . until you are ready to open your eyes and end the reflection.

Buckminster Fuller plummets the inhabitants of the 20th century through the nether regions of time on Spaceship Earth. Optimistically, in his view, *we* control the tools of science and technology which carry us on an adventurous exploration of the universe's as yet untapped resources.

But other thinkers of our time see through a darker glass.

T. S. Eliot sees 20th century humanity as a lost race. Instead of comfort and security, Eliot finds loneliness, meaninglessness, and spiritual death.

> We are the hollow men
> We are the empty men
> Leaning together
> Headpiece stuffed with straw. Alas!
> —"The Hollow Men"

Eliot's voice does not cry alone. Jean Paul Sartre, the existential philosopher and playwright, describes the valueless, emotionally bankrupt characters who search fruitlessly for an escape door from the wasteland of their lives; but, as he describes in his play *No Exit*, the doors open "to nothingness." W. H. Auden,

Albert Camus, Stephen Spender, and Yevtushenko add their voices to the bleak description of the 20th century human condition, a condition which they feel is formed, controlled, and prolonged by the subtle technological powers which have destroyed the human spirit.

The Parable of the Cage

Once upon a time in a far-away land, all the people lived in cages. Each and every cage was furnished with identical equipment. The north wall was a giant, three-dimensional color video screen with multichannel stereo-sound and odor effects. The south wall was a maze of spiggots, slots, and chutes. A soft chair and bedding rested against the east wall and faced the cage bars on the west. The inhabitants lounged motionlessly on their floors, eyes frozen to the giant screens. When the buzzer sounded, the screens blanked, and the caged people rose as one from the floor, sat at the tables which had unfolded from the wall, and waited for the blue-striped straws to funnel the liquidized vitamin food into their mouths. As one, they rose, returned to the video screen and settled down to watch. No one spoke, no one showed any expression as the television flickered on.

One sunny day, a visiting dignitary, guided by a robot, toured the cage-town. Puzzled by the apathy and passive dependence of the cage people, the dignitary asked the robot to explain why the people acted as they did.

"You have not asked a question my program can answer," responded the computerized guide. The dignitary thought a moment. He tried a new approach:

"How did these people so perfect their technology that they can rely totally on machines?"

The robot blinked its lights. "These humans have taken advantage of the freedom we machines have offered. No longer are humans required to engage in physical or mental labor, make choices, or communicate with each other. We feed, clothe, entertain, and maintain all humans in their cages. They no longer suffer — there are no emotional traumas, no personal conflicts, no crises. We can control all tensions and guilts. Nothing will upset them. In the cages they are safe — from themselves and each other. Here you see the ultimate triumph of science. What more could any human want? For the first time in history, humans have complete security. They need nothing else."

Ranking Priorities

Contemporary Issues

INSTRUCTION A. In this exercise, we ask you to rank-order within 10 groups. Each self-contained group will give you (a) a lead sentence, (b) three possible responses, (c) a chance to explain each ranking. Within each group, mark your first priority as #1, your second as #2, your lowest as #3. You may discover that you cannot distinguish among the choices. In that event "pass." Make every attempt, however, to force a ranked choice. The purpose of any priority ranking is to help you examine the fine distinctions among alternatives and make a choice based on _your_ ideas. Finally, completing the explanation which follows each group will help you clarify the idea distinctions you have made. If none of the given alternatives is _your_ top priority, record or create other for that group.

EXAMPLE. I most agree with the concept that
  <u>3</u> technology controls our lives
  <u>1</u> we control our technology
  <u>2</u> technology doesn't affect me.

1. In the parable of the cages, I would prefer to be
  ____in a cage
  ____the visitor
  ____the guide.
  Explanation of my rankings:

2. Most of my students would
  ____enjoy the cage
  ____fight to escape the cage
  ____adapt passively to the cage.
  Explanation:

3. Given patterns of behavior I have observed in my students and other young people, I would predict that
  ____apathy will increase in our society
  ____some individuals will control their own lives

  ____most individuals will control their own lives.
  Explanation:

4. In describing the contemporary human condition, I would most agree with the statement:

  ____"The experience of separateness arouses anxiety; it is, indeed, the source of all anxiety. Being separate means being cut off, without any capacity to use my human powers. Hence to be separate means to be helpless, unable to grasp the world — things and people — actively; it means that the world can invade me without my ability to react. Thus, separateness is the source of intense anxiety. Beyond that, it arouses shame and the feeling of guilt." (Erich Fromm)

  ____"Our official culture is striving to force the new media to do the work of the old. These are difficult times because we are witnessing a clash of cataclysmic proportions between two great technologies. We approach the new with the psychological conditioning and sensory responses of the old." (Marshall McLuhan)

  ____"In many ways, we need a general reorientation. We are all hip to civil and political rights. If there were air pollution that affected only Negroes, there'd be action today. But _everyone_ is beset by constant insults to the body. Air pollution, chemical poisoning of vegetables and of water systems — all of these bring about suffering and death on a greater scale than political injustice. The thing to make people understand and take action on is that the enemy is not "air pollution" or "traffic accidents." These are impersonal results. The enemy is flesh and blood human beings hiding behind the veil of corporate bigness and anonymity." (Ralph Nader)

  Explanation:

5. Our society should give priority attention to
  ____our lost sense of values
  ____our lost command of the ability to municate

_____our lost sense of identity with our natural environment.

Explanation:

6. At present, this attention (above #5) can best be achieved by

_____maintaining the ecological balance of the universe

_____free individuals with a sense of self-worth

_____the lessons of past history.

Explanation:

7. "Freedom" is best described as

_____rebellion against established codes of behavior in order to destroy destructive dependent relationships

_____the opportunity to do, think, or feel whatever one desires at any given moment with no external limits

_____the encouraged opportunity for each person to develop the fullest human potential and to use that potential in a continual sharing of dignity, self-worth, and respect with fellow human beings.

Explanation:

8. In order to fulfill one's potential, it is most essential that

_____the individual have a strong sense of self

_____the individual have clearly established values

_____the individual establish strong relationships with others.

Explanation:

9. The individual potential which traditional schooling most successfully develops is

_____intellectual capability

_____skills in the use of reading, writing, and arithmetic

_____leadership.

Explanation:

10. In future decades, schools will be most helpful to students if

_____improvements in curriculum and instruction are evolved from present practices

_____schools are closed (deschooling society)

_____schools are totally restructured.

Explanation:

As teachers in the last quarter of the 20th century, we face unique challenges which will test our mettle as individuals capable of free choice, self-control, and creative insight. The rank order you completed raises questions about issues which will affect each one of us. Now that you have examined your *ideas* with respect to these issues, focus on how you *feel* about your position.

Reflecting

Meditation on Me

INSTRUCTION A. Allow yourself four to six minutes for this exercise. Before you begin the meditation itself, prepare a dozen small (enough space for a word or phrase on each) sheets of paper and a pencil.

Settle comfortably into your chair . . . relax, close your eyes, and picture yourself standing inside a great, clean, almost sterile factory . . . it is quiet . . . long conveyor belts slip noiselessly down long rows . . . identical glass bottles float past . . . at each centipede-like machine, blinking multicolored lights reach out . . . inject . . . pass on to the next . . . the bottles slide past you . . . a PA system announces: "These are the cloned farm workers; their genes are controlled to guarantee physical strength, resistance to heat, and endurance" . . . you walk on . . . a row of orange bottles . . . the announcer: "These are future surgeons . . ." . . . you move on past rows of red . . . green . . . maroon bottles . . . sunlight as you step outside . . . reflect, examine how you reacted to these images . . . the machines . . . the bottles . . . the announcer . . .

INSTRUCTION B. Take six of the twelve pieces of paper you have assembled. On each sheet, use a word or phrase to describe your feelings concerning the images you have created. Mark the corner of each of these completed sheets with an X.

INSTRUCTION C. Take the remaining six pieces of paper. On each sheet use a word or phrase to describe six attitudes on which you place a high priority in your day-to-day relationships with other people. Mark each of these sheets with a Y.

INSTRUCTION D. Compare the two lists. If any words appear on both sheets, eliminate the duplicate. Rank the words and phrases to complete this statement.

"The feeling in this list which gives me the most satisfaction is . . ."

1. _____
2. _____
3. _____
4. _____
5. _____
6. _____
7. _____
8. _____
9. _____
10. _____
11. _____
12. _____

In addition to perceiving how we think and feel toward ourselves and our environment, understanding the attitudes and beliefs which form the foundation of our value system and clarifying our values become processes significant in our search for self.

A Ranking

A Comparison List

INSTRUCTION A. Use the rankings that you made to conclude "Meditation on Me" — "the feeling which gives me most satisfaction." In the chart below copy your "feeling" rank order. After completing the list, read instruction B.

	feeling	value	belief
1			
2			
3			
4			
5			
6			
7			
8			
9			
10			
11			
12			

INSTRUCTION B. In the spaces which follow each feeling on the above chart, indicate whether the listed feeling is associated with a value or with a belief.

_____VALUES are those actions I have chosen to perform because of import I give to that action.

_____BELIEFS are those self-evident assumptions which I accept without question (they are the first principles without which thinking, valuing, and acting would not develop).

To mark the chart, identify a value or a belief (in some cases both) which you associate with each feeling.

	feeling	value	belief
example	joy	freedom	all men are created equal

You may have found this exercise caused you anxiety. That is not unusual. There are no "right answers." In a task-ordered society "get the job done" is more important than discovering "why do I feel as I do?" If nothing else, this list and the other strategies may help you to see the complexity of the search for self and the important place which your values, feelings, beliefs and attitudes hold in that search.

Ranking

Scale of Priorities

INSTRUCTION A. This is a self-test to help you assess the relative importance you place upon areas of learning. Study the following list of seven words. (Examples are given, others apply, but accept those given for the purpose of this test.) In the left-hand column, rank each word in the order in which you emphasize it in your classroom. #1 would indicate that the item marked received the most emphasis; #7, the least.

_____FACTS (names, dates, places)
_____SKILLS (addition, spelling, welding)
_____VALUES (my family is important, but money is more important)
_____ATTITUDES (you should be on time)
_____BELIEFS (all people are created equal)
_____FEELINGS (love, hate, fear)
_____IDEAS (equality, triangulation)

14

INSTRUCTION B. Rank the seven items in the order in which your students would rank them to describe how you emphasize each in your teaching.

____BELIEFS   ____ATTITUDES
____SKILLS   ____FEELINGS
____IDEAS   ____VALUES
           ____FACTS

INSTRUCTION C. Rank the seven items in the order in which you would prefer to emphasize each with your students if you had the opportunity.

____IDEAS   ____VALUES
____ATTITUDES   ____FACTS
____FEELINGS   ____SKILLS
          ____BELIEFS

INSTRUCTION D. Bring *closure* to the exercise. Complete these sentences. . . .

1. "As I compare the rank orders I made, I see that I. . . ."
2. "On the basis of conclusions I draw from these comparative rankings, I would define 'learning' as. . . ."
3. "On the basis of my definition of 'learning,' I need to. . . ."

Up to this point, the concepts presented were designed to elicit your reactions. Many adults find this approach disturbing. Without an authority figure, the expert who will tell them what and how they *should* think, provide information, and direct them step by step to the completion of a task, they become very anxious.

____"I expect you to give me the facts. You're the expert."

____"Feelings don't belong in the classroom."

____"Why are we fiddling around with this valuing and feeling stuff? Let's get to *work*."

____"Don't ask me questions. Tell me what to do."

You have probably experienced a similar reaction from students, parents, or other teachers. Perhaps you also feel uncomfortable when you are not told by an expert, in this case a book, the specifics of what and how you *ought* to learn. Like the majority of us who achieved success in the traditional educational system which stressed the recall of facts and concepts, adapting to an open system which stresses inquiry, involvement of the whole person, and creative exploration will of necessity cause some stress. The anxiety and discomfort which the change causes, it seems, is almost proportionate to the degree of success an individual experienced in a traditional learning program. Thus, teachers who have adapted their life patterns to the traditional discipline and "A" students who succeed best in meeting the system's highest expectations more usually find first contact most disconcerting. On the other hand, you will discover that a transfer of emphasis which fosters more involvement in decision making, greater creative thought and expression, better interpersonal relations, and increased personal growth will give rise to an excitement and involvement in learning which you may not have experienced previously.

Helping Students

Most young learners, programmed to passive watching by years of TV, will welcome a chance for greater involvement in their learning. You must be careful, however, that you should not be disconcerted by their initial adherence and sometimes reversions to old behavior patterns. If you carefully plan each activity and follow these basic guidelines, you will witness their evolution as involved learners.

1. *Expect from your students only what you would expect from yourself.* If you would not involve yourself in a strategy, do not ask your students to participate in it. As a rule of thumb, you should participate with them in each activity. If you feel uneasy in the water, don't feed others to the sharks.

2. *Encourage each individual to exercise her or his individual right to abstain from participation in any strategy.* You should strive to make the "pass-rule" an accepted norm of behavior. This is an elementary first principle of any classroom that encourages decision making and free choice.

3. *Accept each individual as the person she or he is.* Recognize individual differences — intellectual, emotional, ethical, cultural, attitudinal, physical, and so on. Most importantly, adjust your criticism to fit the child's capability to respond.

4. *Concentrate on trust building.* Traditional attitudes tell teachers, "Don't smile until Christmas." Such an attitude has no place in a supportive learning atmosphere. During the first months, most strategies you select should focus on the trust relationship *among* you and the students.

5. *Prepare to fail.* You are entering a new arena. Explore. Your students will appreciate that you are willing to risk failure. More importantly, they will see in you a model who can fail, recover, and start anew.

6. *Listen.* We teachers tend to talk too much. Sit back and listen. Listen to what the students tell you and say to each other. Listen to their concerns and delights. And when you have the urge to take over a student activity, restrain yourself.

7. *Observe.* Watch student behavior carefully. Notice which students are having difficulty adjusting to the open atmosphere. Watch for small conflicts, explosions generated from frustration, nervousness.

Charting

Behavior Continuum

INSTRUCTION A. "How I act in the classroom will speak clearly about the values and attitudes that I claim." On this continuum, you will rank your behavior in the classroom. Place an X on each chart to indicate how much actual time you give to each of the items mentioned.

1. **I encourage each student to "pass" on any learning activity about which she/he feels insecure.**

always   never

2. **I listen to student concerns.**

always   never

3. **I expect each student, regardless of individual differences, to complete all learning activities, but at her/his time and pace.**

always   never

4. **I observe individual activity.**

always   never

5. **I participate with students as a colearner.**

always   never

6. **I plan strategies to build and maintain a feeling of trust and cooperation between myself and my students.**

always   never

7. **I encourage exploration and risk-taking.**

always   never

8. *En toto*, **my behavior demonstrates encouragement, acceptance, trust, personal risk, listening, and observing.**

always   never

The Stages of Involvement

_____ "Adolescents aren't capable of making decisions by themselves."

_____ "Give them freedom and they'll just run over you."

_____ "You can't let kids do what they want. They don't know what they want."

If a young colt is enclosed tightly in a corral from the time of saddle-training and then suddenly turned loose, it will react in one of several characteristic ways. It may break wildly for the open space before him, bucking and kicking and galloping with wild abandon. Or it may step tentatively, even suspiciously, from the familiar world into the unknown. Whatever the reaction, the colt discovers a new experience and requires careful, skilled handling in order to learn to survive in his new world. Likewise the student. Although each young person who has learned in a tightly controlled normative system may react to the freedom of an open learning system by exhibiting differing extremes of behavior, it is evident that survival depends on the help given by trained, experienced hands. Just as the young colt becomes more valuable because of its training in uncorralled fields, so too the student becomes a fuller, richer person from learning in an open learning environment.

In the process of mastering the stresses and pulls of the open environment, a learning environment system which most closely approximates the choice-dominated society which the student will enter, five stages of development become evident. *What specific form — the open classroom, the pod, the alternative school, the school without walls — the openness takes does not seem to matter, nor does the student's previous degree of success or failure in a traditional program.* Each student who moves from a closed classroom to an open-learning environment spends some time in each of these five stages:

(1) *Initial Anxiety.* New worlds present new threats. Old worlds provide carefully worked-out securities. Like the move to a new house, going to college for the first time, or changing jobs, the concerns about "who I am" and "how I will fit in" unsettle. This stage will last as long as it is necessary for the individual to find friends, "kindred spirits," and trust the teacher. When things begin to click, tension is reduced and involvement begins.

(2) *The Honeymoon.* The joy and enthusiasm which accompany the student's introduction to new-found freedoms are self-contagious. Whether "gallopers" or "toe-testers," the students revel in their learning — "doing my own thing" and "no hassles — what a blast." From the teacher's point of view, the involvement and enthusiasm may create delusions akin to the utopias described in textbooks.

(3) *The Awakening.* In every marriage, the day dawns when the newlyweds awake to discover that the honeymoon has ended. For the first time, the full import of their marriage vows becomes apparent. "Do we want this marriage to work?" "Can we live with each other under these conditions?" So, too, the student discovers the challenges, the difficulties, the hard work implicit in an open-learning opportunity. The questions begin: "Is it worth the struggle to restructure myself so that I take control of what I learn? Or do I want to continue being a spoon-fed learner? I have an inkling of myself and my limitations. How much do I really value learning how to learn?" In most cases, the initial awakening response is 100 percent defensive. The patterns vary in form, but the purpose is one — to deny the snoring, hair-done-up-in rollers, temper-tantrums, no-cap-on-the-toothpaste reality of the honeymoon's end. Some of the patterns are:

a. *The Hider.* Some students, faced with a picture of themselves being devoured by the seemingly monstrous task of overcoming personal inadequacies, both real and imaginary, find ways to hide themselves and avoid confrontation with themselves. Some, who bury themselves in nonessential work, hide behind the task orientation of the work-aholic. Others, refusing to communicate, isolate themselves from human contact and burrow into study carrels, library stacks, and book corners. In programs-without-walls, some students literally fade-into-nothingness.

b. *The Socializer.* A second avoidance personality is the super-socialite. Rather than admit the honeymoon's demise, this student paints on a smile and bubbles through the day with good cheer for all. There are no problems. Life is sunny and beautiful and bright. "God's in his heaven and all's right with — me!" There are many friends, gay ideas, and reports of wonderful, exciting, even thrilling projects *ad infinitum.*

c. *The Dreamer.* Each day brings a new, grand plan for great accomplishments. Yesterday's idea is forgotten in the excitement of today's new concept, ushered in with full pomp and circumstance. "Today, my David; tomorrow, my Sistine Chapel." But tomorrow fades into the illusion of the next dream which also melts without accomplishment.

d. *The Smorgasborder.* Many persons unfamiliar with the experience of an open-learning environment erroneously assume that an undisciplined student will isolate attention on one or two subjects — "I'll just do what I

17

like." If an individual, adult or student, can focus complete attention on one or two subjects for a prolonged effort, that person is NOT undisciplined. For the undisciplined, behaviors contrary to in-depth concentration are the norm: smorgasbording or picking a little bit of everything to avoid significant choices. It is easier to load up with tidbits of irrelevant nothings than make serious choices about important learning. Thus, the smorgasborder avoids choices by tasting every curricular offering, but masters no learning in a 29-hour day.

Avoidance tactics are limited. Like drug addiction, the need for more and more tactics becomes greater and greater, but eventually the student "bottoms out": the student is face to face with the self. The mirror is clear. It only remains for the decision — where to go from here?

(4) *The Struggle.* When the student decides that she or he can accept the image of self, with its limitations and potentials, then begins the fourth stage, the struggle "to become a person." This is the time when a sapling, bent by winds and scaled by insects, fights upward toward the few sun rays which break through the heavily-leaved branches of the mature forest. It is the time when the young learner begins to accept feelings, clarify values, and examine the beliefs that will help attain a self-defined identity with the support and skill of the teacher's expertise.

(5) *Realization and Redirection.* In this stage, which is the omega and the alpha, the end and the beginning, the student discovers the pride of success. A goal is reached, a new dimension added to the self-image, and a new direction assumed with a stronger step.

The degree of support which an individual will need to move securely through these stages will vary. For a few radical risk-takers, the absolute removal of all external structures is most beneficial; for others, only the most gradual transition will lead them into areas of risk. In a conventional honeycomb school, you are not likely to have the resources to allow multiple structures as an initial step. Thus, you will need

to begin with the slow dissolution of external control and implement an open atmosphere with caution for all.

In order to introduce the students to the search for self, use this chapter as a model: a blend of safe, uncomplicated strategies based on the concepts presented. Certain strategies lend themselves well as introductory exercises. When selecting and using strategies, there are two *caveats* to recall:

(1) *Proceed slowly.* You are moving individuals with varying risk-ratios from the known to the unknown. Let one unknown become a familiar, secure known before going on. Blend the strategies with the learning modes students know best: the lecture which gives information and the discussion which *allows* participation. The discussion of ideas is an ideal tool to introduce the discussion of process or "processing." *Processing is the examination of the purposes (why), concepts (what), and strategies (how) that were used to cause change (growth, learning).* In essence, processing is a discussion not only of *what* we learn, but an evaluation of *how* we learn. Initially, it provides "safe" material for a new discussion tack.

(2) *Help students master each strategy.* The first step in becoming the master of one's destiny is to control the tools that help learning. Strategies are a set of tools that can facilitate that task. As the year progresses your students will take greater responsibility for their learning; responsibility implies the ability to control, to steer a course, to direct one's learning. The students cannot achieve this end unless they possess the tools to supplement the attitudes and the desires to control their own learning.

(3) *Fit strategies to issues and concepts that have the most meaning for the individuals involved.* Arthur Combs, the humanistic psychologist who has done pioneering work in self-concept research, points out that relevance has little or nothing to do with current events or contemporary topics, but rather that it deals with information that has personal meaning for the learner. For instance, if you are in the faculty cafeteria and you hear that there is a fire in the

suburbs, you might take a passing interest. When another teacher sits at your table and says, "Two houses burned in Rosedale today," your ears will perk up. Your parents live in Rosedale. When you discover the fire was on Oakwood Avenue, you become concerned. The student mail clerk gives you a note: "Please come to the principal's office. The Rosedale fire department called to inform you about the fire at 730 Oakwood." At this point you excuse yourself and dash to the principal's office. In short, when the information *affected* you, when it became personally meaningful or relevant, you acted decisively. Likewise, strategies which have significance to the learner are most capable of causing active learning.

Much of the information outlined in the last few pages will have less *relevance* for you at this point than after you have helped students in an open-learning experience. As you progress through this book, you can expect that "authoritative" exposition will decline and participatory problem solving will increase. By focusing your attention on this process, as well as the content, you may discover that McLuhan's "the medium is the message" applies to the printed word as well as to the TV and computer.

Processing This Chapter

At this point you may recognize that this chapter was written in two modes: the facilitative and the expository. In the first half of the chapter, your self-definition of values, feelings, beliefs, and ideas was highlighted. Clarifying strategies were used to lead you inductively through your own experiences and responses.

In the second part, the style changed to exposition. You were told how to use exercises, pitfalls to avoid, and reactions to expect if/when you elected to use clarifying strategies in your classroom. To recognize this shift is to perceive not only the shift in style, but also a shift in purpose.

Processing: Step I — Identify Purpose(s) of Chapter
    A. _____
    B. _____
    C. _____

The remaining steps inherent in chapter processing are designed to further your self-definition skills by building the habits of reflection and application. You should concentrate less on what you think the chapter says and more on your understandings and insights.

Processing: Step II — Forming My Ideas in Response to This Chapter.

To leave the chapter with ideas only would leave the task less than half-completed. Having reflected on ideas, you may next process feelings. How did you respond to strategies? What values do you feel most positive about? What feelings did you perceive? The more precisely you can associate these feelings with the values, beliefs, attitudes, and ideas you discovered, the more clearly will you clarify directions you wish to take with your learning.

Processing: Step III — Identifying My Feelings

The final step with processing may be the most important: applying what you have learned (ideas, feelings, values, beliefs, attitudes) through your experience with this chapter to a situation important to you. If, for instance, you discovered that self-examination as suggested in this chapter frightens you, you may decide that you are not interested or ready to learn or teach in the facilitating style, at least right now. Accept that choice and find ways to improve your present style or discover a new style.

Processing: Step IV — Applying My Learning

As a conclusion to each chapter, you will find the formal exercise "processing this chapter." Eventually, I think you will discover that the exercise limits how you may wish to respond to the chapter. Keep in mind with this exercise, as well as all others I have delineated in the book, that the formalized strategies are merely starting points for your creative exploration.

To function well in a
fast-shifting environ-
ment, the learner must
have the opportunity to
do more than receive
and store data; she or
he must have the op-
portunity to make
change or to fail in the
attempt.
Alvin Toffler,
Learning for Tomorrow

2

Beginning The Process

Voting

INSTRUCTION A. In this strategy you will read 10 statements. The questions will deal with the process of education experienced by you as a student. You have four choices: (1) yes, (2) no, (3) maybe or sometimes, and (4) pass. Circle your choice.

(1) In my education, the predominant emphasis was placed on facts, memory, and tests.
Yes   No   Maybe   Pass

(2) In my education, the teacher controlled what I learned.
Yes   No   Maybe   Pass

(3) In my past elementary education, teachers usually lectured or led question-answer sessions.
Yes   No   Maybe   Pass

(4) In my education the final *product* (tests, term papers, essays) determined what I had learned.
Yes   No   Maybe   Pass

(5) In my education, teachers spent at least 50 percent of the time teaching us how to learn.
Yes   No   Maybe   Pass

(6) In my precollege education, I mastered the processes of learning.
Yes   No   Maybe   Pass

(7) In my education, school structures took a variety of forms suited to different purposes (i.e., lecture halls, open classrooms, resource areas).
Yes   No   Maybe   Pass

(8) In my education, I spent 80 percent (or more) of my formal learning time in a four-walled classroom directed by a teacher at the front.
Yes   No   Maybe   Pass

(9) In my education, scheduled bells signaled the beginning and end of each learning period.
Yes   No   Maybe   Pass

(10) In my education, I decided what I would learn, how I would learn, when I would learn.
Yes   No   Maybe   Pass

The conventional honeycombed school works best as a data-processor. Experts, trained in specific fields of knowledge, pass information to the students who are the empty learning banks. To control the information flow the students are key-punched onto a specific terminal — algebra, ecology, English III — to receive the right information in the most efficient manner. In some cases, the data system can track students according to the students' ability to process the information skillfully on tests and exams. The one drawback is that the information system cannot guarantee quality or quantity absorption within a given time parameter. Thus all students, regardless of their information absorption rate, must move to the next terminal at a preprogrammed time.

Clarifying

Ranking Priorities

INSTRUCTION. In this strategy, you will examine the concepts presented in the computer analogy. You are trying to ascertain how you feel about each idea and what importance you place on each.

Within each group of three choices, rank the possibilities in the order of priority. The lead sentence will indicate the basis on which you can decide. A top priority in a group, you will mark #1; the lowest priority, #3.

(1) In my education, primary emphasis was given to
a. ____information
b. ____creative problem solving
c. ____decision making.

(2) In my classroom, I give primary emphasis to
a. ____information
b. ____creative problem solving
c. ____decision making.

(3) In a technological society,
a. ____the schools are the most effective source of information giving
b. ____the electronic media bombard the individual with more information than she or he can process

c. ____technology has created information processing tools such as the computer which have the potential to process information most effectively for the individual.

(4) As an information supplier, the conventional school is
a. ____the best
b. ____in need of improvement
c. ____obsolete.

(5) Students, the adults of tomorrow, need the school's help to
a. ____master learning processes
b. ____learn how to handle "future shock"
c. ____do just what they are doing now.

(6) If I want to prepare my students to survive in their future world, I should give primary emphasis to
a. ____more information
b. ____decision-making skills
c. ____creative problem solving.

Reflecting

INSTRUCTION. Review your rankings. Think about *your priorities* and complete the following sentence. (Write your response. Use as much time as you need to say what you want.)
"In this chapter, I have discovered that I . . ."

Describing Learning

In miniature form, these strategies have reintroduced you to process learning. In schematic, you can see clearly the *cyclical* quality of this process. In this perspective, learning has no clearly defined beginning or end. It is a refining process: the more I learn about who I am, how I think, feel, act, relate to others, and identify my limits, the more clearly I discover what additional needs I have to achieve my potential and what resources, internal and external, I can use to help myself. In short, I define and discipline myself according to my self-identified strengths and weaknesses and decide to act according to my own values and beliefs.

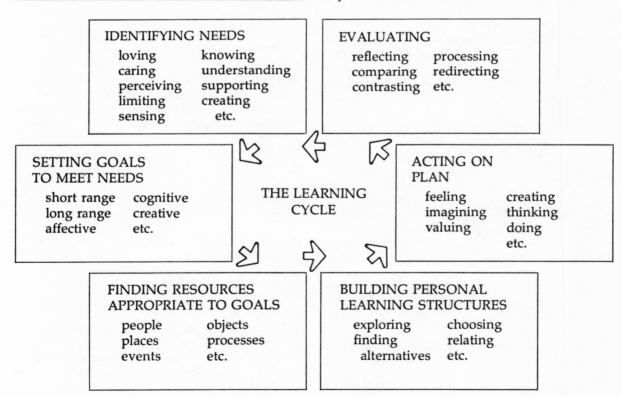

IDENTIFYING NEEDS

loving   knowing
caring   understanding
perceiving   supporting
limiting   creating
sensing   etc.

EVALUATING

reflecting   processing
comparing   redirecting
contrasting   etc.

SETTING GOALS
TO MEET NEEDS

short range   cognitive
long range   creative
affective   etc.

THE LEARNING
CYCLE

ACTING ON
PLAN

feeling   creating
imagining   thinking
valuing   doing
                etc.

FINDING RESOURCES
APPROPRIATE TO GOALS

people   objects
places   processes
events   etc.

BUILDING PERSONAL
LEARNING STRUCTURES

exploring   choosing
finding   relating
alternatives   etc.

STEP I.	STEP II.	STEP III.	STEP IV.	STEP V.
information provided	information gathered according to individual capacity to assimilate	student proves achievement	grade awarded	information provided
textbook		test	A	a new unit
library research		compostition	B	
lecture		report	C	
controlled question-answer			D	
films, slides, tv			F	
controlled seminar				

In contrast, a schematic of the learning process "traditionally" viewed takes on a linear perspective.

The values implicit in each schematic contrast sharply. In the traditional approach, subject matter content and skills are given top rank; the teacher decides what information will be dispensed and how the student will demonstrate achievement in comparison to achievement levels of other students. Of less import is teaching students *how* to learn the selected material; of minimal value is the student's opportunity to define personal learning or to control its selection and use.

A TRADITIONAL RANK ORDER
(1) What is taught
(2) How a student learns
(3) Who a student is

In contrast, the cyclical description of learning assumes that a student must establish personal identity (who am I? how do I relate to my environment?) before undertaking the mastery of subject matter. To the degree that the individual perceives self in control of survival (a positive self-image) to that degree can she or he define *how* her or his learning happens, and apply the attendant process skills to specific course content. Thus, learning how to learn — identify needs, set goals and so on — must precede the "what" in any curriculum.

A CYCLICAL RANK ORDER
1. Who am I?
2. How do I learn?
3. What do I learn?

We hear much talk of negative and positive self-images, drop-outs, and tune outs. But change does not occur; the practiced value remains the same as do skills that have no personal meaning to students. The need exists to examine not the superficial qualities of learning in our schools — but to act on the values that will help students identify and pursue those commitments that will create their place in the sun.

The place to start is your classrooms with your students. This will require a commitment that may place you in conflict with the practiced values of your peers and your community. You alone can make that decision.

If you elect to create a learning environment more conducive to student self-direction, the least risk-laden approach is the introduction of your students to clarifying strategies as a support for subject matter instruction.

In miniature form, this chapter has reintroduced you to process learning. It has applied most of the principles discussed in the preceding chapter. Most importantly, it has outlined some basic processes and simple strategies that will help you introduce process learning to your students.

Begin With

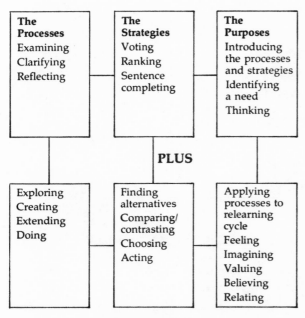

The Processes	The Strategies	The Purposes
Examining	Voting	Introducing the processes and strategies
Clarifying	Ranking	Identifying a need
Reflecting	Sentence completing	Thinking

PLUS

Exploring	Finding alternatives	Applying processes to relearning cycle
Creating	Comparing/ contrasting	Feeling
Extending	Choosing	Imagining
Doing	Acting	Valuing
		Believing
		Relating

EQUALS
THE LEARNING CYCLE

Describing Learning

A schematic of the traditional view of the learning process might look this way:

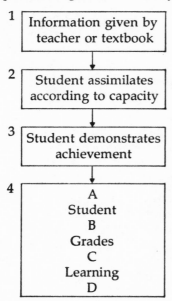

1 Information given by teacher or textbook

2 Student assimilates according to capacity

3 Student demonstrates achievement

4
A
Student
B
Grades
C
Learning
D

The greatest variation in this linear schematic might occur in step 1. In order to distribute the information more effectively, different modes of information-output are used —

The formal lecture

The question-answer session

Selected films, TV, tapes, and slides

The teacher-controlled discussion.

In the open concept, however, learning is not viewed from a linear perspective, but as a *cyclical process.* In the cyclical perspective, learning has no finite beginning or end. While the linear scheme emphasizes "what was achieved" as a terminating point, the cyclical scheme has no terminating point. The process refines itself: the more I learn about who I am, how I think, feel, value, act and relate, the more clearly I discover what additional needs I have to achieve my individual potential. In short, I discover a need to which I must apply the processes I have learned in order that I may achieve my long-range goals. Thus, learning does not end with a test, a grade, or a course's end. It goes on as long as I choose to exercise my freedom to learn.

Introducing Students to Strategies

When *you* feel comfortable and ready, introduce your students to the open process with a few simple strategies. This will give you a chance to check out your own risk-ratio as well as to perceive firsthand the effect such strategies have.

Voting Strategies

Voting takes several forms. The most common is all-class voting by hand-raising. You pose a statement or ask a question —

____How many favor the President's economic plans?

____Who feels that professional sports are too victory oriented?

____Who thinks that the lunchroom needs less supervision by faculty?

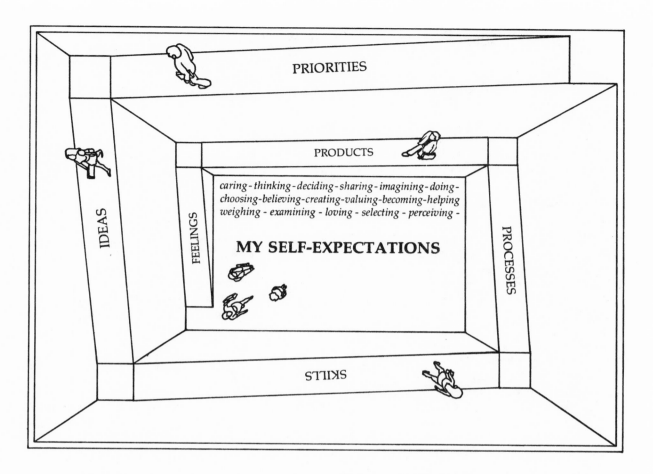

PRIORITIES

PRODUCTS

IDEAS

FEELINGS

PROCESSES

caring - thinking - deciding - sharing - imagining - doing-
choosing-believing-creating-valuing-becoming-helping
weighing - examining - loving - selecting - perceiving -

MY SELF-EXPECTATIONS

SKILLS

Students, informed of the "pass rule," respond favorably by raising hands high in the air, negatively with thumbs down or no response, and so-so with a partially raised hand. Start the voting with light-hearted, safe, but relevant questions. As involvement increases, probe more deeply into significant subject matter, feelings, values, or attitudes related to class work or student interest. Use voting to introduce a new unit, to close out a lesson, or whenever a chance arises.

After the students are familiar with voting, allow teams or individuals to frame the questions for the class. By giving students this opportunity, you help them to learn basic strategies to use later in small groups, to develop positive attitudes about their own decision-making skills, and to identify the needs and concerns *they* feel.

Ranking Strategies

Up to this point, you have used ranking strategies in different forms for different purposes. Like voting, this strategy can help examine, clarify, set priorities, or choose. Values, feelings, ideas, and beliefs make good content for ranking strategies.

A few guidelines will help when you try a ranking strategy.

1. *Don't overload the circuits.* Three choices per group will suffice. If more are necessary, overlap groups.

2. *Encourage but don't force choice.* In every group, there appears someone who resists the distinctions you have given. Get across that this is okay, but that the idea is not a *right answer* or a *right order*, which is usually the hidden concern, but *the reasons for*

25

the person's distinction. Once the hurdle of "being wrong" is cleared, objections usually fade.

3. *Encourage students to make rank orders for each other.*

4. *Participate with students in the rankings.* Share your rank order with them. Your leadership in "risk" will allay their concerns about self-revelation.

REFLECTING STRATEGIES

A task-oriented society may give too little attention to the human need for reflection and self-examination. But reflection, in whatever form, allows us to step out of the race, put aside pressures, and examine the road we have taken. The meditation or reflection exercises provide a framework within which the meditator can move her or his mind and feelings as desired; the meditation may follow the leader's suggestions, or it may wander freely. In the context of these chapters, meditations focus on the self-knowledge process. It is preferable that the teacher participate in the reflection while using the tape recorder to guide the experience.

CHARTING STRATEGIES

More complicated forms of the voting-ranking strategies are the many charting strategies which encourage comparing, contrasting, and opinion seeking.

a. *Lists and grids.* Students are asked to list 10 to 20 items, feelings, values, etc. In adjacent columns, they reflect on responses that apply to each item. For instance, try "ten people I admire." List the persons admired in column 1. In columns 2 to 5 check the reasons which apply in each case.

Name	I admire . . . because she/he is			
	Wealthy	Powerful	Honest	Kind
1.				
2.				
3.				

b. *The circle.* Students are asked to divide a circle. The divisions may show relative importance of items to each other, time spent in activities, and so on. You may compound circles by stacking interrelated circles.

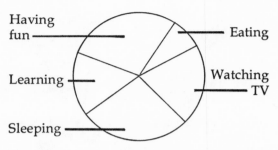

c. *Scale or continuum.* This strategy instructs users to chart alternatives along a scale. Each alternative is visible for examination of its advantages — disadvantages, good-bad points, positive-negative consequences. The scale forces examination of multiple positions before a selection is made.

Example. What is the best argument for price control? (1) Chart alternative arguments.

Saves consumer	Slows growth	Prevents inflation	Pushes inflation

(2) Give support reasons for each argument.

(3) Select the best argument.

STRATEGIES FOR ACTING

In the linear view of the learning process, projects have one purpose: to produce an end result by which the student's achievement can be measured. Thus the graded test, essay, or term project. In the cyclical view, the project assumes an additional function: a strategy to facilitate examining, clarifying, relating, and other processes — a means to an end. Here are but a few:

A chess tournament	A classroom
Poetry writing	government
Building a computer	Role playing

Editing a class
newspaper
Playing a musical
instrument
Equipping a resource
room
Tutoring
Writing a book
Building and using a
telescope
A variety show at a
retirement home

Stream cleanup
Rummage sale
Designing a
playground
Renovating a house
Oral interpretation
A dance program
Lab experiments
Field study

STRATEGIES FOR EXPLORING

The exploring strategies are open-ended spin-offs that facilitate nonlinear thinking. With the exception of whips, all are adaptable to group or individual use, as long as participants will defer making qualitative judgments about the ideas contributed or feelings expressed.

(a) *Brainstorming.* Industry has long relied upon this strategy to invent new ideas and products. Delayed judgment, quantity expectations, a cooperative spirit, and combined energy establish an atmosphere conductive to creative thought. A problem is posed: "How can we improve the taste of our hot dogs?" or "How can we make this a better class?" All ideas are written down. Judgment on the value of any idea is deferred until the possibilities are exhausted. When the brainstorming is ended, other strategies will help select the best ideas.

(b) *Random thinking.* In this strategy, a problem is posed. Five words are selected. Each thinker brainstorms all the ideas she or he can associate with the problem. All ideas are recorded without judgment. Rational problem-solving strategies are applied to the recorded ideas to select the most desirable solutions.

(c) *The whip.* The whip guarantees every individual who wishes it the opportunity to contribute to a solution. Sharing, borrowing, associating, and building on others' input are encouraged.

Problem: How can we improve our group discussion?
First Student: by listening to each other
Second Student: by not talking so much
Third Student: by being more sure of what I want to say
Fourth Student: by being more honest
Fifth Student: by being more accepting
Sixth Student: by accepting and listening . . .
and so on.

The whip, as will each of these other strategies, may serve other purposes. Essentially it is a structure helpful to novice groups which may have a few hesitant contributors. Simpler whips such as "I am proud . . ." whips, "I am most satisfied . . ." whips, or "I need to learn . . ." whips are excellent ways to develop a climate of greater trust.

GROUPING STRATEGIES

The spectrum of group purposes extends from high-task ordered groups which follow specific subject matter study to interpersonal groups which function as support-share-personal growth groups. Groups also differ according to the definition of leadership role.

(a) *Functional differences*
   1. *The subject matter group* functions to solve problems related to course content. The groups may have an outline, prepared by the teacher, which guides the members step by step in the gathering of information and preparing of a report. Such report topics as "The Character Development of Othello" or "Causes of the Civil War" or "A Survey of Flora and Fauna in Northern Illinois" are typical.

   2. *The project group* functions to complete a task with a product that can be evaluated. A play, a scale model, a mural, or a bazaar are possible products derived from the group planning.

   3. *The process group* functions to help the members understand the group process. The group focuses its attention on

the learning cycle. Products and subject matter will resemble those of the product and subject matter groups, but will receive attention secondary to that given the process skills.

4. *The home-base group* functions to create a nonjudgmental relationship among members *assigned* from different social, ethnic, or racial groups. This group provides the opportunity for each student to learn how to solve nonacademic problems with individuals from different backgrounds and outlooks. Each group designs its reason-for-being and plans activities to meet the group needs — picnics, games, social service activities, help-projects, and the like.

5. *The support group* functions to create strong interpersonal relationships among *student-selected* members. The group is selected by one student who respects the insight of those selected. The group acts according to guidelines set up by the student who asks to evaluate her or his learning growth. Trust is built so that the student will solicit the most honest judgments possible concerning the depth, breadth, and intensity of learning, by her/his definition.

6. Leadership role differences
   (a) *The teacher as leader* determines the content, the process, and the outcomes expected and then instructs the class.
   (b) *The teacher as helper* uses strategies that enable the group to move itself through the learning process — from needs assessment to evaluation.
   (c) *The student as leader or as helper* assumes the leadership or enabler role.
   (d) *The group with differentiated student self-guidance* functions to plan and implement a self-determined process. Individuals assume different roles — mediator, conciliator, secretary, subject-matter expert, etc.

PROCESSING STRATEGIES

Processing strategies are informal evaluation tools which have four purposes: (1) to help the learner examine *how* learning occurred; (2) to assess the learning processes which need refinement; (3) to explore alternative ways in which the learner might apply the skills, concepts, and processes mastered to other avenues of learning; (4) to establish closure.

(a) Whips

Use the whip strategy to allow a student to affirm a sentence completion to her or his group or to the class. (Don't forget the pass rule.)

_____ Today, I learned . . .

_____ I am pleased that . . .

_____ I discovered that . . .

_____ A question raised on this discussion is that . . .

_____ I am proud that . . .

Begin the whip by designating a starter, and move counterclockwise. Use a humorous but nonoffensive chance attribute — "the person wearing the most red," "the person with the longest name" — to designate the starter. Be certain that all who choose to receive an opportunity to comment.

(b) Closure Cards

Hand out 3 x 5 index cards. Ask each student to write a statement on the card — no signatures to assure privacy — which will give their final thoughts or feelings on the issue or topic of the class period. Thoughts, feelings, images, titles for the day, associations, and other comments will provide adequate closure material.

_____ I'm glad that our group finished.

_____ I was sorry to see what Reconstruction did.

_____ Today was "Argument Day." Ugh.

_____ I like the way everyone worked hard.

_____ War is rotten.

(c) The Journal

The Journal, a personal diary, is a very private enterprise. Each student decides when to make an entry (you provide abundant daily opportunities and encouragement — the student decides whether to use the opportunity or to pass); what goes in the Journal (you suggest topics, sentence completions, and other strategies, which the student chooses to complete or ignore); how well or how poorly she/he wishes to make entries. (You have no correction power unless the student requests your help or criticism. In any case, encourage students to forget about grammar, spelling, rules, and all the other editorial chains which may block self-expression. It is more important that the student feel comfortable about *what* is said.) Assure the students that no one will see what is written, unless an individual asks another student to read or comment on her or his entry.

When to make entries?

_____ whenever the urge strikes
_____ after a strategy
_____ at the end of a discussion or in the middle
_____ when you give the opportunity at the end of a unit or class period
_____ regularly every morning, noon, or evening
_____ one, two, or three times a day

What form?

___ words	___ epigrams	___ drawings
___ phrases	___ stories	___ charts
___ sentences	___ sketches	___ grids
___ paragraphs	___ cartoons	___ forms
___ essays	___ songs	___ exercises
___ novels	___ watercolors	___ nonforms
___ poems	___ collages	

What content?

___ me	___ my beliefs	___ my hang-ups
___ my feelings	___ my questions	___ my good points
___ my values	___ my ideas	___ my successes
___ my attitude	___ my statements	___ we, us

How I relate to my friends?

___ my family	___ my support group
___ my teachers	___ my state
___ my neighbors	___ my nation
___ my school	___ my environment

Just as it is valuable for you to participate in strategies with the students, it is valuable to keep your own Journal. Join with the class in making entries and in sharing, when you are ready, what you have written. The students will take their cue from your leadership. Your attitude, your openness and trust, your willingness to share your feelings and values, your discipline in making regular, even daily, entries will encourage imitation. You may wish to set a specific time each day for Journals.

As the trust climate builds, you will find more and more students who are willing to share entries. Be careful that all who wish receive equal chance, even over several days or weeks, to receive recognition by sharing their Journal entries. Gradually, you will find the climate conducive to round table discussions of the ideas and feelings which individuals have expressed.

(d) Closure Continuum

This strategy will help you and your students provide support and positive feedback to each other. Do not attempt this until you and the students have a firmly rooted trust relationship. Use this strategy as a follow-up to a clarifying strategy. Give each student two copies of the feedback sheet. On the first sheet, the student signs her or his own name; on the second, the name of a designated or a self-selected partner. Each student — include yourself — will (a) self-evaluate, (b) evaluate another student. The topic extremes on each continuum should indicate various aspects of the issue, question, or subject under discussion, or it should be left open for the individual to construct personal criteria. In the latter case, the student would make duplicate entries on each continuum before the exchange.

Name. _____

INSTRUCTION A. Seven items are listed on the scales. You may add as many additional scales as you wish. When you have added the scales, exchange one sheet with any other person. After the discussion, complete both sheets. Return the other person's completed sheet.

1. **Understands self**   Lost in a maze
   1   2   3   4   5

2. **Sensitive to others' needs**   A cold fish
   1   2   3   4   5

3. **Clearly defined values**   In a values crisis
   1   2   3   4   5

4. **Respects and trusts**   Callous and
                                    vindictive
   1   2   3   4   5

5. **Strong beliefs**   Wishy-washy
   1   2   3   4   5

6. **Committed and involved**   Apathetic
   1   2   3   4   5

7. **Constructive problem-solver** Sloppy thinker
   1   2   3   4   5

8.
   1   2   3   4   5

9.
   1   2   3   4   5

10.
   1   2   3   4   5

11.
   1   2   3   4   5

12.
   1   2   3   4   5

INSTRUCTION B. After you have rated yourself and your partner, reexchange the feedback sheets. Compare the responses.

INSTRUCTION C. In your Journal, comment upon the comparison. "In this feedback, I learned that I . . ."

Processing this Chapter

PURPOSES: _____
_____
_____
_____
_____
_____
_____

CONCEPTS: _____
_____
_____
_____
_____
_____
_____

FEELINGS: _____
_____
_____
_____
_____
_____

APPLICATIONS: _____
_____
_____
_____
_____
_____

"Whether or not you return is thoroughly unimportant," he finally said. "However, you now have the need to live like a warrior. You have always known that, now you're simply in the position of having to make use of something you disregarded before."

Carlos Castaneda, *A Separate Reality*

3

Assessing Needs

INSTRUCTION A. After each statement, there are four given positions: strongly agree, agree, disagree, strongly disagree. Circle the symbol that indicates where you stand on that needs issue.

1. Needs assessment, a diagnosis to determine what skills or concepts are necessary for the student's learning improvement, is an integral phase of the learning process.

   SA   A   D   SD

2. My students are not *capable* of assessing their own needs.

   SA   A   D   SD

3. Under present conditions, my students lack the skills for self-assessment.

   SA   A   D   SD

4. Needs assessment *requires* exact, scientifically validated measuring instruments.

   SA   A   D   SD

5. Individual learning needs are so unique that standardized measuring instruments are no help to me or my students.

   SA   A   D   SD

6. Standardized diagnostic tests can help in some needs assessment situations.

   SA   A   D   SD

7. Needs assessment is not the concern of a classroom teacher.

   SA   A   D   SD

8. Due to the complexity of my students' needs, I am not capable of helping them assess their learning needs.

   SA   A   D   SD

9. Needs assessment should be limited to the basic skill areas (reading, writing, computing) because these areas cover the obligation of a school to educate.

   SA   A   D   SD

10. I have the responsibility to help each student assess any need that *affects* her or his learning.

    SA   A   D   SD

11. The assessment of individual needs to learn how to learn is a necessary step in any student's learning.

    SA   A   D   SD

12. The assessment of individual needs to learn how to clarify values, examine feelings, or establish relationships is as important as needs assessment of the basic skills (reading, writing, etc.).

    SA   A   D   SD

ASSESSING SELF

My Needs Grid

INSTRUCTION A. Brainstorm 10 to 20 needs which you determine for yourself (my needs as a teacher, a parent, a daughter, etc.). As in group brainstorming, suspend judgment while you make your list. Don't worry about priorities, validity, or accuracy. Limit yourself to five minutes for making the list.

My Needs	Physical	Emotional	Social	Intellectual	Ecological	Personal Growth	Aesthetic	Other	My Comment
1									
2									
3									
4									
5									
6									
7									
8									
9									
10									

INSTRUCTION B. After you have listed your needs as best you could determine them, begin working on the grid. At the head of each column on the grid is a title. Column 1, for instance, is labeled physical, column 3 is labeled social, and so on. If *you* feel the first need listed is a physical need, check the box after that need under "physical." If it is also a social need, check the box under "social." Complete your list in this manner. Use the comment column to make notes, if you so desire.

INSTRUCTION C. After you have completed the grid, rank order the five needs you feel are *most necessary* for you to fulfill.

1. _____

2. _____

3. _____

4. _____

5. _____

INSTRUCTION D. In your Journal, comment on *why* you selected these five needs.

Let's Talk About It
(A Simulation)

SETTING: An educational TV studio. The participants, seated in a half circle, flank the reserved moderator, Dr. O.B. Jective.

CAST: *DR. O. B. JECTIVE, former school superintendent and now TV moderator.*

COL. K. P. STILL, Principal of Valley View Military Academy

MS. MARSHA McLUHANITE, open-classroom teacher in Waukesee Elementary District 107

DR. SUE TESTEM, Professor of Educational Psychology at City U

MR. BUCK STOPPER, Director of the Career Alternatives Program, Mission High School

DR. JECTIVE: *I'm so glad that you have joined us for tonight's topic, "Do the schools meet individual needs?" As is our custom, we will first ask each of our panelists to respond briefly to the question. Then, we can light the fireworks up, so to speak. Why don't you begin, Colonel?*

COLONEL STILL: *I'd be glad to start. Let me begin by pointing out that at Valley View we do meet our students' needs. Our students' parents pay good money for us to teach reading, writing, and math. Students get a good preparation for college and build a firm character. Their needs are simple; we give them ample food and shelter, and the uniforms take care of clothing. Beyond that any child needs only to get good grades, become disciplined, and learn to obey. Whenever a child graduates from the Academy, the parents are assured that the Academy has met those needs and the child is ready for real life.*

MS. MARSHA McLUHANITE: *The children I teach are not living in a prehistoric cave. They are the inhabitants of a global village. Many are near "future shock." Technology and electronic media bombard their senses with values, images, and ideas which conflict and confuse. In my classroom, I try to give the children many options. The devices I have to assess their needs are very primitive. Waukesee doesn't have the money to buy fancy tests, so I have tried to make my own diagnostic tests. The parents insist on reading and math. I have concentrated on these areas. If a child has a talent in some other area, say art or geography, I'm really just guessing. And when it comes to non-cognitive needs, like Joanne's being too shy to talk after three months, I'm lost. Needs assessment needs a lot of work, even on the basics.*

DR. SUE TESTEM: *In my experience, most teachers expect too much. They compound simple problems. I have concentrated my research in the last three years on needs assessment. I agree that the tests so far devised are restricted and somewhat primitive. But we must be careful. We know more about the skills which are necessary to learn reading and mathematics. Therefore, we can form reasonable* behavorial objectives and sound tests. These objectives enable us to identify the measurable needs and construct appropriate diagnostic tools. If you will be patient, we will develop needs assessment instruments that someday will help us determine the most complex needs. For now, we must focus the students' attention on skills which we can measure and scale; any attention given to other so-called "needs" will raise unfulfillable and highly subjective expectations.

MR. BUCK STOPPER: The students in CAP have not had their needs met. And we aren't going to claim success with every kid who walks in our door. But they wouldn't come into CAP if something weren't missing in the traditional program. I've heard much emphasis on reading and writing. Our kids don't see reading and writing as "needs," but as skills that will help them get a job. They want to make a living. I know that may be a subtle distinction, but that's the way they see it. I think the problem comes from our ivory tower smugness which says, "I'm a trained teacher. Therefore, I know best what you need." Obviously, that attitude is all wet. If we would listen more to what the students say about their own needs, we wouldn't need CAP or have so many pushouts.

DR. O. B. JECTIVE: I'm a bit confused by your different uses of the word "needs."

DR. TESTEM: Yes, if we are going to conduct a rational discussion, I should expect some basic, objective definition with which we can all agree.

MS. McLUHANITE: All the behavioral objectives that purport to meet individual needs not withstanding, my students can't afford to wait for your research. They are not rats or monkeys and they aren't cave dwellers. In prehistoric times, the need to survive encompassed every breath, every action. Total concentration of energy went to survival skills. But that's not the 20th century. Survival today is more complex.

MR. BUCK STOPPER: I agree. The students I see in CAP and around Mission are the best examples of unmet needs. At one time, the correlation between knowing how to read and write and a job or college was clear and direct. But today's generation re-

minds me of a pinball, bounced and jostled by bright lights and clanging bells. Which direction, which slot, which bumper is not in their control. That's the nature of an electronic society. What I'm saying is this generation is hunting for basics more essential to their survival than reading and writing. It would be well for us to listen.

COL. STILL: You can't tell me that any child or adolescent is capable of determining what she or he needs.

MR. STOPPER: At what age would a person be capable, Colonel?

COL. STILL: That depends on the individual. Everyone matures at a different rate.

MR. STOPPER: I agree, but that doesn't answer the question.

COL. STILL: It is not the school's job to run a psychiatric clinic.

MS. McLUHANITE: You're clouding the issue, Colonel. I'm not describing emotionally disturbed children. I'm talking, and I think Buck is too, about the plain, ordinary, everyday kids in my class who have been raised on a diet of violence, war, and crime since they could lift their heads to see the TV, about kids who have been disillusioned by the hollow authority of Captain Basher-Dasher Cereals and Suzy Home-Styler Dolls and all the other empty dreams they've been promised. They can't believe authority because every time they do, they get taken. The only people they can trust are themselves. That's their age and they are its victims.

COL. STILL: I still must insist that this does not make them capable of deciding what they need to learn.

MR. STOPPER: I agree, Colonel. Given an educational system that strives inordinately to measure each and every individual by rigidly established norms, that condones brainwashing under the abstruse title of behavorial modification, that keypunches kids into computerized statistics to proclaim "accountability"; given all this, what can you expect but passive resistance and apathy?

DR. TESTEM: I take exception, Mr. Stopper, to your attack. Children work best when they can readily perceive our expectations. Behavioral modification techniques, which you reject, are the logical implementation of that concept. Learning objectives delineate precise, measurable expectations which the child can readily obtain. Industry has already demonstrated that objectives make good management.

MR. STOPPER: Very good, Doctor. I understand the theory. But what you forget, Doctor, is the attitude that behavior mod reinforces — passive independence.

DR. TESTEM: I don't understand.

MR. STOPPER: I think you can agree that we live in a society saturated by machines, computers, electronic media. Machines serve us well, but in one respect, we are blinded by their benefits; each invention, each tool has a built-in independence factor. Air conditioning comforts us from sweltering heat, but when a brown-out strikes, how easily can we readjust? Trains and planes transport food from distant states. Suppose an energy shortage incapacitated all planes or trains? What would happen in our urban cities without massive daily delivery? TV turns dull subjects into entertaining specials. But what happens when the TV addicts get to school? What I'm arguing is that our technology creates an addiction more pervasive, more insidious than heroin or cocaine. Behavior modification is no more than another nail in the coffin. You brainwash a child to depend on your assessment, your expectations, your decisions. If successful, you will have a perfectly controllable child who abides by your every whim. Welcome, Doctor, to 1984, the ultimate triumph of scientific objectivity.

DR. O. B. JECTIVE: You have been very critical, Mr. Stopper. If we had more time, I would hope you would give us some positive solutions. Our time is up. Thank you for your ideas.

Finding Immediate Needs

INSTRUCTION A. Using the five needs you ranked as MOST NECESSARY FOR YOU TO FULFILL, list those needs in ranked order. Use column I, "needs."

INSTRUCTION B. In column II, "immediate needs," list two necessary steps that you must take or two subneeds possibly helpful as a means to meet the major need listed in column I. For instance, in column I, you might list (a) "being more open with my students," (b) "saying what I really think to my boss." Add an entry in column II for each entry in COLUMN I.

INSTRUCTION C. In column III, "means to get," list two means you might employ to obtain each immediate need listed in column II. For instance, after "saying what I think to my boss," you might list (a) tell her off at the next department meeting, (b) make an appointment to discuss our disagreement. Complete all entries in column III.

INSTRUCTION D. Check one box in the "DO" column against each need listed in column I. This will give you five action projects to complete as a means to fulfill assessed needs.

EXAMPLE:

NEEDS	IMMEDIATE	MEANS	DO
1 sharing	(a) open to students	(a) participate in groups	
		(b) conferences with each	
	(b) telling boss what I think	(a) telling her off	
		(b) make appointment	

RANK	NEEDS	IMMEDIATE NEEDS	MEANS TO GET	DO
1	A			
	B			
2	A			
	B			
3	A			
	B			
4	A			
	B			
5	A			
	B			

Reflecting

Needs Meditation

INSTRUCTION A. Follow the procedures you have developed for using self-reflection exercises.

Relax yourself . . . find a quiet spot to slow down . . . get yourself comfortable . . . settle down . . . close your eyes . . . recall the needs you assessed for yourself . . . what were they? . . . were the priorities real or a cover-up to avoid a need you won't admit? . . . have you done anything about the needs you identified? . . . why? . . . was the needs assessment helpful to you? . . . how did you react to the process? . . . how do you feel about what you decided? . . . think about your classroom? . . . as you organize it now? . . . what changes would you introduce to facilitate your students' needs self-assessment? . . . could they? . . . do they need self-assessment? . . . what are your students' needs? . . . improved skills? . . . a subject mastery? . . . success? . . . motivation? . . . belonging? . . . picture individuals . . . what needs do you see for each? . . . pick out a student who has special needs . . . what are those needs? . . . is the student aware of those needs? . . . or are the needs buried behind other concerns? . . . defenses? . . . how can you help that student? . . . can the student assess those needs? . . . can you find a resource person with special expertise to help? . . . what needs have you identified for yourself in this reflection? . . . do you need to learn assessment skills? . . . to relate more openly with your students? . . . to focus more attention on individual needs? . . . to give more attention to basic skills? . . . to help individuals relate more openly with the class? . . . to help individuals get in touch with their feelings? . . . to clarify values? . . . to identify assumptions? . . . to think more creatively? . . . to become more independent? . . . to help yourself in these areas? . . . pick out another student who is much different from your first selection . . . review her or his needs and how you meet those needs in your class. When finished, end the reflection.

Examining Practices

Areas of Need

INSTRUCTION A. On this scale, mark the amount of attention you actually give to each need area listed. The scale moves from very much (VM), to much (M), to some (S), to little (L), to none (N).

1. **Basic skills (reading, writing, computing) relevant to my discipline**

   VM   M   S   L   N

2. **Content (information, concepts) relative to my discipline**

   VM   M   S   L   N

3. **Valuing (clarifying, examining)**

   VM   M   S   L   N

4. **Thinking creatively (brainstorming, random idea-searching)**

   VM   M   S   L   N

5. **Thinking logically (problem-solving, inquiring)**

   VM   M   S   L   N

6. **Feeling (getting in touch with feelings, accepting feelings)**

   VM   M   S   L   N

7. **Believing (examining basic attitudes)**

   VM   M   S   L   N

8. **Relating (with other persons, the environment)**

   VM   M   S   L   N

INSTRUCTION B. In your Journal, complete this sentence: "I discovered that the areas of need which I should consider with my students are . . . "

As a first step to implement whatever decisions you have reached about needs assessment in your classroom, adapt the strategies that have helped you in this chapter. If you have decided that student self-assessment is important — *and that you are capable of guiding that process* — the strategies you used are ordered so that you will need only adapt the question content to your students. Here are some additional strategies which may help.

Needs Voting

Use the voting strategy (or adapt a whip, sentence completions, or rank orders). Review the procedures for voting in Chapter II.

How many need to review the quadratic equation? (content)

How many feel uncomfortable with the seminar? (relating)

How many need more practice with . . .? (skills)

How many are concerned that . . .? (believing)

Who is satisfied . . .? (attitude)

Overview

Overview is a small-group needs assessment or a subject-matter review strategy at the end of a study unit. Divide the class into small groups. Write the unit objectives on the chalkboard. Inform the class that each group should select three objectives from the list which ought to receive major attention on the unit exam. Mimeograph and hand out the following instructions for the strategy to each group. Distribute newsprint and magic markers to each group.

INSTRUCTION A. Select the three objectives for this unit which the group feels should receive major attention on the exam.

1._____

2._____

3._____

INSTRUCTION B. For each objective, list what facts, ideas, or skills a test taker will need to show proficiency.

OBJECTIVE	1	2	3

Processing This Chapter

PURPOSE: _____
_____
_____
_____
_____
_____
_____

FEELINGS:_____
_____
_____
_____
_____
_____

CONCEPTS:_____
_____
_____
_____
_____
_____

APPLICATIONS:_____
_____
_____
_____
_____
_____
_____
_____

Breath in my nostrils this breasty spring day
shouts a jubilee
like one of my old sweaty fathers:
in the surge of song and
sweetness of green trees and
the steaming blacky earth,
he lifted his head to a wildhorse tilt
and forgot that he was a slave!

Lance Jeffers,
"Breath in My Nostrils"

4

Getting In Touch

From the New Orleans slave markets to Buddy Bolten, from Coltrane to Louis Armstrong and James Brown, the blues of Black America have filtered passion and pain onto the contemporary musical scene. Soul music initiated the renaissance of feelings in America.

But can soul-sense survive in an insta-do, no-sense environment?

_____ Microwave ovens for insta-eat gourmet dinners

_____ Music synthesizers for insta-make symphonies

_____ Videotape machines for insta-replay family discussions

_____ Computers for insta-write novels

_____ Telstar for insta-surveillance

_____ Closed-ciruit TV for insta-pornography

When Did I Last . . .?

	Yester-day	Last week	Last month	Never
Cook myself a gourmet meal?				
Smell a rose bud?				
Touch a cheek?				
Listen to a symphony?				
Soak in a tub?				
Pick a daisy?				
Roll in the snow?				
Cry in a crowd?				
Scream with delight?				
Laugh in a theater?				
Savor a glass of chablis?				
_____?				

INSTRUCTION A. Complete the grid by checking the most recent time that answers each question.

INSTRUCTION B. In your Journal complete this sentence: "I observed in this grid that I . . ."

1. _____

2. _____

3. _____

4. _____

5. _____

INSTRUCTION C. Beginning with the top priority, brainstorm 5 to 10 ways that could make that experience more accessible or more regular to you or to persons you know well. Repeat the procedure for each ranked experience.

INSTRUCTION D. Mark the chart below. Apply the question to the brainstorming you just completed. Evaluate your performance by placing an X on the scale in the appropriate space between the extremes.

In the brainstorming I used —

1. _____
   reason   springboarding ideas

2. _____
   immediate judgment   deferred judgment
   (good idea, bad idea)

3. _____
   ordered selection   random responses

4. _____
   sensible answers   reckless abandon

5. _____
   pure logic   analogy

INSTRUCTION E. Examine your thinking process. In the Journal, describe how you think, what values control your thinking process, what ways of thinking make you uncomfortable, and the consequences of your thinking process on what you do and how you operate in a problem-solving situation.

If you use these strategies with your students, you will want to adapt the list content in "When did I last . . .?" To facilitate the brainstorming and processing activities, you could introduce both the "List" and the "Thinking Cap" as group strategies. Change the instructions and content to fit a group situation.

Ballot Box

INSTRUCTION A. In this voting strategy, check the answer that best approximates your classroom practice.
In my classroom, I encourage —

	YES	NO	SOME-TIMES
1. Cooperation	☐	☐	☐
2. Logical reasoning	☐	☐	☐
3. Instant solutions	☐	☐	☐
4. Acceptance	☐	☐	☐
5. Springboarding	☐	☐	☐
6. Use of metaphor	☐	☐	☐
7. Expression of feeling	☐	☐	☐
8. Deferment	☐	☐	☐
9. Competition	☐	☐	☐
10. Brainstorming	☐	☐	☐

INSTRUCTION B. Ask the class to rate you. Give each student a copy of the ballot. Tally their responses. As you study the tally, be aware of the feelings their responses generate in you. *What are the feelings? Which are the most intense? How are you reacting to those feelings? Can you detach your self and brainstorm multiple responses to this idea? "I could be more in touch with my feelings if I would . . ."*

Sensing

Sensations-I-Enjoy List

INSTRUCTION A. Allow yourself 60 seconds to list as many sights, sounds, tastes, smells, touches which you enjoy. Stop after 60 seconds if you have not completed 20 sensations. Complete the remaining columns. Use a "+" to indicate "yes" and "−" to indicate "no."

	I enjoy	today	this week	I pursued	I told someone*
Example: Smell of fresh spring rain		−	+	+	+
1. _____					
2. _____					
3. _____					
4. _____					
5. _____					
6. _____					
7. _____					
8. _____					
9. _____					
10. _____					
11. _____					
12. _____					
13. _____					
14. _____					
15. _____					
16. _____					
17. _____					
18. _____					
19. _____					
20. _____					

* "Today" — I enjoyed that experience today.
"This week" — I enjoyed it this week.
"I pursued" — I went out of my way to experience this sensation.
"I told someone" — I expressed my enjoyment to someone.

What does the list tell you about yourself? Are you a no-sense person? Do you use some senses more than others? How aware are you of the sense zones in your body? Your skin? . . . Your toes? . . . Your tongue? . . . Your lungs? . . . Your stomach? Is one sense more sharply tuned than others?

Fruits and Vegetables: A Blind Walk

Bring a variety of fruits and vegetables to your class. Scatter pairs of students around the room. Be sure that you participate. Give each pair one blindfold large enough to cover both eyes *and* nose. One student in each pair will volunteer to be blindfolded and guided by the partner. If neither wishes to volunteer, switch some pairings. After the volunteer has covered eyes and nose, ask the guide to lead the blind person past your desk. Organize the movement so that only one or two pairs are moving at once. Spread the fruits and vegetables on the table. You should have one or two vegetables for each pair. Have the guide place the blind person's hand on each vegetable or fruit. Encourage the blind person to feel the size, shape, texture, distortions, protrusions and so on. After all items have been examined, ask the student to select one item with which to become familiar. Back at the seat, the blind person should — *without removing the blindfold* — (1) sketch the favorite object with as much detail as possible, (2) identify by name the fruit or vegetable drawn, and (3) identify by name as many other items from the desk as possible. The guide will write down the names. Finally, the pair should return to the desk and find the favorite object without removing the blindfold. (Vary this exercise by changing the objects or the senses used.)

After all pairs have completed the exercise, gather the class in a seminar circle for a discussion:

1. Record the number of items correctly identified in each drawing. Share the drawings.
2. Record the number of items correctly identified by name.
3. Record the number of items correctly found in the second blind walk.
4. Discuss the procedures that individuals used to select and identify objects.
5. Draw conclusions from the experience about the sense of touch (or whatever senses were used).
6. Ask individuals to draw conclusions about their own sense awareness and make entries in their Journals.

Perceiving

Seeing is not believing. How often have you been fooled by an optical illusion? How many times have you looked at an object with a friend and discovered that your impressions differed radically from what the friend perceived? The trained first violinist of the Cleveland symphony will hear Beethoven's Fifth more precisely than a tone-deaf preschooler or an amateur pianist. A socialite collector's view of a Rodin exhibit will not approximate an art critic's perception.

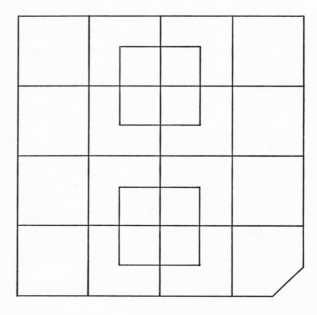

How many squares do you see on this drawing? Record the number. Instruct your class to do the same and record the number. Instruct your class to do the same and record the individual counts on the board — "How many see 1? 2? 3?" — until all possibilities are exhausted. Diagram a curve that charts the differences. What accounts for the difference? Ask the students to explain counts. (Write responses on the board as a discussion.)

As a follow-up to this discussion, project an ink blot on an overhead screen. Ask the students to list the images each perceives in the blot. Put the responses on the board, brainstorm possible reasons for the variances, and select the most probable. Conclude the activity by using the Journal.

———write a poem that uses the images
———write a story based on one image you saw
———make your own ink blot and pick out the images

The Color Game

Divide the class into four teams: red, blue, green, and purple. Each team will plan one day's class activities to demonstrate the cultural heritage and identity of the color-group. The activities should include the following:

1. Room decorations in the color, a national flag in the color, and a coat of arms in the color
2. Student art work in the color
3. A meal in the color
4. Costumes in the color
5. A play or film about the color
6. Magazine or newspaper with ads on the color
7. Songs and poems about the color
8. History book of the color
9. Famous people who wore the color
10. And whatever else can be used to demonstrate pride in the group color.

While one group has its day, the other groups are required to think the day-color. After each group has completed its day, a fifth day should be given to processing the activities. Build on the insights learned from the perception strategies:
What good qualities did you perceive in your own color? In the others? How did you feel about your color? About the others? Why are there different points of view about the colors? What experiences gave you the most pride? What other feelings did you experience in this exercise?
Close the activity by using the Journal. "In this color game, a new experience for me was . . ."

Focusing

Two high school English teachers in Evanston, Illinois, snared the newspaper headlines several years ago when they were accused of using "unauthorized sensitivity sessions" with their students. The furor, which eventually caused the teachers' dismissal, stormed around misconceptions by other faculty members and, soon thereafter, by the administration and community. Each group, relying on a narrow perspective, focused not on the facts, but on what it wanted to see. As a consequence, a profitable learning situation, supported by the participating students and parents, was destroyed.

A Focus Game

Assemble the class in a multisound environment (a park near a busy street, a cafeteria, the classroom with several records or tapes going in each corner). Get everyone comfortable and relaxed. In your softest voice, take them on a sound tour. Focus their listening on individual sounds. As they become aware of the multitude of aural stimulations, help them to control which sounds come to the foreground and which are pushed into the background. Process the experience:

1. What sounds did you hear?
2. What sounds did you like? Can you talk about that feeling?
3. How do you react to the process of focusing?
4. What are the implications of this exercise for you?
5. How can you improve your ability to focus?

As you become more skilled in controlling your ability to focus, you will discover a greater awareness of both external stimuli and internal reactions, a more sensitive response to both, and an acceptance of the feelings which you experience.

Body Mirror

Get yourself into a comfortable position. Lie down or sit in an easy chair. Close your eyes and get in touch with your body. Feel the uncomfortable zones. Adjust your position until these zones are relaxed. Focus on the rhythm of your breathing. Feel the body parts which rise and fall, the muscles which help you inhale. Take five slow deep breaths. Feel the change in your nostrils . . . your chest . . . your diaphragm . . . what muscles move . . . continue breathing . . . inhale as deeply as you can . . . hold your breaths for longer periods . . . notice where you feel strain . . . pressure . . . release the tension . . . what are you experiencing? . . . what images of yourself do you see? . . . be your own mirror . . . continue your deep breathing and observe your face . . . what muscles tighten? . . . what ripples can you sense? . . . survey the rest of your body for five to ten minutes . . . control your focus as you move from part to part . . . notice when discomfort sets in . . . begins to pervade other parts . . . let it develop . . . focus on your reactions to it . . . what changes take place within you until you need rest . . . refocus on your breathing.

Self-Dialogue Scripts

After you have completed the Mirror exercise, select the feelings that were dominant. In your Journal, write a play script. Personify two feelings in a situation that allows you and your mirror image to discuss your feelings. Have the actors speak in the first person ("I", "we") and present tense.

Feelings Are Facts

It was not too long ago that teachers were trained to ban feelings and emotions from the classroom. "Thou shalt not destroy objective knowledge with personal feelings." While most students discovered the rules of that no-emotion game, few were prepared to handle the absurdity of the institutional schizophrenia which the behavior mod fad promotes: "Yes, there are emotions, but not on this side of the room. Affective objectives are scheduled for Mondays and Thursdays in the reading corner. Everything in its place, please." (And we wonder why students feel fractured and boxed.)

Precision: A Play

Sam Superintendent:
  Togetherness? Horror of horrors.

Carol Curriculum Director:
  We must maintain our standards. We have clearly defined each objective. No curriculum has ever seen such detailed breakdowns.

Tom Teacher:
  I think the pen-holding objectives for advanced writing are brilliant. At last we are assured all students will place their little finger at the correct angle when holding the pen to write the word "is."

Sam Superintendent:
  Such wonderful exactitude. The board will surely grant my raise now. We are models of measurable efficiency. Our assembly line is perfect.

Carol Curriculum Director:
  Ford, move over.

Sam Superintendent:
  I just don't understand those students who object to our precise methods.

Sound and Sense

For this exercise, you will need a classical dance recording, some finger paints (crayons or water colors will do), newsprint, and three pictures. Turn the record to a comfortable volume. Spread the newsprint, paints, and photos in front of you. Beginning in the upper left-hand corner, sketch as rapidly as possible images of the feelings you experience from the combination of the music and the three pictures. As your emotions change, move to a different blank space and begin a new sketch. Work in pace with the music. Let the sound and your feelings carry you to the end of the record. Conclude the exercise by transcribing your experience to your Journal. Describe the feelings, thoughts, and images you experienced.

Proud Sculpture

Take some modeling clay to sculpt a statue of yourself. Create an image that accentuates the positive feelings you have toward yourself. In effect, make the statue a sentence completion, an "I am proud that I . . ." statue. Describe to the class the feelings that you have communicated in your completed work. (This exercise is also helpful when discussing feelings of inferiority brought on by racial, ethnic, or social bias. Have the class discuss the positive aspects of darkness, womanhood, and the like. Then ask individuals to sculpt or paint an "I am proud" work.)

"Media, by altering the envoronment, evoke in us unique ratios of sense perceptions. The extension of any one sense alters the way we think and act — the way we perceive the world. When these ratios change, men change."

  Marshall McLuhan,
  The Medium Is the Massage

Experiencing

Seeing is not always believing. Optical illusions such as the window swinging on a fulcrum cause the viewer to blink twice. "If the senses are not trustworthy, what then?"

The American mania for objectivity and validity has created this paradox: Instead of learning to trust sense experience, students are taught to observe stringent adherence to measurement of the objective facts. Facts, of course, never lie. To counter this miseducation, teachers and students must sensitize themselves not only to sharpened sense awareness, but also to open acceptance of emotional experiences that flow, move, and change as the environment flows, moves, and changes.

Walking Alone

An Awareness Experience

Loneliness and aloneness are feelings that a technological society fosters in its giant, impersonal institutions. For all the crowds, hustle and bustle, and talk of personal interaction, many individuals — especially the young and the very old — are left alone and isolated to deal with feelings of loneliness and aloneness. If the lonely can conquer and control the despondency that stalks the empty nights, there is no fear of being alone.

Send the members of your class on an afternoon walk — alone. Tell each person to find a place to walk (to and from) which is at least three miles away. When each returns, she or he should use the Journal to recall the feelings, events, and places experienced. On the school day following the walk, assemble the group into a tight circle. With eyes closed and hands interlocked with the person on either side, the group should review the journey. One by one, let each describe what she or he did, saw, or experienced on the walk alone. Descriptions should be graphically detailed. After the last description, keep eyes closed but separate hands and move apart. Once again, ask each student to describe the walk, but focus on the feelings recalled. Most importantly, ask each to speak in the first person ("I") and present tense. ("I'm feeling carefree and excited . . .") as the feelings are described. After each has described the journey-feelings, open eyes. In the final whip ask each to describe her or his feelings during this experience. Keep comments in the first person, present tense. When all who wish have responded to the question, open the discussion to the directions it flows. Conclude the exercise by using Journals to record personal feelings and re-sponses to the walk alone, the group experience, the discussion, or the feelings of trust that were demanded by the exercise.

Processing This Chapter

PURPOSE: _____

_____

_____

_____

_____

_____

FEELINGS: _____

_____

_____

_____

_____

_____

CONCEPTS: _____

_____

_____

_____

_____

_____

APPLICATIONS: _____

_____

_____

_____

_____

_____

We hold these truths to be self-evident, that all men are created equal, that they are endowed by their Creator with certain inalienable Rights, that among these are Life, Liberty, and the pursuit of Happiness.

Declaration of Independence

5

Questioning Assumptions And Beliefs

The Declaration of Independence announced to the Western world a new set of assumptions defining the essential rights of individual citizens. What were declared as self-evident truths in 1776, the Constitutional Convention adopted as the supreme law of the land in 1787. Since its ratification, the Constitution has sustained itself as the final protector of individual rights. As the nation evolved, contradictory state laws, attempts to usurp power, and historically ingrained, counterconstitutional values have dissolved under the just authority that declares by action that "all men are created equal."

But is the dream fulfilled for all Americans? Do those who share the dreams in the comfort of the good life assume that their life-style is the norm? How often, how intensely, do we question the assumptions and beliefs that we value? How aware are we that historically ingrained, counterconstitutional values have dissolved too slowly for many native Americans? Tacit assumptions do not give way to facts, logic, persuasive skills.

The Matchstick Puzzle

INSTRUCTION A. Give each student six matchsticks. The task is to construct four congruent equilateral triangles with the six matchsticks. Allow 3 to 5 minutes. As soon as one person succeeds, or at the time limit, stop all activity. Demonstrate, or have the successful experimenter do it, how to solve the problem. The false, tacit assumption is that all triangles must lie on the same plane. Solve the problem by forming a pyramid base with three matchsticks and three to define its sides. The result is a tetrahedron.

INSTRUCTION B. Discuss the implications of this solution for human relations problems caused by tacit assumptions that receive an affirmative answer. For students, change column III to "student."

INSTRUCTION C. After you have checked each appropriate column (II-VII), rank order those rights from which you or other persons are excluded. Make the rank according to the seriousness of the destructive effect which the exclusion has on the self-image of the excluded person or group. In the last column identify those who are excluded. (For students, change III to read "adult" and IV to read "student.")

I My rights	II As human	III As citizen	IV As teacher	V I exercise	VI I am excluded	VII Others excluded	VIII Rank	IX The excluded
1.								
2.								
3.								
4.								
5.								
6.								
7.								
8.								
9.								
10.								
11.								

INSTRUCTION D. Isolate the three rights that you ranked "most serious." For each, give two or three reasons that might account for an excluded individual's *not seeking actively* to exercise the right.

Indicate whether *you* can substantiate that person's assumption with fact, or whether it is an opinion that neither you nor the person can counter with fact.

Excluded right	Reason I	Fact	Opinion	Reason II	Fact	Opinion
1.						
2.						
3.						

What conclusions can you draw from these guides? Have you assumed that some rights which are denied you are not worth the bother? What other limiting assumptions have you or others you know made about yourselves? What reinforces these assumptions? What beliefs about your own capabilities might chart new horizons for you? How do you extend yourself to achieve your goals and fulfill your capabilities?

Positive Assumptions Inventory

INSTRUCTION A. Brainstorm 15 or 20 of *your* personal capabilities (cooking gourmet seafood, mountain climbing, doing needlepoint, teaching slow learners, and so on). Remember that brainstorming calls for nonjudgmental thinking. Think as quickly as you can; write down or tape record each response. *After the list is complete,* or you have exhausted all possibilities, select the best ideas.

Name

Assumptions	Explicit	Me	Them	Implicit	Me	Them

48

INSTRUCTION B. Ask one or two other persons to do the brainstorming exercise with you. They, however, are to focus on *your* capabilities.

INSTRUCTION C. Compare the lists. What capabilities appear on all lists? Which of these common capabilities are based on *explicit* assumptions? What *implicit* assumptions are made in each list? Match the explicit and implicit columns.

Students may complete these strategies in small groups. If brainstorming is used as a group strategy, take care to instruct the participants in the ground rules for effective brainstorming:

    (1) Have a student recorder. Every idea suggested must be recorded. Make no qualitative judgments. Go for quantity.

    (2) Build ideas one on another or make spin-offs. Help each other to add ideas.

    (3) Work quickly and cooperatively.

Separating Fact from Fiction

The Delphic oracle was called the fount of truth: her prophecies never failed. When Oedipus learned from the oracle that the plague would lay waste to Thebes unless the polluting cause were removed, Oedipus, the king, relentlessly pursued the facts until the horrible truth faced him: he alone was responsible. Having killed his father and married his mother unknowingly, he, the king, had defiled the country.

The Oedipus story symbolizes the unusual enigma which each person must face in the search for self: are the assumptions I make about the forces which I believe control my life based on fact or fiction? When others see me differently than I see myself, am I suffering, Oedipus-like, self-delusion which rejects all advice as blind and misbegotten? Or have I distinguished clearly between fact and fiction?

Proof of Validity

INSTRUCTION A. Select one of your basic assumptions about which you and your group members cannot agree. Those who agree that the assumption is valid for you will construct one list; those who disagree will construct a second list. You join one group or the other. Each group should list in the first column 5 to 10 examples of behavior (specific incidents) or attitudes expressed (specific quotes) that illustrate support for the position being argued. In addition, in the column headed "Would Do," list what behaviors or attitudes not demonstrated would be necessary to prove the opposite point.

	VALID LIST		INVALID LIST	
	What She/He Does	Would Do	What She/He Does	Would Do
1.				
2.				
3.				
4.				
5.				
6.				
7.				
8.				
9.				
10.				

INSTRUCTION B. On the basis of observed behavior, which assumptions made in prior strategies hold up in fact? *To what degree do you (or the student in question) act on your capabilities? What appears to be the relationship between performance and assumptions about limits and capabilities?*

INSTRUCTION C. Use your strongest communication skill (writing, painting, dancing, sculpting, weaving, photographing) to create a self-portrait that communicates your five strongest talents. This might take the form of a symbolic painting, a descriptive essay, or a poem. You decide.

or

Select your five most hidden talents, take them from under the bushel, and devise a way to show a good friend what these talents are. For each talent you should have one product which either depicts the talent or is a result of that talent.

Perceiving Beliefs

The Declaration of Independence speaks of the "Creator"; the Constitution separates church and state; the American flag hangs in churches and synagogues; the Supreme Court bans classroom prayer. How can such opposites coexist? Surrounded by such paradox, what and who can be believed?

Agreement Continuum

INSTRUCTION A. Respond to the statements listed below by marking the spot on each continuum that most accurately reflects your position.

1. The founding fathers separated organized religion from government to protect each from the restrictive power and control of the other.

   Strongly agree   Strongly disagree

2. The separation of church and state limits the right of individuals to believe in a supreme being.

   Strongly agree   Strongly disagree

3. The separation of church and state limits the right of the individual to practice a religion.

   Strongly agree   Strongly disagree

4. Schools should help each student clarify her or his religious beliefs as a way of attaining a positive sense of self.

   Strongly agree   Strongly disagree

5. Schools should help each student to question her or his beliefs in the "self-evident" truths outlined in the Declaration of Independence.

   Strongly agree   Strongly disagree

6. My beliefs in no way affect my sense of self.

   Strongly agree   Strongly disagree

7. The search for personal meaning may take many forms.

   Strongly agree   Strongly disagree

8. There are no universal truths.

   Strongly agree   Strongly disagree

9. Questioning basic tenets leads to trouble.

   Strongly agree   Strongly disagree

10. What I say I believe could be reflected in what I do.

    Strongly agree   Strongly disagree

Personal Declaration of Independence

INSTRUCTION A. In your Journal, write your own Declaration of Independence. Make it as accurately reflective as you can of the basic tenets or principles of life that are evident in the way you live. (These may or may not have religious connotations.) "When in the course of human events, it becomes necessary for me to dissolve the false assumptions that have bound me to others. . . ."

Commiting Self to Action

"Man is the kind of creature who cannot be whole except he be committed, because he cannot find himself without finding a center beyond himself. In short, the emancipation of self requires commitment."

Reinhold Neibuhr,
Religion and Freedom of Thought

Your Choice for Action

INSTRUCTION A. Pick one of the topics listed in group 1 and match it with one of the strategies in group 2.

GROUP 1

trust, religion, humanity, freedom, nature, life, equality, charity, liberty, work, God, pursuit of happiness, property, sensitivity, or your own option.

GROUP 2

(a) ALL THE NEWS. FIT TO PRINT — Edit a two- or three-page newspaper built on the theme word you have selected. Show examples from cultural-historic characters who exhibited the quality or its opposite, make ads selling the quality, report events, crate a cartoon, and write an editorial with concrete suggestions to implement the value.

(b) WRITE A LETTER to your senator and congress person. Frame your letter's topic around the theme you selected. Give suggestions for how she/he might use personal influence to further your ideas.

(c) CREATE AN EDUCATIONAL GAME based on the concept you have selected. The game might create a path to a goal (such as liberty) with the obstacles that will hinder player progress and aids to help players to reach the goal.

(d) MAKE YOUR OWN . . . First make a list that describes every facet of the idea you selected. (Use brainstorming rules.) For instance, list every idea or statement about freedom that you can. (All people are free, freedom will destroy humanity, etc.) Secondly, select those ideas *which make most sense to you.* Organize these ideas into an institution (a city, a religion, a commune). Make the laws or rules, symbols, flags, constitution, and so on of your institution. Post your completed description.

(e) WRITE AND PRODUCE A DRAMA based on the concept selected. Plot the play about a conflict which, when resolved, will reveal your position.

(f) PAINT A MURAL depicting your feelings and beliefs related to the concept.

(g) OTHER ACTION PROJECTS

____Volunteer to work in a hospital emergency room, a nursery school, or retirement home.

____Compare prices in supermarket chains and publish your results.

____Volunteer to campaign for a candidate who reflects your political beliefs.

____Organize a church group to identify a common belief and find a way to practice that belief together.

Processing This Chapter

PURPOSES:_____
_____
_____
_____
_____

FEELINGS:_____
_____
_____
_____
_____

CONCEPTS:_____
_____
_____
_____
_____

APPLICATIONS:_____
_____
_____
_____
_____

6

For no one desires any-
thing nor rejoices in
anything, except as a
good that is loved.
Thomas Aquinas,
On Charity

Perceiving Relationships

A Relating Continuum

Care, responsibility, respect and knowledge are mutually interdependent. They are a syndrome of attitudes which are to be found in the mature person; that is, in the person who develops his own powers productively, who only wants to have that which he has worked for, who has given up narcissistic dreams of omniscience and omnipotence, who has acquired humility based on the inner strength which only genuine productive activity can give.

Erich Fromm,
The Art of Loving

A person who has been educated for living freely in community will be self-directed without being self-centered. He will be other-centered without being other-directed. He will be free from the domination of others' wills but able to give himself fully in the terms of insight, sympathy, and talents to fill others' needs.

Paul Nash,
Authority and Freedom in Education

Love is an active power in man; a power which breaks through the walls which separate man from his fellow men, which unites him with others; love makes him overcome the sense of isolation and separateness, yet it permits him to be himself, to retain his integrity.

Erich Fromm,
The Art of Loving

INSTRUCTION A. Reproduce and distribute these statements to *three* representatives of each group: administration, teachers, parents, students. Ask each *group* to complete the following scales so that the extreme opinions (marked with X's) and the consensus opinions (marked with O's) are indicated.

e.g. Students should supervise cafeteria.

(Teacher Response)

X   O   X
_____
Strongly agree   Strongly disagree

(Student Response)

           X   O   X
_____
Strongly agree   Strongly disagree

Your task is to observe each group as it completes the scales. Use the observation tool that follows the scales.

1. Care, responsibility, respect, and knowledge are mutually interdependent.

_____
Strongly agree   Strongly disagree

2. The students in this school are disrespectful, disobedient, and irresponsible.

_____
Strongly agree   Strongly disagree

3. The students in this school need close supervision to prevent damage to property.

_____
Strongly agree   Strongly disagree

4. Students should take the responsibility to supervise each other in the enforcement of school rules that the board and the administration have devised.

_____
Strongly agree   Strongly disagree

5. A person who has been educated for living freely in a community will be self-directed.

_____
Strongly agree   Strongly disagree

6. This school educates its students to live freely in a community.

_____
Strongly agree   Strongly disagree

7. Students are given multiple opportunities to learn how to make intelligent, free choices.

_____
Strongly agree   Strongly disagree

8. Faculty in this school give top priority to helping students become self-directed.

_____
Strongly agree   Strongly disagree

9. Most students in this school use talents to help each other by choosing to help faculty and peers in concrete ways such as tutoring, reorganizing classroom materials, maintaining nonpersonal records, decorating, mutual courtesy and learning, material sharing, etc.

_____
Strongly agree   Strongly disagree

10. One can merge one's self in ecstasy only as one has gained the prior capacity to stand alone, to be a person in one's own right.

Strongly agree   Strongly disagree

11. The programs and structures of this school encourage students to develop personalized learning goals.

Strongly agree   Strongly disagree

12. The programs and structures of this school help students to share learning with each other.

Strongly agree   Strongly disagree

13. The programs and structures of this school help students to share talents with the communities in which they live.

Strongly agree   Strongly disagree

14. The programs and structures of this school help students to build positive working relationships with their families and other adults.

Strongly agree   Strongly disagree

INSTRUCTION B. Gather the responses and chart the consensus view of each group on the "opinion horseshoes." Chart your own response to each question and add it to each horseshoe (you should have 14).

EXAMPLE:

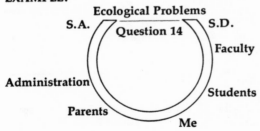

INSTRUCTION C. In your Journal, complete this sentence: (1) "From the relationship horseshoe I discovered . . ."

There are many variables in this strategy. You may wish to vary the small group size or makeup by mixing students, teachers, administrators, and parents together or add questions that question relationship patterns and structures in your school with more specific topics. For instance, if your school has a multiracial or multicultural student mix, questions should deal directly with issues common to those groups, such as, "In this school, teachers give respect and recognition to the racial/cultural heritage of Indian Americans" (or whatever racial, cultural, ethnic groups are represented). If the exercise is used exclusively with students, or if the climate is conducive to open discussion among students, faculty, parents, and administrators, a discussion should follow the posting (use newsprint) of the horseshoes. You should moderate the discussion.

Group Roles

In order to acquire the skills that will help students work more effectively in problem-solving groups that are dependent upon cooperative relationships, you must spend some time observing the behaviors that individuals adopt in a group situation. You can communicate your observations to the groups or to the individuals, whichever is necessary to help students improve their group skills.

The Dictator — dominates the group, constantly interrupts to give the correct answer, insists on maintaining her or his point of view, pouts when challenged.

The Compromiser — attempts to resolve arguments by synthesizing polar points of view, suggests alternate positions, coordinates process of reaching the goal.

The Arguer — loves to fight, will take opposite position of the group majority just for the joy of battle.

The Clarifier — raises questions, examines all different points of view with consequences and obstacles relevant to each.

The Isolate — withdraws from active participation, may listen or may dream, but says as little as possible, may respond to a direct question.

The Doubter — constantly raises questions of a theoretical nature, "yes, but what if . . .?"

Seldom contributes helpful movement to the group goal.

The Defender — rallies to the support of individuals placed on a hot seat, provides comfort, respect, and warmth.

The Follower — a "yes" person who relies on everyone else to think, moves with the majority.

The Attacker — challenges ideas and personalities, can cause deeper thinking or bruised feelings.

The Orator — loves to talk, but says nothing that helps the group.

Side-Tracker — never stays on the point, especially skilled at changing the point when the issue gets hot, avoids all tension.

The Destroyer — will hold side conversation, walk around, make wisecracks, or use any means to destroy group unity.

INSTRUCTION A. Make a chart that lists the *good* and *bad* characteristics of each role. Give a number to the name of each person in the group. (Keep groups small when you first observe.) As you observe group behaviors (note the plural — seldom will one student exhibit only one behavior), match the student's number on the chart noting the appropriate behavior.

EXAMPLE: THE DEFENDER

Good Reactions I Observed	Exhibited by Students #	Destructive Reactions I Observed	Exhibited by Students #
Support student being attacked	3, 5, 3, 1	Over-protective	3, 1, 1
Verbal comfort given	3, 1, 3, 1, 5	Defensive posture	4, 2, 1, 4
Prevented scape-goating attack	2, 3	Verbal attack	4, 4
Warm smile to defensive student	1, 3, 3	Scapegoating	4
etc.			

Developing Group Relationships

Group relationships are formed with great care and much apprehension. Time is an essential ingredient. Pressuring the development of relationships in learning groups is more disastrous than trying to bake a pie quickly by turning up the oven to 950°. Your eye, enriched by experience, will give you the sensitivity to recognize the stages of development through which group relationships evolve. No group will evolve in the same way, at the same pace, or to the same degree. Some will flop 100 percent. Your support and care, however, will help, especially in the beginning stages, or when a group regresses, as all do, into an earlier stage.

STAGE 1: *Who's running this ship?* Imagine the presidents of GM, Ford, DuPont, and GE forming a group to institute industrial reform. Used to exercising powerful control, each would insist on being ship's captain. In practice, every group begins with a battle for control. The defensive scoffers will assume that you have abandoned ship. Their untrained eye will have missed the *more* demanding, more intensive leadership that you provide to help each group succeed at its task. The teacher who acts as a learning facilitator does not abandon responsibility for curriculum and instructional leadership; instead she or he makes skilled use of those learning tools and strategies that research has demonstrated are most effective. Simply stated, between the extremes of moral authoritarianism that dictates how and what all must learn, and *laissez-faire* abandonment that naively lets everyone "do their thing," there exists a third alternative, that of the clarifying helper who understands and practices creative learning techniques.

STAGE 2. *Cooperation.* When members of the group acknowledge that their task goals are more readily attained by synergetic effort — the cooperative union of skills — they can differentiate roles according to talent and group need. At this stage the seeds of trust, mutual respect, and personal responsibility begin to form. This is the crucial time in the group's formation. Any group can survive as an amalgamation of individuals ruled by an authority figure, but the cooperative group requires what Fromm calls "individual inner strength." Unless each individual has the courage and capacity to carry her or his own responsibility, unless each member has "gotten her or his head together" to work within the group consensus, the group will collapse. When Tom agrees to record the finances or Sue to lead the Wednesday discussion, that commitment weighs far more heavily than mere obedience to a teacher's command.

The failure to meet commitments will strain the group at this stage. Strong members will revert to control and evasion tactics. "Teacher, give us the assignments. Tell us what to do," or "John and Mary always do their jobs. Let them run the group," or "Just tell me what to do and I'll do it. If you don't put me under a threat, I won't perform." The resolve at this point must focus on helping individuals who lack that inner strength rather than on the group's goals. How can helping-sharing relationships provide the support needed? What strategies can the group learn from the teacher-helper so that each member *feels* wanted, necessary, even indispensable?

STAGE 3. *Intimacy.* The more deeply the group involves itself in the cooperative effort, the less it will need to rely on your facilitating skills. You will know that the group has entered the third stage when the group no longer needs your input. Rather than feel rejected, you should recognize that the group has achieved the internal cohesion it needs to stand alone. Although you may receive an invitation to suggest materials or give formal evaluations, recognize that the independence was caused by the group's successful attainment of a caring-sharing relationship. As that relationship deepens, you will find yourself more and more an "outsider," welcome only by invitation.

STAGE 4. *Dissolution.* Time and circumstances such as graduation, end of semester, or a family move will eventually force a group to dissolve itself. As the facilitator, you will need to help the members with "reentry." As in each stage, your main function is to help the group examine its own processes and to draw conclusions applicable to new situations. You are the mirror of the group's learning, not only of the formal content, but also of the relationships it has created.

Organize your class into groups. Plan for each group to work together at least one class period each week for a two-month period. Allow groups to self-select membership, but make sure that all students are included in a group of four to six students.

SESSION I: Reintroduce the brainstorm strategy. Review brainstorming rules.

(a) Have each group select one problem from a hat or box.

_____find five new uses for (1) an empty shoe box, (2) a wine bottle, (3) a broken TV. Record ideas.

_____Find ten ways to improve the kitchen knife.

_____Find ten ways to improve this class.

_____Find ten ways to improve the lunchroom.

_____Find ten ways to improve the basketball team.

_____Find ten ways to improve TV for kids.

_____Find five ways to (a) make money, (b) spend money, (c) save money.

(b) After each group has selected a task, allow three minutes to define the problem. Tell the groups to agree on understanding the task. Signal the time.

(c) Brainstorm possible solutions under the suspended-judgment rule. Allow five minutes.

(d) Examine each suggestion for all its good and bad properties. Decide which properties would make this suggestion helpful to the final solution. Allow 15 to 20 minutes.

(e) Rank order your solutions. Redefine the problem in the light of the top priority. Allow 5 minutes.

(f) Have groups process their activity. Allow ten minutes.
   1. What difficulties hindered the group at each step?
   2. Who played which roles? What destructive strategems appeared? How were they resolved?
   3. What parts of the process worked well? Why?
   4. What relationships did you perceive among group members? How can these relationships be strengthened?

(g) Process the activity with a class discussion of each group's strong and weak points.

SESSION II. Reassemble the groups and repeat the think-cap strategy used in Session I. Before the groups begin, have each one review the self-processing that concluded the first session.

SESSION III. Reassemble the groups. Give each group a dictionary and have each select a problem from the Session I list and complete steps (a) and (b) of that Session.

(c) Instruct each group to select five words at random from the dictionary. Beginning with the first word, see what words, images, phrases, and feelings are ignited by its association with the problem. Defer judgment and record all responses. Repeat the procedure with each word and allow ideas to build through association and spring-boarding. Allow 15 minutes.

(d) Using the listed results of step (c), create three or four possible solutions to the problem. Work by consensus. Allow 15 minutes.

(e) Process the group relationships in this session. What improvements are evident? Allow five to ten minutes.

SESSION IV. Continue the problem begun in Session III. Begin with (a) a review of the process content, and (b) a review of process evaluation. Allow five minutes.

(f) Chart the proposed solutions on a continuum. (Use the newsprint and magic markers.)

1	2	3	4	5

(g) Brainstorm the advantages and disadvantages of each proposed solution. Allow 15 to 20 minutes.

(h) Rank order the solutions. Give top priority to the solution which the group agrees is the *most imaginative*. Post worksheets and selections.

(i) Process group procedures. Identify problem areas in the group's relationships. Allow ten minutes.

SESSION V-VI. Reassemble the groups. Give each group a dictionary, newsprint and magic markers.

(a) Define the relationship problem that most hindered the group in completing its tasks in Sessions III-IV.

(b) Randomly select five words from the dictionary. Brainstorm associations with each word *as that word relates* to the group's relationship problem. Create several possible solutions. Make a continuum and discuss the advantages — disadvantages of each proposed solution. Rank order by group consensus.

(c) Process the group procedures and examine its relationships. Compare group interpersonal relationships of the first session with those now established.

(d) Make a group contract to discuss "unfinished business" over lunch.

SESSION VII: *Creating from Junk.* In this session, the established groups can firm up their relationships and prepare to work at a subject matter task. Begin by asking each group to gather *for itself* these materials:

string, rope, thread	rubber bands
paper cups, bowls, plates	toothpicks
rubber glue	cloth scraps
styrofoam cups	wallpaper
small boxes	paper clips
pencils, crayons, magic markers, chalk	wood
rulers	newsprint
wire	nails, tacks, staples
rods	cardboard
construction paper	egg crates
old pictures	plastic freezer
magazines	containers
buttons, beads	and so on

Remind the group that it made some internal commitments regarding relationships. Review those relationships and decide responsibilities for this task.

Pile the materials on a table or desk. Instruct groups to create an objet d'art from the junk. (You may wish to structure the exercise more rigidly by calling for a specific art form such as a mobile or sculpture.) Allow 25 minutes for the construction.

After the construction is complete, instruct the groups to process the activity:

1. How successfully did the group accomplish its creative task? Evaluate the completed work.

2. How successfully did the group accomplish its agreed upon process goals?

3. To what extent was the group successful in maintaining a support climate and a creative atmosphere?

4. What effect did the task have on relationships within the group?

By this time the groups should have identified control issues. They are now prepared with the skills and basic relationships to work on content tasks related to the subject matter of your course. As the groups work on each task, include the following guidelines:

1. Begin each task with a review of the interrelationship goals established after the previous task.

2. Conclude each task with evaluation of the product and the process. Use guides from previous sessions.

The Facilitating Teacher in a Support Climate

As the groups function more and more independently of your control, you may wonder about your role in the classroom. As students learn to define their intragroup roles, you will see coordination, support, resource expertise, and critical evaluation tasks move from your grasp to theirs. What do you do?

Carl Rogers contrasts traditional teaching, which he calls the "mug and jug" method to the facilitative approach which might be called the "climate control" method. The mug and jug teacher is concerned with holding the mug in place long enough to fill it with facts from the jug; the climate control teacher is concerned with creating a creative atmosphere and finding the resources that will enable the learner to feel free to master, to experience, and to discover. The former uses grades, rules, and normative standards to mold the student; the latter seeks techniques, strategies, and tools that will help each student discover, use, and evaluate inherent talents. In place of a control-role, the facilitator teacher builds an atmosphere of trust, support, and creative discovery.

The helper teacher listens sensitively to ideas, values, and feelings.

The helper teacher shares feelings, values, ideas, and skills.

The helper teacher accepts each individual's total person as it is without judgment.

The helper teacher encourages participant involvement.

The helper teacher provides learning based on real choices.

The helper teacher responds to wants, needs, and concerns.

The helper teacher focuses learning on processes as well as products.

The helper teacher co-participates in all activities.

To encourage the environment of trust and support, the facilitating teacher will help the learners grow in their concern and respect for each other. As groups improve their skills, they can be introduced *inductively* to several *rules* which the teacher has practiced daily:

(a) *The Pass Rule* — each individual decides when, where, how, and to what extent she or he will become involved in any learning activity. If the student chooses to bypass an answer, an activity or strategy, that is the student's prerogative. The support climate says, "You are capable of deciding. Therefore, decide."

(b) *The Respect Rule* — each student respects the quantity and quality of every remark made by each person in the classroom. In turn, the child *feels* the respect given to her/his ideas, feelings, and comments.

(c) *The Focus Rule* — every day, each student receives the opportunity to be the focus of attention for a designated period of comment. A support teacher uses a variety of strategies to make the focus times significant moments of learning.

(d) *The Compliment Rule* — positive reinforcement (giving compliments) is crucial to the support climate. Each child is expected to observe polite amenities and acknowledge successes of peers. In turn, each can expect both peers and teacher to acknowledge her or his successes. Negative comments, sarcasm, and harsh criticism, especially from the adult, have the same effect on the learner as a pinprick has on an amoeba.

(e) *The Honesty Rule* — false compliments hurt more than lies. Basic to a trusting relationship is the expectation that all interpersonal transactions will be honest, open, and straightforward.

The Creative Atmosphere

The creative act cannot be dictated; it must spring full-blown from the individual. This does not mean, however, that the teacher cannot encourage creativity. Research has shown that creativity is most prone to appear in situations in which the facilitator establishes an atmosphere which gives highest value to imaginative and original problem solving.

Atmosphere Assessment

INSTRUCTION A. Complete this assessment by a double rank order. Within each group, first rank the items according to what you think *should* happen in your classroom. Second, rank the items to describe what *does happen* in your classroom. After you have given yourself this test, ask the class to rank you and/or itself.

	Should	Does
1. Student relationships work best with		
competition	———	———
cooperation	———	———
isolation.	———	———
2. I feel most positive about students who		
challenge ideas	———	———
accept and obey	———	———
reject all order.	———	———
3. To solve a problem, the best tool is		
a rational mind	———	———
a mind free of all controls	———	———
an imaginative mind.	———	———
4. In group work I encourage		
trusting feelings	———	———
organizing plans	———	———
following instructions.	———	———
5. I think creativity is best judged		
on the basis of the product	———	———
as a process	———	———
on the basis of established talent.	———	———
6. I think creativity is best fostered in an		
atmosphere of some tension	———	———
atmosphere of support-trust	———	———
atmosphere of much stress.	———	———

INSTRUCTION B. Complete this sentence in your Journal: "In my classroom, I am pleased that I . . ."

The number and variety of strategies which will help to build the support climate, enhance trust relationships, and encourage creative thought are legion. Rather than isolate each strategy which will help you or your students to understand the numerous concepts outlined in this chapter, you will find it more valuable to apply some principles of creative self-direction to your own learning.

Processing This Chapter

PURPOSE: _____

_____

_____

FEELINGS: _____

_____

_____

CONCEPTS: _____

_____

_____

APPLICATIONS: _____

_____

_____

_____

_____

He who knows
nothing, loves nothing.
He who can do nothing
is worthless.
But he who understands
also loves, notices, sees . . .
Paracelsus

Deciding

Personal Preferences

INSTRUCTION A. Make a choice between the two preferences in each question. Circle your choice.

I am more

1. a thinker — a doer
2. an extrovert — an introvert
3. a carrot — a stick
4. a smiler — a frowner
5. a picker — a pickee
6. a tiger — a pussycat
7. self-assured — insecure

I prefer to

8. avoid causes — fight battles
9. lead — follow
10. help others do for themselves — do for others
11. rank priorities — confuse priorities
12. select from alternatives — ignore alternatives
13. avoid choices — make choices
14. move with the flow — act decisively

INSTRUCTION B. Make an entry in your Journal. Complete this sentence, "When it comes to choices, I usually . . ."

Discovering Choices

INSTRUCTION A. As you have noticed, the strategies and exercises you have used encourage you to make choices. On this chart, check the boxes after each entry that apply to the choices you have made.

I freely choose to	YES	NO	SOME-TIMES
read this book	——	——	——
read the strategies	——	——	——
try the strategies myself	——	——	——
lead individual students through strategies	——	——	——
try strategies with small groups	——	——	——
keep a Journal	——	——	——
make up my own strategies	——	——	——
share the book with a friend.	——	——	——

INSTRUCTION B. List the strategies or exercises in this book that helped you or your students to make meaningful decisions.

1. _____
2. _____
3. _____
4. _____
5. _____
6. _____
7. _____
8. _____
9. _____
10. _____

Personal decision making is integrally related with the thinking and valuing processes. The thinking processes help the decision maker to understand WHAT and HOW. The valuing processes help the decision maker to understand WHY?

Assessing Thinking Processes

How do your think? Are you aware of your own thinking style? of the patterns you have established for problem solving? for inquiry? for organizing? for creating?

When you think about thinking, you most likely focus attention on the inductive and deductive processes which you mastered in school.

Inducing

STEP 1. DEFINE THE PROBLEM (This water looks polluted; this horse appears dead; this man seems to be dead.)

STEP 2. GATHER THE EVIDENCE. (Water samples, vital life signs, clues.)

STEP 3. STUDY THE EVIDENCE. (99 out of 100 samples show excess microbes; there are no vital signs in the horse; there is a knife in the man's back and a broken window nearby.)

STEP 4. DRAW A CONCLUSION FROM THE EVIDENCE. (pollution! dead! murder!)

Deducing

STEP 1. MAKE A GENERAL STATEMENT. (A triangle has three connected sides.)

STEP 2. PROVIDE SPECIFIC EVIDENCE. (This figure B has three connected sides.)

STEP 3. DRAW CONCLUSION. (Figure B is a triangle.)

The inductive and deductive processes are visible, although not explicit, in any well-taught classroom. In biology or chemistry labs the students investigate the world of science. They carry out the prescribed experiments inductively. In literature, the students analyze famous books in order to induce an author's main ideas. In algebra and geometry, students construct syllogisms by the deductive model; in English composition they write deductively organized essays.

More Choices

INSTRUCTION A. This is a multiple choice strategy. Circle the answer that best describes your thought patterns.

1. **In my thinking, I usually think**
   (a) inductively; (b) deductively; (c) a combination of the two; (d) I don't think.

2. **In my teaching, I present material**
   (a) inductively; (b) deductively; (c) in a combination of the two.

3. **I encourage students to improve**
   (a) inductive skills; (b) deductive skills; (c) both.

4. **The strategies in this book are examples of**
   (a) induction; (b) deduction; (c) both.

5. **This book is organized**
   (a) inductively; (b) deductively; (c) both

By definition, a patterned thought process has several limitations. As patterns, induction and deduction are *closed* processes which operate in a lockstep sequence. Once the sequence begins, the process follows step-by-step in a controlled, logical order which locks out information of concepts not *previously* judged as integral. The fault at each step of these processes is found in this lock out *based on prior judgment.* Review, for instance, the inductive process:

STEP 1. Define the problem. Define connotes "limit," "narrow," "distinguish," or "select," all of which instruct the problem-solver to filter or narrow thoughts to that which fits or adjusts within a conceptual framework.

STEP 2. Gather the evidence. The only valid evidence is that which fits the definition. Since the definition has established the control parameters, only information which *clearly fits* under the defined categories is worth consideration. It is, therefore, very easy *to reject* any information that does not clearly and exactly fit the already narrow definition agreed upon before the process began.

STEP 3. Study the evidence. Once again, prior selection is implied.

These limitations do not suggest that either the deductive or inductive process is "bad." Both induction and deduction are essential to most learning situations. What the limitations do suggest, however, is that thinking involves much more than the categorizing-refining-defining thrust that induction and deduction both require. That "much more" consists of exploratory thinking processes which thrive under suspended or deferred judgment. Without the control imposed by prejudgment, exploratory thinking frees the mind to create alternatives that the closed deductive-inductive definition would easily pass by without notice.

Both the inductive and deductive processes can be enriched by exploratory thinking. In essence, exploratory thinking is a preamble. Before refinement, before definition, before categorization come spin-offs, brainstorms, random exploration, and any activity that will cause the mind to reach out and *make* new possibilities which the thinker may include in the definition, the evidence, or the conclusion being formed.

Exploratory Strategies I've Used

INSTRUCTION A. List in your Journal 10 to 15 exploratory strategies you have read about or used in this book. Exploratory strategies have these qualities:

    (a) A quantity of responses are encouraged

    (b) Quality judgments are suspended

    (c) Spin-offs, trades, random searches, and other cooperative tactics are encouraged

    (d) They are open-ended.

Random-Word Brainstorming

HOW CAN I MAKE SOMETHING FROM NOTHING?

INSTRUCTION A. Use this strategy with your class. Divide the class into *two* teams. Team A will observe in round one and perform in round two. Team B will use the opposite pattern.

Instruct Team A to select *ten* words from the dictionary. The team should use the *random* method. List the *ten* words on the blackboard and gather team A in a semicircle around the list. Instruct the team to *brainstorm* all thoughts or images that they can construct for each word. (One or two team members should record the responses.) Allow three to five minutes on each word. *When brainstorming, exploratory thinking will focus on the problem: how can I make something from nothing?* All responses initiated by each random word should deal with that problem. Keep brainstorming until the given time has elapsed.

Instruct Team B to observe Team A, and list behaviors that are exhibited. Team A should *NOT* see this list.

Checklist

(If you see the members of the other team thinking in a way that is listed, make a mark for each incident.)

Made a positive comment about another's idea _____

Made a negative comment about another's idea

_____

Used one idea in combination with another _____

Used one idea to spark a second idea _____

Helped others make ideas _____

Stuck to the tried and true _____

Invented a new word or object _____

Withheld judgment _____

Made many suggestions _____

INSTRUCTION B. After round one is finished, reverse the tasks. Let Team B conduct the random search and Team A observe.

INSTRUCTION C. Before discussing the *products* of the brainstorming, consider the behaviors observed.

1. Which behaviors on the check list were conducive to open-ended thinking and which were a hindrance?

2. Which helpful behaviors did each team show?

INSTRUCTION D. Instruct each team to synthesize the brainstorming results by forming three or four solutions to the problem, "How can I make something out of nothing?" (If the first two rounds were not productive enough, the teams might use two additional rounds to get more ideas.) Give 20 to 30 minutes for this activity. At the end of the time ask each team to self-evaluate its process. Use the checklist from above and then these questions:

1. How successful were we in finding solutions?

2. How open-ended was the process in contrast to the brainstorming? What did we do differently in this stage?

3. How do we suppose our solutions would have agreed or differed if we had *NOT* brainstormed with the random words?

4. What are the advantages/disadvantages of randon-word brainstorming?

Computhink

Efficiency ratings are computhink

Accountability is computhink

Grades are computhink

Standardized tests are computhink

Memory exams are computhink

Behavioral objectives are computhink

Tracks and levels are computhink

* Computhink is the belief that objectivity is the standard by which a "quality education" is measured.

In Computhink

_____A school is an assembly line to mass-produce a 3R product.

_____Boards of education represent the stockholders. Their motto: "getting better readers through accountability controls."

_____Administrators are quality control supervisors.

_____Teachers run the assembly line.

_____Behavioral objectives establish clear efficiency standards.

_____Tests and exams are the optical scanners plugged to the computer to avoid human error. The scanners measure products for placement.

_____Tracks and levels are the assembly lines that separate prestige models from the economy lines

_____The computer, operating efficiently without human error caused by subjective judgment, stamps a grade on each finished product and reports product deficiencies to the accountability supervisor, the director of personnel.

Objectivity

INSTRUCTION A. **Mark each scale at the spot that reveals your position on the statement.**

1. **My grading is the result of an objective assessment of student performance.**

Strongly agree   Strongly disagree

2. **My tests are objective measures of what students have learned.**

Strongly agree   Strongly disagree

3. **Students who think without feeling achieve higher grades on my tests.**

Strongly agree   Strongly disagree

4. **Responses 1 through 3 in this strategy were based on factual, objective evidence.**

Strongly agree   Strongly disagree

5. **What I value in the learning process has no bearing on student grades.**

Strongly agree   Strongly disagree

6. **My feelings and values influence how I think.**

Strongly agree   Strongly disagree

7. **My feelings and values influence what I think about.**

Strongly agree   Strongly disagree

8. **By clarifying my values and examining my feelings, I can better control my thinking.**

Strongly agree   Strongly disagree

9. **By understanding how I think, I can better understand my values.**

Strongly agree   Strongly disagree

Valuing

Valuing is a process inextricably interwoven with thinking and feeling.

Thinking = Problem solving
Valuing = Deciding importance
Feeling = Accepting inclinations

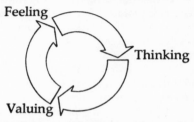

Thinking helps us to solve problems that we feel are important; feeling inclines us to respond to personal needs important to the problem; valuing helps us to establish priorities among our feelings so that we can decide how to solve the problem in a way that suits our needs.

PROBLEM:

How do we rescue my cat from the neighbor's tree?			
Think about possible solutions and consequences	_I climb ladder_	_I leave cat_	_I call animal warden_
	I break a leg	cat freezes	I get fined
Identify feelings	I'm scared	I'm concerned	I'm frustrated
Clarify values	most important that I don't break leg	moderately important	least important

SOLUTION: Call the animal warden.

Valuing Is Thinking Is Feeling

We Are Proud

How free is your school from racist and sexist stereotyping? How often do you contribute to a child's negative self-image by ignoring or degrading her or his ethnic or social heritage? How many of your students are proud to acknowledge their background and culture?

INSTRUCTION A. List the title of every ethnic or racial group represented in your class. Write across the board Asian American, Polish American, Black American, or whatever designations the students give you for their own groups.

INSTRUCTION B. Divide the class into self-selected groups. Each group will center its attention on the heritage of one listed nationality or racial background. Present the problem with careful instructions that groups must observe the valuing steps outlined above. Finally, present the problem: (1) Who are we, and (2) why are we proud of our origin? (The student group will solve the problem by assuming the identity of the racial or ethnic group that was selected.) As part of the solution, each group must demonstrate its answers to the two questions. Here are some possibilities for demonstration: (1) Paint a mural on a wall or newsprinted bulletin board. Show scenes, faces, and words that depict the reasons you are proud. (2) Construct and administer a survey test to find out what other persons in your school or community know about famous persons from your "proud group." (3) Write and illustrate a magazine with ads, stories, drawings, etc., for your "proud group." (4) Make a film, videotape, or audiotape about the historic contributions of the "proud group." (5) Produce a play about famous representatives from the "proud group." (6) Devise your own demonstration.

INSTRUCTION C. After the demonstrations have been completed, gather the groups in a circle to process their work.

(a) How are feelings, values, and thinking interrelated?

(b) In this strategy, how were the thinking, feeling, valuing processes improved?

(c) What did individuals learn about their own feelings, thoughts, and values? (The pass rule applies.)

INSTRUCTION D. At this point there are several options.

(a) Begin a new round of "proud groups." Have students select a new group.

(b) Bring closure on the discussion by using "thought-feel" closure cards. Give each student a 3x5 index card. On one side students will write a thought about the "proud group" discussion. On the other side they will write a feeling. No names. Collect the cards and read responses back to the class.

Valuing Is Deciding

Choices are made in the context of feelings, thoughts, and values. A person who controls these processes will respond to self-assessed needs and make decisions that will enhance her or his personal growth. The more positive an individual feels about the ability to control decisions that affect her or his personal growth, the more capable and sure that individual feels in deciding to act on those values, feelings, and thoughts. For instance, if Jimmy Thompson's self-image tells him that school has no value, that life is hopeless, and that his only recourse is escape from pressure, Jimmy will fall into a pattern of helpless escapism — drugs or alcohol or delinquency. On the other hand, if Jimmy feels respect for himself, he will reflect that feeling by making choices that further enhance his self-respect. If that means selecting a course of study which will prepare him as a carpenter, he will do what is necessary to complete that course; if it means medical school, he will select the courses and practice the discipline required; if it means touring Europe, Jimmy will make those choices that will guarantee his goal. In essence, the degree of meaning *felt* by an individual determines what is valued; what *is valued* determines the choices made. When the choice brings success, the feelings are enhanced and the learner has strengthened her or his self-image. The more positive the self-image, the more assured the choices.

Implications

INSTRUCTION A. List five statements that reveal your thinking about relationships among values, feelings, self-images, and choices. In columns 2 and 3, check boxes which apply to you. In column 4, give a specific example of a practice you have used in class to illustrate the statement.

1 STATE- MENT	2 I agree strongly	3 I practice regularly	4 Example
1.			
2.			
3.			
4.			
5.			

INSTRUCTION B. Ask your students to assess you. Give each a copy of the chart with the statements column filled in. Compare their charts with yours. In your Journal, draw conclusions from the comparison.

Degree of Decision Making

INSTRUCTION A. Complete each sentence three times, ranking from the most appropriate (#1) to the least appropriate (#3).

1. In my classroom I feel that *I should*
   ____encourage individuals to make choices
   ____allow individuals to make choices
   ____help individuals to make choices
   about their own learning.

2. In my classroom, *I do*
   ____allow individuals to make choices
   ____encourage individuals to make choices
   ____help individuals to make choices
   about their own learning.

3. In my classroom I
   ____structure group activities which require group decision-making skills
   ____structure group activities which facilitate the learning of group decision-making skills
   ____help groups structure and process the decision-making skills they use.

4. In my classroom, I help students master decision-making skills by
   ____planning strategies for individuals
   ____planning strategies for small groups
   ____planning strategies for the class to facilitate these skills.

5. In my classroom, I help students apply decision-making skills
   ____in activities planned and structured by me
   ____in activities totally planned and structured by students
   ____by sharing equally with them the planning and structuring of activities.

6. In my classroom, I help students use decision-making skills
   ____in curricular choices
   ____in instructional style
   ____in material selection.

7. Outside my classroom, I believe students in my school
   ____should have greater choice in extracurricular matters that affect their learning
   ____should vote on student-teacher-administrator planning committees for curriculum and instruction
   ____should participate in the disciplinary processes of the school by having a full voice in all judgments and punishments given to students.

8. Outside my classroom, I believe students in my school should
   ____take greater responsibility in the *enforcement* of Board policies that affect students (hall duty, etc.)
   ____receive the opportunity to help formulate Board policies that affect students
   ____have no participation by enforcement or by formulation of policy.

Valuing Is Acting

If not acted upon, value-decisions have no value. If you or a student claims a value without acting on it — "honesty," "full student involvement," "being responsible" — it is a dead gesture, the "words without meaning" which T. S. Eliot refers to in "The Hollow Men." The test of valuing is acting on those values with consistency and intensity. If a school administrator tells a state senate committee: "The major cause of the vandalism and drug abuse that have inundated our school is the low self-esteem, the meaning-lessness which the students find there, the inability to find any reason for attending . . ." and then returns to his desk to comment on a community-based grading committee's recommendation to abolish grades: "I recognize your arguments. I agree with the theory that grades destroy self-image. But we need grades to keep good records for colleges and employers. Sorry." No change is possible; the asserted concerns are a front, not a value.

A Final Assessment

INSTRUCTION A. For each item listed, give a grade in each column that follows the item. Grades will be determined by you in response to these questions. Add others to the list if you wish.

Column I: To what extent do I feel this value is important to me?

Column II: To what extent do I act on this value consistently and intensely?

Column III: To what extent do I help students act on this value consistently and intensely in their learning?

Column IV: To what extent do the school board and administration act consistently and intensely to implement this value for faculty or students?

Your Scale: Very Much — A Sporadically — D
Much — B Never — F
Somewhat — C

Proclaimed Value	I	II	III	IV
building trust				
assessing needs				
building positive self-image				
controlling my life				
establishing my identity				
strengthening relationships				
mastering content/basic skills				
clarifying values				
improving thinking skills				
getting in touch with feelings				
learning how to set goals				
seeking resources				
self-evaluating				
becoming self-directed				
acting on values				

Self-Contract

INSTRUCTION A. Complete this self-contract in your Journal. Examine the Final Assessment chart and draw conclusions. Find several values which you claim are important to you and devise a plan to put those values in action. Write out the self-contract. Check up on yourself at the completion date.

SELF-CONTRACT
Name_____Date_____
What value claimed_____
What I will do _____

Completion date_____

Processing This Chapter

PURPOSES:_____

_____

_____

_____

_____

FEELINGS:_____

_____

_____

_____

CONCEPTS:_____

_____

_____

_____

APPLICATIONS:_____

_____

_____

_____

America is like a student who is proud of having somehow survived without serious work, and likes to imagine that if he really put any effort into it he could achieve everything, but is unwilling to endanger so lovely a dream by making an actual commitment to anything.

Philip W. Slater,
The Pursuit of Loneliness

8 Setting Goals

"Teenagers are totally unrealistic."
"She hasn't got the faintest idea what she wants."
"He walks around in a daze."
"Kids don't know what they want."

How often have you heard similar frustrations aired? Think about your students. How many fit the description of "lost souls" wandering aimlessly through life? Is there a greater or lesser number of adults whom you know who live without purpose or direction? If there's a difference, how do you account for it? What about yourself? Are you going in any direction? How firmly do you control what happens to you? The way you feel and think and act? What and how you learn? . . .

A REFLECTION ON A SUMMER'S DAY

INSTRUCTION A. Relax and make yourself comfortable. Close your eyes and concentrate on your internal self. Get in touch with your breathing . . . listen to the rhythm of your body as you inhale and exhale . . . Concentrate on your feelings . . . focus on now. Imagine that you are walking alone down a quiet deserted road, hear the crunch of gravel under your feet . . . feel the warmth of the sun on your neck . . . hear the sounds in the fields . . . notice the colors . . . return inside yourself . . . to your feelings as you walk . . . what are your reactions as you pass the wild flowers? . . . as you watch the white clouds billow against the blue sky? . . . as a fly buzzes around your head? . . . as roadside poplars sway in the slight breeze? . . . as you wave casually to the farmer jockeying his combine down the narrow furrows? . . . what is his reaction to you? . . . stop to chat with him . . . tell him why you are walking down the road . . . what is his response . . . talk about his obligations . . . why is he out working on such a beautiful summer day? . . . if he had a chance, would he trade places with you? . . . would he choose some other way to live? . . . tell him why you are out walking today instead of working . . . do you have a destination, someplace you are going, or somebody you want to see? . . . or are you out to enjoy what you can see and smell and feel as you walk? . . . or are you getting exercise? . . . does this walk fill some other need? . . . after you have talked awhile, say goodbye and head back down the road . . . what's the difference now? . . . what new feelings are you experiencing after your talk with the farmer on his tractor? . . . can you see any consistent pattern in your purposes? . . . how do you respond to felt needs? . . . are you a precise preplanner who maps out each detail? . . . do you point yourself to a specific end? . . . a place to go? . . . a person to meet? . . . an object to acquire or a product to complete? . . . or do you focus on the rich experience, the joy of doing? . . . or do you react on the spur of the moment, enjoy the moment, and move on? . . . recall other instances which reflect your pattern . . . what made you feel good about those experiences? . . . dissatisfied? . . . how do you feel about your pattern? . . . what concerns you? . . . what makes you feel pleased? . . . proud? . . . savor an experience that made you feel good about your way of doing what you want . . . as you reflect, continue your walk until you arrive at your destination.

INSTRUCTION B. In each group, rank each statement according to which most accurately describes your practical use or nonuse of goals. *Apply all statements to yourself, based on the reflection you just completed.*

1. ____I always set my goals in response to felt needs.
   ____I sometimes set my goals in response to felt needs.
   ____I never set my goals in response to felt needs.

2. ____I feel that goal setting is essential to my learning.
   ____I feel that goal setting is a waste of my time.
   ____I feel that goal setting can help me learn.

3. ____A goal is more effective if the individual sets it for herself/himself.
   ____A goal is more effective if a knowledgeable person, such as a teacher, sets the goal.
   ____Goals have no effect on learning.

4. ____Roles are more important than goals.
   ____Goals are more important than roles.
   ____Roles result from goals.

5. ____The experience of reaching a goal is more important than the goal itself.
   ____The goal is more important than the product which results.
   ____The product is more important than the experience.

INSTRUCTION C. Mail yourself a telegram. Announce what you have discovered about yourself and your goal-setting pattern.

TO:

FROM:

RE: MY GOAL-SETTING PATTERNS

In addition to your patterns and attitudes toward goal setting, most likely you have recognized some of the key problems that are involved.

1. *When is a goal most helpful to learning?* It is not important that you formalize a goal in a written contract by stating what you plan to accomplish, how you plan to accomplish it, and the method of measurement. The contract, either with yourself or a second party, merely provides a written commitment that reminds you of your intent. In the traditional climate of distrust that pervades a highly competitive school, contracts are perverted so that the paper statements outweigh the goals, the products, and the experiences of learning. As a device *to help students and teachers organize a learning experience* or *to keep clear records of who is learning what,* the contract has a valuable function; the contract, however, is not the goal.

As a first step in learning how to set goals, it is helpful to differentiate the *types* of goals that are most suitable to each learner's pattern.

The Type-Choice Ladder

INSTRUCTION A. Read each description given below.

a. **The goal as a product.** Artists, composers, carpenters conclude with a product. Some students receive most satisfaction by setting products as a tangible end result.

b. **The goal as process.** "Learning for the sake of learning," "sailing because I love it" and similar statements indicate an individual whose goal is the enjoyment of participating in an action or process.

c. **The goal as prize.** The race car driver, the professional tennis star, and the owner of a racing stable compete in order to win a prize — a ribbon, money, or a headline.

d. **The goal as acquired skill or knowledge.** The student who learns to type 40/wpm or to use a slide rule or to list three causes of the Civil War has mastered taught material.

e. **The goal as place.** Ulysses and Aeneas wandered around the Mediterranean world before each found a homeland. For Ulysses, the place was a precise, well-remembered location — his home island, Ithaca. For Aeneas it was a dream, a promise of the gods, which was reached on the shores of Italy.

f. **The goal as personal identification.** "Who I am?" "searching for my identity," "getting my head together" are frequent explanations by today's young people who try to characterize their goals. Some, disillusioned by political charlatanism of the late '60's and early '70s, others beleaguered by the false authoritarianism of mass media, make role-identification their goal. Theirs is a search for personal meaning-values, beliefs, relationships, a positive self-image which is not a beautifully photographed, precisely edited supersell of "the real thing." It is their thing. The goal is a role.

g. **The goal as a personal relationship.** A couple who give themselves fully win each other's love, friends who are happiest sharing together, or parents who struggle to build strong family ties are examples of persons for whom the relationship itself — not the reward, not the product, not any other reason — is the prime goal.

INSTRUCTION B. When you have completed reading each type description, use the stepladder that follows to rank the five types that best characterize your learning style. No single type will divide itself precisely and absolutely from the others, so do not be disconcerted by any overlap. At the bottom rung, place the goal-type that most often characterizes your pattern of goal setting. Move up the ladder to the fifth rung where you will place the least characteristic type.

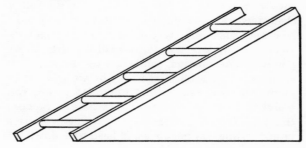

INSTRUCTION C. Write a letter to a friend. Describe what you have discovered about your own goal-setting patterns. Be sure to include one or two examples of goals you set and met that illustrate your most characteristic patterns.

When is a goal realistic? The sad tale of Icarus is well known. Enraptured by his father's dream that humans could fly, he stole away with the waxed wings Daedalus had created. The higher he flew, the more venturesome he became. He soared closer and closer to the sun, realizing too late that the sun's hot rays were melting the wax wings.

Unfortunately, the moral of Icarus' fall is too often used to dissuade adventurous minds from taking risks. "Be realistic; you can't possibly succeed." For whatever reason, the 20th century shortcoming is not Icarus' overreaching, but an excessive caution which avoids risk and dotes on security and conformity. "Better the astronauts risk their fool necks; I'll get my kicks watching splashdown on TV."

A goal is realistic when an individual, having weighed the positive and negative consequences of her or his action, her or his own capability, and her or his need, implements a plan to reach a goal. The infant who spies candy on a table will decide whether it wishes to take the first steps and walk to the candy. The stockbroker will choose to advise a client to sell; the client chooses whether to ignore the advice or not.

Alternate Strategies

Take a Chance

INSTRUCTION A. This is a game that requires moderate risk testing. Distribute or ask each student to give you 25¢. Sit the students in a circle and pile the money in the center. Make two piles worth $1, one worth $2, and scatter the rest inside a ring drawn on the floor.

Allow any student who wishes to withdraw the 25¢. Stress that this will be the last chance anyone has to get out of the game. If anyone takes out 25¢, she or he will not participate, but will keep the 25¢. Give no game instructions until each has decided about participation.

INSTRUCTION B. After the withdrawals are complete (don't disturb the $1 or $2 piles), give these instructions.

1. Each participant draws a number from a hat. The highest number will begin the game. The second highest will go second, and so on.

2. Blindfold all participants. Nonparticipants will help the blindfolded players sit around the money, outside the ring.

3. Give the first player a token marked #1. She/he will throw the token toward the area she/he thinks is the ring. Have each participant do the same with an appropriately numbered token.

4. After the last token is thrown, decide which one is closest to each money pile. Begin with the lowest amounts. A token must have the lowest amount and may only win one pile. Continue until all money is awarded.

INSTRUCTION C. Repeat the game. Allow students to enter any number of 5¢ pieces up to 25¢. For each 5¢ a student has one token. Make the piles in multiples of 5¢ with no more than 30¢ in any one pile.

1. Repeat the draw. If there are 20 participants, and number 1 has entered 15¢, he has tokens 1, 21, 41.

2. DO NOT BLINDFOLD ANYONE. Tokens may be tossed from any spot outside the ring.

3. Award money prizes in the same manner as above.

INSTRUCTION D. Seat the students in a circle and process the money toss.

1. Begin with a "I was most pleased when . . ." completion and whip clockwise until each student has completed the sentence or passed.

2. Repeat the whip with each of these completions: "I was most anxious when . . ." and "A difference between the two games which I felt was . . ."

3. Build on the sentence completions. As the discussion evolves, focus attention on these issues:
   Which game did you prefer?
   What risks were involved?
   How did you react to those risks?
   What planning did you do?
   What did you want to accomplish?
   What would you do differently given another opportunity?

INSTRUCTION A. Have each group hide the product somewhere in the school. They must next draw a treasure map with devious clues and obstacles to avoid. After all groups have completed maps and placed clues, exchange maps and send each group to find a "treasure."

INSTRUCTION B. Process the treasure hunt with the class. In the discussion (use either a large circle or keep the small groups), cover these points:

What was the goal you planned?

What other goals emerged to help you reach your main goal?

What obstacles did you meet?

How did you overcome the obstacles?

What were the frustrations? What were the successes?

How did the goals for making the map differ from those in the hunt?

What would you do differently to reach your goals if given another chance?

INSTRUCTION. Ask the students to relax and get comfortable. Have them concentrate on the quiet in the room. When their bodies are still and the room silent, begin the meditation. Talk softly and slowly. Allow sufficient time for your lead statements to create images and reactions.

Close your eyes . . . hear the quiet . . . get yourself quiet . . . imagine that you are climbing a steep mountain . . . you are searching for something that you have wanted a long time . . . your goal is now reasonably close . . . you may have a very clear idea of what it is and why it is important to you . . . what are some obstacles that are hindering you from getting to the top? . . . how do you get around these obstacles? . . . what alternatives are you using? . . . what changes occur in your plans? . . . what new information do you have about your goal? . . . can you see it more clearly? . . . as you reach the top, you find the object of your search . . . how do you feel about being on top of the mountain? . . . about the object you found? . . . what do you have to say about

INSTRUCTION A. Give each student a sheet of paper. Mark in the following chart:

GOALS	IMMEDIACY	ME	OTHERS	RISK	TIME	HELP	ORDER
1.							
2.							
3.							
4.							
5.							
6.							
7.							
8.							
9.							
10.							
11.							
12.							

your feelings? . . . examine the object . . . how do you feel about it? . . . are you satisfied? . . . or is the goal you have reached going to lead you elsewhere? . . . to another mountain? . . . to another goal? . . . what would you say to a news reporter about your triumph? . . . talk to her or him about the process, your feelings, and reaching the goal . . . say all you feel at the moment.

My Dozen Goals List

1. *Goals* — In the next year, list twelve goals in any order that you would like to achieve.

2. *Immediacy* — Mark A if the goal is short range; Z if long range; J if medium range.

3. *Me* — Check if you feel that you will impede yourself.

4. *Others* — Check if you feel external obstacles will impede you.

5. *Risk* — rank the risk ratio from 1-12.

6. *Time* — rank the time ratio from 1-12.

7. Indicate plus (+) if help is available.

8. Rank order the goals in the order of possible achievement. #1 is most possible.

INSTRUCTION B. Either process the chart results with the class or ask each individual to devise a written plan/self-contract to achieve one or more of her/his goals.

Processing This Chapter

PURPOSE:_____

_____

_____

_____

_____

_____

FEELINGS:_____

_____

_____

_____

_____

CONCEPTS:_____

_____

_____

_____

APPLICATIONS:_____

_____

_____

_____

_____

I sang
to the warm sun
and cold moon
this morning
and offered
myself
to the land
and gods
for them
to
teach
me
the hard ways
of living
all over again
Ray Young Bear,
"Four Songs of Life"

9

Finding Resources

A Dependency Quotient

INSTRUCTION A. Circle the percentage that most closely approximates your response to each statement.

1. My students depend upon *my knowledge* of subject matter as their major source of information.
   All the time   75%   50%   25%   not at all

2. My students depend upon prescribed *textbooks* as their major source of subject matter information.
   All the time   75%   50%   25%   not at all

3. My students depend upon other *printed materials* as their major source of subject matter information.
   All the time   75%   50%   25%   not at all

4. My students depend upon *classroom TV* as their major source of subject matter information.
   All the time   75%   50%   25%   not at all

5. My students depend upon *classroom films, film loops, or slides* as their major source of subject matter information.
   All the time   75%   50%   25%   not at all

6. My students depend upon *me to select and organize the use* of learning resources (books, magazines, films, etc.) *to meet class needs.*
   All the time   75%   50%   25%   not at all

7. My students depend upon *me to select and assign the use* of learning resources *to meet individual needs and goals.*
   All the time   75%   50%   25%   not at all

8. My students depend upon *me to assess all individual or class needs and set the appropriate goals for learning.*
   All the time   75%   50%   25%   not at all

9. My teaching style, attitudes, and needs *encourage* my students to depend upon me.
   All the time   75%   50%   25%   not at all

10. My students' *dependency quotient* average is

    _____
    100   90   80   70   60   50   40   30   20   10   0

THE ALL-PURPOSE LAYER CAKE

INSTRUCTION A. The cake symbolizes the school day. It has four layers. Before you put the layers together, divide each into the sections described below.

LAYER I: Resource use[1]

(a) Slice the percentage of time in which *you are a learning resource* in your classroom. Mark it "me."

(b) Slice the percentage of time in which *other persons* (students, faculty, staff, community volunteers) are used as resources in your classroom or outside the school walls. Label it "persons."

(c) Slice the percentage of time during which the students use *locations* in the school building or in the community other than your classroom for learning. Label it "places."

(d) Slice the percentage of time during which the students use *printed or visual materials as* resources for learning. Label it "things."

EXAMPLE:

LAYER II: Resource Persons

(a) Slice the percentage of time in which *you* are the *primary subject-matter resource person.* Label it "me."

(b) Slice the percentage of time in which *other faculty or staff aides* are the primary *subject matter resource.* Label it "faculty."

(c) Slice the percentage of time in which *community volunteers* (parents, retirees, tradespeople, business persons, professionals) are the *primary subject matter resource.* Label it "volunteers."

(d) Slice the percentage of time in which *students* (cross-age, peer) are the *primary subject matter resource.* Label it "students."

---

[1]A resource is (a) a person who shares expertise upon request with one or more individuals, (b) an object or tool that is selected to help learning, or (c) a place that offers learning opportunities.

(e) Shade in the percentage of each slice (me, faculty, volunteers, students) in which the person or persons serve as a resource for *other than primary subject matter.*

LAYER III: Resource Places

(a) Slice the percentage of time in which the students are gathered together in your classroom as a *single instructional group.* Label it "classroom."

(b) Slice the percentage of time in which students are using *resource corners, learning stations, or small group spaces* in your classroom. Label it "stations."

(c) Slice the percentage of time in which your students use the *school library, departmental resource rooms, materials centers* (with or without your direction but pursuant to individual learning style and/or subject matter under your guidance). Label it "IMC."

(d) Slice the percentage of time in which your students use *community libraries, agencies, museums, office buildings, laboratories,* etc., as learning resources (the location itself, such as an architectural monument or fire station, provides the learning experience, or makes learning more easily available, such as an architect's office or a research lab facility). Label it "community facilities."

(e) Shade the percentage of time in which individuals use each location pursuant to learning experiences that meet assessed needs. (The unshaded area represents time used by the class as a unit in the location.)

LAYER IV: Resource Materials

(a) Slice the percentage of time in which students use *printed materials* available in the classroom for individualized instruction. Label it "print-in."

(b) Slice the percentage of time in which students use *nonlinear materials* available in the classroom for individualized instruction (TV, films, film loops, tapes, etc.), Label it "video-in."

(c) Slice the percentage of time during which students *experiment* with or use equipment/materials such as 8mm film, clay, microscopes as tools to learn about subject matter. Label it "experience."

(d) Slice the percentage of time which students use to *construct* or create a product from found materials as a means to master a concept. Label it "junk."

(e) Slice the percentage of time during which students use *printed* instructional materials obtained from sources outside the school. Label it "print-out."

(f) Slice the percentage of time during which students use *visual* instructional material obtained from sources outside the school, Label it "video-out."

(g) Shade in the percentage of time which your students devote daily to noninstructional TV or film.

INSTRUCTION B: Layer your cake. Compare and contrast each layer. Rank order the three most significant conclusions you draw from this observation of your students' use of resources.

1. _____
2. _____
3. _____

Let Your Fingers Walk

How do you find persons who can help your students meet their learning needs? . . . where do you find a Mandarin gourmet cook? . . . an authority on English common law? . . . a lateral thinking expert? . . . an architect knowledgeable about Frank Lloyd Wright? . . . who can help you find and contact businesses and museums? . . . organize and supervise your vocational skills station? . . . give advice on a career as a tradesperson or dentist? . . . demonstrate filmmaking or yoga? . . . check in/out your cameras, pamphlets? . . . help small groups plan and discuss? . . . talk about old age? . . . train peer tutors? . . . tutor? . . . help plan a learning fair? . . . visit sites of potential internships? . . . whatever . . .

A. *Volunteer Talent Pools.* Many communities have created a resource pool. (Federal funds are available.) The pool consists of an office, a telephone, stationery and stamps, and enough volunteers to run the office at least two or three days each week. Any service agency (a school, a retirement home, a hospital) that identifies a need (a lecturer, a tutor, a nurse's aide) contacts its VTP. The pool staff uses its expertise and time to seek out a person in the community who will meet the need and sends the volunteer to the agency. VTPs usually construct resource files which grow thicker and more useful as they gain experience and recognition. Some use weekly news ads (often donated by the community newspaper), radio and TV spots (also donated), personal contacts (friends of friends of friends), and the yellow pages. ("Perhaps you could suggest . . . ") As demand for VTP service grows, the "search staff" (those who volunteer time to seek out other volunteers) grows. In some cases, demand from a single agency or school may necessitate a "search volunteer" in that location. (The school provides a small office and phone.) Teachers contact the building VTP rep. who relays the requests to the search staff. In addition, the building rep. can counsel both the teachers and the search staff and assure a smoother linkup and more successful use of the volunteer. When a special program or a single teacher uses the volunteer rep. to the degree that a second building rep. will enhance that special need, the program or teacher should find a parent or community volunteer to fill that function. For instance, an open classroom teacher may have six or seven volunteers who tutor weekly, plus request demonstrations and minicourses which use volunteer leaders. The teacher might train an additional volunteer who will organize and coordinate the others. The class rep. might work through the building rep. or directly with the search staff.

B. *Learning Exchange.* Several communities have instituted Ivan Illych's learning exchange idea: individuals in a community make themselves available to teach a specific subject or skill. The barter rates are money or a reciprocal skill. The exchange harnesses a computer's memory to match teachers and learners. Thus, if I could teach Hindustani and wished to learn plumbing, I would express my needs to the exchange computer. (The exchanges usually publish a resource index.) The computer would tell me who wished to teach plumbing, the barter conditions, and phone number. If possible, the computer would link me with a plumber who wished to learn Hindustani.

C. *Resource Files.* Any school or individual could maintain a file of resources (name, skill, phone, address). Each time an outside resource person is used, the information is recorded in a central, alphabetical, skill/topic file. When a resource is needed, the teacher goes to the file in a procedure no more complicated than going to a library for a book.

D. *The Yellow Pages.* When all else fails, follow Bell Telephone's advice: "Let your fingers do the walking." Look up the topic or general interest area needed. Find a name within a reasonable driving distance and call. Explain your need. If the party called can't help, ask for a referral. Two words or warning: (1) be clear about the *volunteer* nature of the request (if funds are available for travel expenses, say so) and (2) be prepared to make calls.

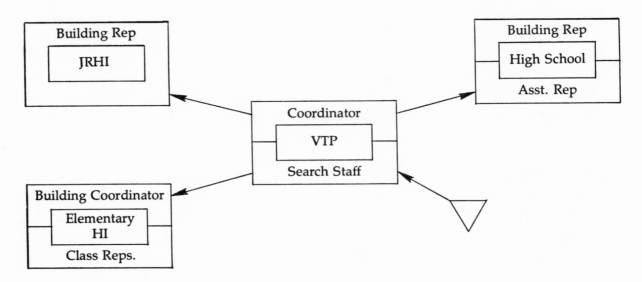

First Steps

INSTRUCTION A. In order to use resources effectively, you will need to plan the steps.

STEP 1. Build on the needs assessment that you completed with your students. Start with the priority needs that you have identified as easiest to fulfill.

STEP 2. Rank order the four resource-organizing tools. Which of the tools can you implement now? Which will be most helpful to the class? (Obtain class consensus, if possible).

____talent pool
____learning exchange
____resource files
____yellow pages

STEP 3. Rank order the possible persons who will have responsibility for running the selected resource tool. (Obtain class consensus, if possible.)

____yourself
____a student or student committee
____a parent(s)
____community volunteer
____student teacher
____other

STEP 4. Make a "Resource Persons Needs Grid." In column I, list the functions for which resource persons are needed. In column II, list what is needed (e.g., money, transport, special scheduling) to obtain those persons' help. In column III, list the first steps to take. In column IV, note the deadline for each step. In column V, list the student responsible.

STEP 5. Vote "yes-no" on the statements that follow. If you cannot distinguish your feelings on a question, pass it.

1. Resource persons are an intrusion into my professional territory.

                Yes   No   Pass

2. If I use resource persons to meet my students' needs more effectively, I will have nothing to do in the class.

                Yes   No   Pass

3. If a student takes the responsibility for implementing any aspect of Step 4, the whole idea will collapse.

                Yes   No   Pass

4. I feel that resource persons could enrich the learning of my students.

                Yes   No   Pass

RESOURCE PERSONS NEEDS GRID

Functions	Needed	1st Step	Deadline	Responsible
1. Lecturer				
2. Mini-course				
3. Tutor				
4. Building rep.				
5. Small groups				
6. Field trips				
7. Seminars				
8. Learning stations				
9. Organize records				
10. Check-out equipment and materials				
11. Make contacts				
12. Train peer tutors				
13. Repair equipment				
14. Career advice				
15. Demonstrations				

Alternate Strategies in the Beginning
or
How To Make Something for Nothing and Learn While Doing

Visit any bedroom suburb aglitter with the denture gold mines and you will find at least one school building elaborately adorned with the latest trinkets, modular variations on the box theme, and innovative spaces that school architects can use to spend a million dollars or two. Inside, the odds weigh heavily that what and how the students learn and teachers teach is less productive and more frustrating that what goes on across town in the traditional school boxes. It is said that in the beginning came the theory, then came the school board's innovative design to pass the referendum, and then came the beautiful and very impressive building. Education as product earns its "A" for show.

Try a different tack. Forget the money. Forget the budget. Forget the pretty colors and stamped posters and expensive publishing house materials and fancy machines. Just ask the principal to remove your desk and the kids' desks down to basement storage. In the beginning, there is only you and your 30 to 35 soon-to-be friends whose names are stamped on the computer cards in your hand.

In case the principal wants to know what you're planning, try this explanation:

"The students in this class will create one of the following:

——a. a preschool playlot
——b. a nursery playroom
——c. a kindergarten circus

by using trash, junk, and miscellaneous odds and ends that will provide mastery of the problem-solving process with special emphasis on resource identification and utilization."

STEP 1. Divide the class into three groups. Each group will select one of the three projects. (It doesn't matter whether one, two, three groups select one option. Make it clear, however, that only one design will be constructed, if that is your intent.)

STEP 2. Instruct each group to design the project. The design should include a scaled drawing of layout and all constructs, a materials list, job assignments, and resource helpers.

a. Finding a location. The group must seek a suitable lot, room, or open area in which to build a project. It is advisable that they secure the aid of a real estate agent, the city clerk, a lawyer, and a landscaper who can advise them on site-procurement (free), legal restrictions on use, design possibilities and restrictions, and a formal use contract with city approval.

b. Making a design. With the help of an architect, the group should design the project under the restriction that all materials must be obtainable without cost. (If some costs are unavoidable, the group must plan how it will obtain the monies.) The plan should contain a "what we want to happen" proposal. The proposal should be organized with the aid of a child psychologist who can help the group to understand the special play needs and physical capabilities of each group. The "what we want to happen" proposal will guide the group's plans for the functional equipment they build.

c. Obtaining materials. With the functions wanted (involvement, creativity, private worlds, swinging, climbing) the group can brainstorm the forms and shapes needed. A needs grid will help plan "how to get 'em." Boxes, barrels, ropes, old railroad ties, sand, telephone poles, drums, tractor tires, potato sacks, auto parts, crates, cable spools, old fences, ice cream cartons, carpet roll ends, attic junk, basement junk, foam packing, yard-sticks, and so on . . . Who has them? How can you get them free? What will you build with them?

d. Putting it together. Where can you find the tools and the experience to teach the groups how to use each? Fathers, uncles, older brothers and sisters, mothers, neighbors, and the yellow pages make good resources. "If Aunt Jane doesn't know how, she must know somebody." Let the group line up its resources and organize the division of labor.

STEP 3. Have the class review all proposals and select one project. (The class will need to pick a procedure for this last task. If they don't know the options, send them off to find someone who does.)

STEP 4. Complete the project. (If you planned to go only as far as the complete proposals, don't wait until now to say so.)

STEP 5. Process the experience. Although you may process the group learning process, it is more advisable to focus on each individual's experience. Use strategies that will help each student perceive how she/he identified needs, set goals, selected resources, related with group members, and so on.

STEP 6. Have each individual design, carry out, and process a project that (1) requires use of at least one costless resource person, as well as places, and materials from outside the classroom and (2) will help the student overcome weaknesses identified in the group project just completed.

_____Write and produce a three-minute radio vignette characterizing a historic figure.
_____Draw a cartoon strip with an ecological theme.
_____Produce a one-act play.
_____Design and equip a learning station for the classroom.
_____Build a free-form chair from scrap plywood.
_____Weave a rug from pink rope.
_____Design and sew an animal costume from material scraps.
_____Renovate an old house and sell it.
_____Invent a word game with cardboard pieces.
_____Build a cardboard dollhouse with furniture.
_____Build a tree house with scrap lumber.

Continue this list.

Me: My Ultimate Resource

INSTRUCTION A. Plan a nonverbal project or select one from the foregoing list. Your restrictions are (1) that no money is to be spent and (2) that you must find one person who can help you master a new skill or solve a problem. After you have completed the project, process what you did with the help of the following spectrum.

A. To solve the problems inherent in my project I discovered my responses were basically:

1. Intuitive _____Logical
   1 2 3 4 5
2. Synergetic_____Analytical
   1 2 3 4 5
3. Visual_____Verbal
   1 2 3 4 5
4. Sensory _____Intellectual
   1 2 3 4 5
5. Simultaneous _____Sequential
   1 2 3 4 5
6. Image Making_____Order Making
   1 2 3 4 5
7. Hunches _____Linear Thought
   1 2 3 4 5

B. I learned that I am essentially

1. dependent _____independent
   1 2 3 4 5
2. acquiescent to   questioning of
   authority_____authority
   1 2 3 4 5
3. subservient to preestablished   accepting of my
   modes of learning _____learning style
   1 2 3 4 5
4. locked into logical   exploring alternative
   order _____resources
   1 2 3 4 5

INSTRUCTION B. Complete this statement "In this chapter, I noticed that . . ." Use your Journal.

Processing This Chapter

PURPOSE:_____
_____
_____
_____

FEELINGS:_____
_____
_____
_____

CONCEPTS:_____
_____
_____

APPLICATIONS:_____
_____
_____
_____

10

To be responsibly self-directing means that one chooses — and then learns from the consequences.
Carl Rogers,
On Becoming a Person

Controlling Learning

INSTRUCTION A. On the agree-disagree spectrum, mark your position for each statement. (SA — strongly agree; SD — strongly disagree).

1. If I can assess accurately my learning needs, I can determine what skills or knowledge I must acquire to meet those needs.

   SA   SD

2. If I am capable of determining what skills or knowledge I need to reach my goals, courses required by law or school policy may become major obstacles to my learning.

   SA   SD

3. In an educational environment which successfully facilitates process learning, there is no need for required courses; each individual will make her/his own requirements based on accurate needs assessment.

   SA   SD

4. A measure of traditional education's adolescence is its adherence to outmoded requirements formulated to protect the poor and disenfranchised from biased neglect.

   SA   SD

5. Due to the complexity of technological society, the traditional basic skills — reading, writing, computing — are no longer the *most essential skills.*

   SA   SD

6. More universally needed in the 1970's and 80's and more basic than the 3R's are the process-learning skills — "learning how to learn."

   SA   SD

7. A person who can assess needs, set goals, and control the other learning processes is more likely to survive in a 1990 society than one who has merely learned the rudiments of reading and writing.

   SA   SD

8. A person who has mastered the process of learning is more likely to achieve her/his full potential than a person who acquiesces to dominant adults.

   SA   SD

9. A person who has mastered the process of learning will select the skills and subject matter, as well as the style, most appropriate to her/his goals.

   SA   SD

10. Any student can learn to direct her/his own learning. Self-direction does not depend on sophistication, achievement, intelligence, or personality.

    SA   SD

The Model T was a magnificent car. Imagine that Henry Ford, so enamored with the perfection of his car, decided that the motor should never change. A new body, yes; new interiors, yes; new tires, yes; but the same engine. Imagine yourself chugging through city traffic or jouncing and jerking down the expressway in your sleek, shiny Model T with that motor. Outlandish? Perhaps, but consider that the educational system, which is preparing this generation to live in the 21st century, fits the analogy.

In spite of the historic extremes in educational thought, the practical methods of teaching and learning have changed little — some patches, some paint, a new fender, new body designs — since Socrates dialogued with his pupils. The centuries-old Model T chugs along: "What was good enough for me is good enough for my kids."

College of Complexes

INSTRUCTION A. Read these descriptions.

THE CASTOR OIL COMPLEX "A spoonful of sugar makes the medicine go down." In some locales, the medicine is enough; no sugar. Because a child "doesn't know what's best," state legislatures, federal agencies, school boards, administrators, pressure groups, and parents prescribe the medicine: required courses, hours in school, places of study, textbooks, and so on. Instructions to the student on what must be learned and how are clear and specific. After all, "It's for the child's good."

THE BASICS COMPLEX. No one can learn anything unless the basics come first. Definition of the basics will vary according to time and circumstances. Usually, the definition depends on the parents' goals. For most, the basics complex equals wealth and success: good reading will assure good grades will assure good college will assure good job will assure great success.

THE PRESSURE COOKER COMPLEX. "What that kid needs is a good swift kick." When the kick fails, try other goads: rewards (an "A" grade merits 25¢, $1, a sports car), punishments (an "F" merits grounding, hassles, cutting the lawn). "Life is pressure so learn to take it while you're young. It's the best motivator."

THE LITTLE BOXES COMPLEX. Pete Seeger's song characterizes the categorizing organization of schools from time immemorial. "Everybody in its place, and a place for everybody." Subjects, courses, tracks, levels, ability subgroups, behavioral objectives, programmed learning, etc. Refine, organize, categorize, define, refine, reorganize. With each decade, the boxes get smaller and smaller, the expectations more and more refined.

THE FOUNTAIN OF KNOWLEDGE COMPLEX. The teacher is the trained expert, the authority in her or his field, the master of knowledge. It is the teacher's task to pour the knowledge into the empty pitchers, the students.

THE WAR CAMP COMPLEX. The school is the battleground. On this side, we teachers; on that side, the enemy students. The dividing line is clear. Cross into enemy territory and you are committing suicide.

INSTRUCTION B. Select the three complexes described that you feel are *most characteristic* of conventional schooling as you know it. Brainstorm the positive and negative effects of each complex on today's students.

INSTRUCTION C. Write a description of a 1980 society, as you imagine it might be. Specifically describe the conditions of survival (physical, economic, and social) that individuals will have to learn to face.

INSTRUCTION D. Return to the three complexes you selected. Brainstorm the positive and negative effects these complexes will have on students in your future society if those complexes continue to dominate educational practice.

INSTRUCTION E. Design a model schooling program for your future society. What attitudes toward learning will formulate classroom practice and school organization? What instructional and curricular modes will dominate? What roles will the teacher have?

Looking Ahead

Unlike traditional education which structures and controls each detail of what (content) and how (style) students learn, schooling in the 80's and 90's will need to focus on helping students take control of their own learning. Without the skills of self-direction, individual learners will have great difficulty withstanding the information bombardment that can only intensify as technology improves mass media.

In practice, what will schooling for self-direction mean to a student?

Superficially, the school building will look the same, but it will function differently; instead of new body designs for the Model T, a new motor will be installed. With this *essential* change, individualized instruction will be a reality for each student. Consider two contemporary students who enroll in an open school without walls.

Case 1. Carl claims that he wants to become a carpenter. Already goal-oriented, Carl easily seeks out what he will need in order to reach his goal. He goes to his math resource teacher to discuss specific skills, sequence, and math applications. With this information, he is able to plan out an independent math study that will help him reach his goal. In addition, he discovers that practical experience as a carpenter's apprentice will prepare him more thoroughly. He makes arrangements with a local cabinetmaker to work as an apprentice three days a week. The cabinetmaker suggests he learn more about woods and finishes. Carl's adviser steers him to a science-lab resource person who helps him set up a study that will teach Carl about the woods and finishes. Finally, Carl goes to the writing skills lab to arrange for tutoring help with his letter writing. In planning this work, he discovers that he needs more help with reading skills also. He arranges to join a literature seminar.

CARL'S SCHEDULE

	M	T	W	T	F	S
8	Support Group			Support Group		
9		Science Lab			Science Lab	Carpentry Apprentice
10	Math Lab		Math Lab			
11	Ind. Study		Ind. Study	Carpentry Apprentice		
12	Writing Lab		Writing Lab			
1						
2	Carpentry Apprentice	Carpentry Apprentice	Home Base		Science Seminar Writing Lab	
3						
4		Lit Seminar		Lit Seminar		
5						
6						

Case 2. Lee Ann is an 18-year-old near dropout. She has floated through school with D's and F's. She transferred to the open school because "I got nothing else to do and there you ain't gotta do nothin'." Her initial conferences affirm her low self-image, her passivity, and her nonexistent interests. Six or seven conference hours pass before she will lower her defenses, trust her adviser, and pick a support group. As the trust solidifies, Lee Ann talks about "animals" and "sick people." On this basis after three months of talking and sharing, she takes the step to design an intern program which will "try out" working with people and animals, "as long as it don't cut into my part-time job."

LEE ANN'S SCHEDULE

	M	T	W	T	F
8	Nurse's Aid Hospital	Dr. Smith's Animal Hospital	Nurse's Aid Hospital	Dr. Smith's Animal Hospital	County Forest Preserve
9					
10					
11					
12	Support Group		Home Base	Support Group	
1					
2					
3					
4			W A I T R E S S I N G		
5					
6					

From this point, Lee Ann embarks on a course that reveals increasing commitment. At first, she changes her schedule regularly; the hospital internship is the first to drop. As the months pass, however, she solidifies her plans around her success experiences at the animal hospital and the forest preserve where she also cares for animals. She finds a third internship at a school for handicapped children and, for the first time, communicates a sense of purpose. By June, she talks openly and sincerely about possible careers: teaching, psychology, medicine. One year later, Lee Ann's program reflects the changes which took place within her:

	M	T	W	T	F	S
8	Support	Psych Seminar		Support	Psych Seminar	
9	Algebra	Lake Forest	Home Base	Algebra	Lake Forest	Nurse's Aide
10			Psych Lab			
11	Lit. Seminar		Lake Forest	Lit. Seminar		Children's Ward Hospital
12		U.S. History Seminar			U.S. History Seminar	
1						
2	Internship	Psych. Ind. Study	Internship	Animal Behavior	Writing Lab	
3						
4	Teacher Aide		Teacher Aide	Lincoln Zoo		
5						

Carl's learning, as reflected in the schedule he made, and Lee Ann's, as reflected in the second schedule, appear to take very traditional forms: scheduled classes, subject matter courses, boxes. The content of the courses may also appear traditional: spelling, writing skills, algebra, grammar, carpentry. The appearances, however, belie essential differences.

1. When needed, Lee Ann received many hours of intense support from her adviser and her peer support group. This guidance was open-ended, nonjudgmental, and respectful of Lee Ann's decisions. The emphasis was not upon telling her what was good or bad but on supporting her decisions and helping her to learn from the consequences of actions she took.

2. Both students learned to control their own choices. They formed goals, found resources, and designed individual or group learning experiences with the resource persons. At each step, both Carl and Lee Ann participate in any and all decisions which concerned their goals, style, readings, or whatever else was necessary to what each wanted, and both learned from the consequences of choices.

3. Bureaucratic rules or budgetary limitations did not prescribe what or how learning should occur. Each selected (a) what to learn, (b) how, (c) when and where, and (d) who would help.

Lee Ann's Choices

(a) *What did she select?* The high school had the resources to provide instructional assistance in algebra, history, and literature. Her very special interest in psychology, however, was beyond the school's capability. Instruction was available if Lee Ann wished to travel to a nearby college.

(b) *How?* Lee Ann's program encompassed a wide range of learning styles. She was not trapped in the walled classroom for a steady RLT (Read the book, Listen to the teacher, Take a test) diet.

1. *Internship.* Lee Ann apprenticed herself in three different situations. She worked as a teacher's aide with mentally retarded second graders, she fed and cared for newborn animals at the local zoo, and she tutored and entertained children at the town's hospital. In each instance, she planned and evaluated her learning with her "master," a practicing professional who not only supervised the work but also discussed career possibilities, suggested readings, and instructed skills.

2. *Classes.* Lee Ann's classes took a variety of forms. Child Psychology 107 was a college lecture-seminar. Her literature seminar was a small group which selected its own curriculum and shared leadership responsibilities. On several occasions, different teachers were invited as guest lecturers. In U.S. history, the large group was guided by a faculty resource person. The curriculum was organized around simulation games and discussion of related readings.

3. *Lab Courses.* Lee Ann chose a writing lab that would allow for guided individual study in expository writing skills. She began her math study in a similar lab, but later helped to form a class when enough students with similar needs were assembled. The lab gave her the support and external structure in a skill area for which she had not developed sufficient self-discipline.

4. *Independent Study.* The most difficult selection was Lee Ann's independent study in psychology. Because of her intense interest in child development, she sought out a psychologist who could meet with her once a week to discuss readings. The success Lee Ann showed in this election demonstrated the strength of her self-direction. Independent study requires the most sophisticated degree of control and motivation. Although many naively assume that independent study is the easiest, they soon discover, as Lee Ann did in her first attempt, that "avoiding hassles" is a shallow definition of independent study.

(c) *Where and when?* Time and place should never limit learning. Conventional education has locked itself into boxes and buildings. Lee Ann's schedule found free time available in the day. She chose how to use or not use that time. The schedule caused her to learn in the school building where she had one class in a box room, one in a quiet resource room, and one in a multipurpose lounge. In addition, she attended a lecture course on a college campus, a seminar in a home, and interned at a zoo, a hospital, and a school. She sought out the places and people she needed in order to learn.

(d) *Who?* Lee Ann's subject resources were experts in practicing their fields, as well as certified staff. The most important resource, however, was the adviser who spent long hours in one-to-one counseling, in the support group which met with Lee Ann twice weekly, and in the home-base group that gave her a sense of belonging.

Adapting Futures to the Present

What's Possible Now

INSTRUCTION A. Here are some ideas to which you can respond. Use voting: *yes, no, with some work* are the choices you will have. Check the appropriate response to each statement.

In my classroom, I have the power to

	YES	NO	WORK
1. Give students more choices in the curriculum	—	—	—
2. Give students more choices in reading materials	—	—	—
3. Give students more choices in classroom behavior policies	—	—	—
4. Give students more choices in style alternatives (small groups, independent study, going to library, etc.)	—	—	—
5. Bring guest "experts" into the classroom	—	—	—
6. Take the class to outside-the-school learning experiences	—	—	—
7. Design learning units that will help students learn process skills	—	—	—
8. Help students break the RLT mold by encouraging inquiry projects, action projects, and visual-aural products (films, murals, sound tapes)	—	—	—
9. Build subject-matter learning centers in my classroom	—	—	—
10. Form support groups and schedule time each week for support group meetings.	—	—	—

Taking Action

Alternatives for Deciding

INSTRUCTION A. On this chart, list in column one the administrative restrictions over which you have no power but which restrict student decisions in the classroom (i.e., every student must have five hours of spelling instruction each month).

1 Administrative Restrictions	2 Now Organized	3 Alternatives for Deciding	4 Alternatives for Deciding

INSTRUCTION B. In column 2, describe *how* you presently comply with that restriction so that your students learn what is required. In columns 3 and 4, invent two alternatives that will allow you to comply with the administrative requirement, but which will help you to design *learning experiences based on student choice.*

EXAMPLE:

1	2	3	4
specified hours for each subject	box schedule, all instructed at same time in each subject	small groups with peer tutors	learning centers with individualized materials

INSTRUCTION C. After considering (1) administrative restrictions, (2) your readiness to change, (3) your alternatives for deciding, design three classroom practices that you can implement and that will allow students to *learn from the consequences of their own choices.*

Self-Contract

INSTRUCTION A. Complete this Self-Contract in your Journal.

Name: _____ Date _____

The alternatives for decision I will implement are:

_____

My helping resource person is: _____

Completion Date: _____

Processing This Chapter

PURPOSE: _____

_____

_____

_____

_____

FEELINGS: _____

_____

_____

_____

_____

CONCEPTS: _____

_____

_____

_____

APPLICATIONS: _____

_____

_____

_____

To open the mind, to correct it, to refine it, to enable it to know, and to digest, master, rule and use its knowledge, to give it power over its own faculties, application, flexibility, method, critical exactness, sagacity, resource, eloquent expression is the object.

John Newman,
The Idea of a University

11
Evaluating

A Final Test

INSTRUCTION A. Answer each question. If true, mark T. If false, mark F. Record your answers in the blank spaces. Each correct answer is worth 10 points.

1. ____Grades are necessary for college admission.

2. ____Grades are the traditional evaluation tool.

3. ____"The Eight Year Study" demonstrated that students who were evaluated with normative grades were more successful in every aspect of college life than students who were evaluated in a self-selected manner.

4. ____Grades based on objective norms prevent the fulfillment of the "self-fulfilling" prophecy.

5. ____Teacher evaluation would benefit from the reliability of normative-based grading scales.

6. ____Grades are excellent motivators for learning.

7. ____Recording and reporting considerations are the best arguments to support the retention of normative grades.

8. ____Competition, induced by grades, prepares students for the realities of a competitive society.

9. ____Without grades there is no viable way to evalute student progress.

10. ____Normative grades support mastery learning processes.

INSTRUCTION B. Match your answers against the correct answers given below. (Do not confuse self-marking with self-evaluation.) Each answer is fully explained. Deduct 10 points for each incorrect answer or unanswered question.

1. F (false) The National Center for Grading Alternatives surveyed every junior college, college, and university in the nation. Twenty-five hundred responses demonstrated conclusively that grades are *NOT* a precondition for college admission. The survey results, plus each college's criteria for "non-normative credential review," are described in the Center's *College Guide for Experimenting High Schools (AMHEC, 1973)*. Essentially, less than 8 percent of the 2,500 responding institutions would refuse to review any transcript that did not include grades, a grade-point average, or rank in class. A like percentage indicated preferential treatment for written teacher evaluations. In practice, high schools that evaluate and report in nonnormative forms have experienced little or no difficulty in the placement of graduates in college programs. The Shanti School in Hartford, Metro in Chicago, SWAS in Minnetonka, Minnesota, John Adams in Portland, Oregon, and hundreds of others in big cities, in rural towns, in bedroom suburbs have had a like experience.

2. F (false). The words "traditional" and "nontraditional" are loaded, especially when a school board or administration wants to resist change. Historically speaking, the most traditional evaluation procedure in American education has been the log discussion, a discussion between pupil and teacher on what was learned and what was not. Conferences were employed to inform parents of pupil progress up until the democratization of education swept into the expanding urban centers. As the one-room school gave way to P.S. 101 and more efficiency was needed to keep track of large numbers of students, grade records were introduced. Increased complexity of curriculum, size of schools, and improved technology have enshrouded the grade report in so-called tradition — "the way it was when I went to school."

3. F (false). "The Eight Year Study" (1942) matched 1,500 students who were free to plan their own high school curriculum with 1,500 students similar in all background respects except the high school curriculum. In *every* aspect of college life — scholastic achievement, sociability index, extracurricular achievement, and so on — the experimental group, in which individuals and groups planned their own curriculum, eliminated grades, and prepared for college in a self-devised way, did just as well or slightly better than the control group which received normative grades for traditional achievement. In addition, the experimental group exhibited superior patterns of curiosity, resourcefulness, objective thinking, creative endeavor, and personal motivation (*Adventures in American Education: Did They Succeed in College?* Harper and Brothers, 1942).

4. F (False). Rosenthal's *Pygmalion in the Classroom: Self-Fulfilling Prophecies and Teacher Expectations* (Holt, Rinehart and Winston, 1969) demonstrated how teacher expectations dictate student performance. Although this study was based on IQ tests, the correlation with grades is not difficult to perceive. Last year's teacher, an older brother, a race or ethnic bias, sex — all are factors

that build expectations and the student performs accordingly. Grades solidify an average student, or a "dumbbell." Listen to teachers' dialogues in the lounge: "Boy, is that Smith kid a loser." "Oh, Mary is just average." "What numbskulls those Santos kids are."

5. F (false). Imagine how you would react to your supervisor's sitting in the back of the room with this checklist:

_____relaxes the students by perpetual smiling **B**
_____asks perceptive questions **B**
_____speaks grammatically **C**
_____gives clear instructions **A**
_____dresses neatly **B**

Final Grade **B—**

On Fridays, the staff gathers in the auditorium. The principal distributes the weekly tests and collects lesson plans for the next week. The total of your supervisor's observation (46%), the weekly test (34%), and the lesson plan evaluation (20%) will determine your placement on the month's salary scale. The scale, of course, places you in dollar competition (the real world, remember) with your fellow faculty members. What other evaluation system could provide a more reliable measure of your teaching performance?

6. F (false). On a normative curve, most students end in the C area. The only positive motivation goes to the A and B students; D and F students obviously do not respond to grade motivation. On the other hand, there is positive proof to indicate whether this or some other parental-reward-punishment factor is the principle motivation. The work of Maslow, Rogers, Combs, and other humanistic psychologists argues strongly that learning and growth occur most successfully when individuals are free to discover a meaningful relationship between what they need and what they learn. Rogers' *Freedom to Learn* (Columbus, Ohio, 1969) is an excellent primer.

7. T (True) When considering the pros and cons of normative grading, no other practical (or theoretical, for that matter) argument carries the weight of the recording/reporting position: "We must use grades to evaluate because grades are the most efficient, easily transcribed, and clearly read method of keeping school records, reporting those records to parents, college admissions officers, and future employers." *In effect, this position argues that the recording and reporting needs of an academic bureaucracy determine what and how students learn, and that they must learn through a normative system in which acquired knowledge and skills are reducible to a numerical or letter code.*

8. F (false) First, those who argue that competition is essential to survival ignore the fact that the human race's greatest advances came from cooperative effort. Witness the wheel, the lever, anaesthetics, the discovery of America, wagon trains crossing the continent, the moon landing. Secondly, those who argue that grade competition builds character ignore its effects on the "losers." What happens to the D and F students? Where do they go with their scarlet letter blazoned on their credentials? What other institution in our society has such sweeping power to predetermine an individual's self-image and future life? Thirdly, those who argue that competition singles out the brightest, most capable students who will provide leadership and brain power supportive of "our national interest" ignore their own very narrow definition of "bright" and "capable". How has competition fostered the creative arts and provided the painters, the musical composers, the writers who transcribe the "national character" in brilliant works or art?

9. F (false) There are many options which are more conducive to learning (by whatever definition) than normative grades. The best options distinguish between evaluation and reporting/recording procedures in a way that normative grades cannot. For elementary systems there exist checklists and computer-assisted procedures to record and report each skill, concept, or behavior a student has mastered. After the student *demonstrates* proficiency, the record is noted and the student moves on to the next level. The record is used to *report* progress to parents (using a checklist sheet, a computer printout, a parent-teacher conference, or some other reporting system) and to help both teacher and student evaluate strengths, weaknesses, and new directions. In effect the student-teacher conferences use the specific records to help the student see what she or he has learned and has not learned and to correct the deficiencies. No competition is involved; the student masters what she or he can in a speed and style that produces proficiency in the areas of need.

Secondary school systems do not yet have available refined academic need-assessment tools to record or report a mastery approach. However, in those programs, notably in the alternative schools, in which the students are taught self-evaluation skills and teachers receive the time and training to help students self-evaluate, the combination of teacher-written/student self-evaluation has provided a noteworthy improvement over "traditional" normative grades. *WAD-JA-GET: The Grading Game in American Education* (Hart, 1970) and the *College Guide to Experimenting High Schools* provide comprehensive discussions of these and other evaluation options. Both provide extensive bibliographic references for every facet of grading reform.

10. F (false). The purposes and practices of mastery learning contradict those of normative based learning. Mastery learning individualizes instruction with clearly defined, specific criteria (either student- or teacher-made), and gives the opportunity for each student to form or select objectives conducive to needs, and the resource help to fulfill those objectives with a personalized program. Therefore grades, based on a normative curve which uses *comparative* judgments, are rendered unnecessary, inappropriate, and illogical.

INSTRUCTION C. Tally your grade. Place it on this curve to see how well your results measure against the established standards.

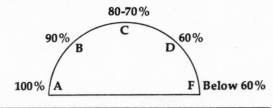

Reacting to Grades and Norms

Feelings About Grades Grids

INSTRUCTION A. In the first column list the feelings and reactions you experienced during the test and the grading. In the succeeding columns, check the appropriate box(es) after each entry if you think that the column-statement applies to the entry.

Feelings List	I Feel Negative	I Feel Positive	Good Students Would Feel Positive	Poor Students Would Feel Positive	Overall Feeling + −	
1.						
2.						
3.						
4.						
5.						
6.						

INSTRUCTION B. List the advantages and disadvantages that you ascribe to normative grading practices.

Advantage	Disadvantage

Passing or Failing?

INSTRUCTION A. Complete this task. You have two options.

1. Refer to the advantage-disadvantage list you just completed. If more than 30 percent of your listed advantages or disadvantages check out against research findings, you pass. Use the resources described earlier in this chapter or find other resources to validate your list.

2. Ask another teacher, friend, or student to take the "Final Test" on grades. If your score was higher, you pass.

INSTRUCTION B. If you "passed" the option you selected, move to the next strategy. If you "failed," you must *complete.* one of these options.

1. Do the option above that you did not select.
2. Ask another teacher, friend, or student to read the answer sheet to the "Final Test." Construct a test. If you can "fail" the testee, you "pass."
3. Challenge someone to an arm wrestle. You make the rules. If you win, you "pass."

Resent-Appreciate

INSTRUCTION A. In column 1, list the *resentments* you have toward the pass-fail options. Include immediate reactions to the "tests," as well as philosophic disagreements. In column 2, list the qualities of the pass-fail option which you *appreciate.*

Resent	Appreciate

INSTRUCTION B. Construct two rank orders. Each rank order should include three items from the resent-appreciate list. Make one rank order question the priorities for the positive consequences of pass-fail grading. Make the other question the priorities of its negative consequences. In areas of doubt, refer to bibliographic material described in the answers to Final Test.

Evaluating Mastery

What Behaviors?

INSTRUCTION A. In the left-hand column, indicate to what extent a behavior is integral to the evaluation of mastery learning: Very Important (VI), Important (I), Slightly Important (SI), or Not Important (NI).

_____1. To make clear and exact performance expectations based on a careful assessment of each student's needs.

_____2. To assess individual needs according to explicitly defined and communicated personal standards.

_____3. To assist the student in setting clear, specific learning objectives which meet assessed needs.

_____4. To assist the student in identifying and finding resources.

_____5. To assist the student in selecting and organizing appropriate learning resources.

_____6. To select clear and exact evaluation procedures that indicate how, to what extent, and what products or processes will be used to evaluate performance.

_____7. To acquire specific communications skills — oral and written — that will ensure each student the help to complete a personally meaningful evaluation.

INSTRUCTION B. Rank order the three most important items from the above list.

1. _____
2. _____
3. _____

INSTRUCTION C. Complete each item given below for each item you ranked.

	A	B	C
1. Evaluation skills I need to improve.			
2. Write an objective which will help you meet each need listed in number 1.			
3. Describe the methods you will use to attain that objective.			
4. Describe your resources.			
5. Describe the criteria you will use to evaluate your performance.			
6. Describe the procedures for evaluation. Include terminal dates, product, and responsibilities for evaluation.			
7. Name your primary resource person/evaluator.			

INSTRUCTION D. Implement the project you just outlined. Construct strategies and procedures that will help you to attain your goals. If you discover your goals are too narrow or too broad, make adjustments in the objectives, methods, criteria, or any other aspect of the plan you select. *Consult your primary resource person about changes before you adopt the plan.*

INSTRUCTION E. After you have completed your project, *evaluate* what you have done.

A Self-Evaluation Tool

1. To what extent did I accomplish my objectives?

   1   2   3   4   5   6   7   8   9
   Unsatisfactory   Satisfactory

2. To what extent did I feel positive about this experience?

   1   2   3   4   5   6   7   8   9
   Negative   Positive

3. To what extent did I achieve my expectations?

   1   2   3   4   5   6   7   8   9
   Poorly   Exceedingly well

   List and chart each expectation:

   a. _____

   b. _____

   c. _____

   d. _____

4. Describe the learning which occurred, but which you did not expect.

5. Describe what you *did.* (Include a resources-used list, processes, and products).

6. List test results, written comments, skill-mastery check-off sheet, or other measurement results.

7. What newly discovered needs were brought to your attention by this learning experience?

8. Attach your original plan, products (such as essays, films, paintings), and give the complete package to your primary resource person for her/his assessment and recommendations.

INSTRUCTION F. Devise a strategy that will enable you to assess the positive and negative qualities of the mastery evaluation that you just completed.

A Final Perspective

INSTRUCTION A. Rank order the three evaluation procedures: normative grading, pass-fail, and mastery evaluating.

1. Which evaluation procedure best reinforces the learning values in my classroom as that classroom is now organized?

   ____normative   ____pass-fail   ____mastery

2. Which evaluation procedure would I prefer to use if I had the opportunity to organize my classroom as that procedure would require?

   ____pass-fail   ____normative   ____mastery

Processing This Chapter

PURPOSES: _____

_____

_____

_____

_____

FEELINGS: _____

_____

_____

_____

_____

CONCEPTS: _____

_____

_____

_____

APPLICATIONS: _____

_____

_____

_____

_____

The facilitator helps to elicit and clarify the purposes of the individuals in the class as well as the more general purposes of the group. If he is not fearful of accepting contradictory purposes and conflicting aims, if he is able to permit the individuals a sense of freedom in stating what they would like to do, then he is trying to create a climate for learning.

Carl R. Rogers,
Freedom To Learn

12
Facilitating The Learning Process

Looking at Style

The Fable of Zenodes

Once upon a time there was a queen bee named Aster. Aster ran a very efficient hive. When she buzzed, the drones and workers hummed. Whatever other complaints the young bees had against Queen Aster, they could not say "Aster is unfair," or "Aster doesn't teach us to become good honeybees." Aster, well schooled in traditional norms of beehive management, ran the most successful hive in the state. One day, a young worker named Zenodes discovered a different, and for him (or so he thought), more successful way to gather honey. He explained his idea to Aster. Being all-wise and capable, she gave Zenodes permission to perfect his method under two conditions. First, during working hours, Zenodes must use the traditional methods. If he wished to experiment, he could do so during lunch break or after 4 p.m. Second, Zenodes had to file weekly progress reports to her, single-spaced and typed on lined paper in triplicate. If the experiments seemed to have any merit, she would ask the Research and Development Office to take over.

"Someday," Aster told Zenodes, "when you are grown up, you will make a fine scientist. I hope you will continue your experiment. Meanwhile, don't neglect your good bee duties."

For several weeks, Zenodes tried to follow the queen's advice. Each day at 4 p.m., he finished his assigned duties and flew off to continue his experiment. The double labor, however, proved too strenuous. Saddened, Zenodes stopped his experiments, decided he could never be a scientist, and concentrated on his daily task. Aster, who had watched Zenodes try to do double work, nodded her wise head.

"These young bees always seem to prefer the hard way. If Zenodes had listened more attentively to my lectures on efficient honey-potting techniques he would know that there is just one correct method for gathering honey."

A Reflection on Style

INSTRUCTION A. Use the procedures you developed with previous reflections.

Relax . . . close your eyes . . . be comfortable . . . visualize yourself in the classroom . . . what do you see? . . . rows of desks? . . . students listening to your lecture? . . . or tables, chairs, pillows, and work spaces scattered? . . . students at work in small groups or individually? . . . you moving quietly from cluster to cluster? . . . what are you saying? . . . "That's not the way. Let me show the right way."? . . . prejudging? . . . giving instructions? . . . lecturing? . . . asking questions? . . . processing a problem? . . . picture yourself helping one student for an entire period . . . visualize the relationship . . . what are you discussing? . . . how? . . . continue the reflection until you end the discussion.

The Spectrum of Style

A Self-Comparison

INSTRUCTION A. Five famous teachers are described in the paragraphs which follow. Read each description and imagine yourself as that person.

DEMOSTHENES THE ORATOR. Skilled in the formal delivery of ideas, you stand before the students who are assembled silently at your feet. Neither the number of students present nor the amphitheater's size affects your polished delivery. At your right hand, the AV board with multicolored buttons and switches awaits your selection of slides, films, or overhead projection on the great rear-projection screen. Rhetorical questions, humorous anecdotes, sardonic asides punctuate your cogent insights at the most illustrative moment. Your students listen attentively. As words trip brilliantly from your tongue, the students transcribe each nuance, each inflection. A head stirs to show a furrowed brow; another flashes a quizzical smile. The bell rings. You fold your notes, switch off the projector, smile to the class, and steal quietly into the hallway.

SOCRATES THE QUESTIONER. The students gather in a circle. When all are seated, you direct your attention to the auburn-haired young woman in the second row. As befits your style, you begin the session by asking her a review question. In chronological sequence, she covers the issues you have elicited carefully each day. She concludes with an apt distinction between stolen government property and unauthorized security leaks to the media.

At this point, you interrupt her discourse and direct a new question at a young man with wire-rimmed glasses seated at your right hand.

"John, what is the difference . . .?"

As he responds, you lead his thought: he clarifies vague wordings, defines his terms, and illustrates until he reaches your conclusion. You summarize the point to clarify a few ambiguous terms and end the session with a question for all to ponder.

ABELARD THE SEMINARIAN. You seat yourself at a large round table. Having announced the next week's agenda devoted to "Women's Rights in a Free Society," you ask Heloise to begin with her presentation. As she reads, you listen, jot down a few questions, and watch the reactions of her 25 co-seminarians.

"Finally," she intones, "in the light of my previous arguments, I would assert that Lake Michigan is doomed."

Hands raise. You direct Scot to ask his question. You observe, control the questions, and occasionally comment. When the clock indicates 10 remaining minutes, you halt the discussion. Correcting two factual errors, one logical fallacy, three grammatical lapses, and praising the thoroughness of her research, the subtlety of her examples, and the precision of her conclusion, you end the session promptly with the bell.

MARTIN THE CLARIFIER. When you enter the classroom, students are clustered in fives and sixes. You interrupt their social chatter.

"Each group should begin where it ended yesterday. If there are questions, call me over."

You circulate from group to group. At the second group, you stop to listen. As they brainstorm alternatives to impeachment, you suggest additional areas to consider. Another group requests help with reporting methods. You help design a values continuum strategy. You listen as a third group rehearses a role-playing skit and modify a technique. Priscilla, working alone at the carrel, beckons. You discuss her questions. You notice that she is squinting.

"What about those glasses, Pris?"

She smiles apologetically. "I forgot 'em today."

You note the time and issue the five minute reminder. The groups scurry to clean up.

"Tomorrow," you instruct, "we'll want to post our positions and discuss each issue." The bell rings.

FREDERICK THE FACILITATOR. No bell sounds. Each student enters, marks herself or himself present, picks up a folder, and selects a work area. You sit with six students who are assembling an American-inventions time line with photos and drawings. They ask about the placement of radio; you discuss Marconi and his wireless. Two students submit their math work for evaluation. You review the work, process the next skill, and illustrate examples on three-dimensional geometric board. You stop at Tom's carrel and discuss the book he is reading. Meanwhile, the choral poetry group indicates that it is ready to present the class with its reading of Frost's "Two Roads." You invite any who are interested to gather in the reading corner. Tom stays with his book, and the time-liners decline. The others drift over. You sit down to listen. "Two roads . . ."

INSTRUCTION B. On a sheet of paper, mark out five columns. Head each column with one famous-teacher name. Under each name, list four characteristics that describe that person's teaching style. (One characteristic is already attributed to each.)

Demosthenes	Socrates	Abelard	Martin	Frederick
1				helps
2			clarifies	
3		guides		
4	questions			
5	delivers			

INSTRUCTION C. In the space that follows, you will find the Spectrum of Style. Reflect on the character descriptions and the words you selected to characterize each style. First, mark the Spectrum under the name that represents *your* dominant teaching style. Indicate the approximate percentage of the time that you use that style. Next, mark each of the other styles you use with approximate percentages.

EXAMPLE:

Demosthenes	Socrates	Abelard	Martin	Frederick
15%	75%	10%	0	0

In my class, I am

Demosthenes	Socrates	Abelard	Martin	Frederick
%				

In my class, I think my students learn best when I am

Demosthenes	Socrates	Abelard	Martin	Frederick
%				

Having turned the mirror on your style, ask the students to look at your teaching style. Give each student a copy of the Spectrum descriptions. Rank the characters in two columns: column A will rank "style most descriptive of my teacher" and column B will rank "style that helps me learn best."

____Demosthenes	____Aristotle
____Aristotle	____Martin
____Martin	____Frederick
____Abelard	____Abelard
____Frederick	____Demosthenes

The general instructions for this strategy are identical to those for the "Scale of Priorities":

1. Don't give the Spectrum to students unless your self-image is solid.

2. Structure the discussion. So that all who wish may contribute, use the Whip strategy (without editorials) to report each rank order. Select a representative to explain each point of view, and finally, if time allows, move to open discussion.

If you prefer, collect the rank orders for scrutiny in the comfortable privacy of your kitchen. Whichever conclusion you select, give the bulk of your attention to the differences between your perceptions and those of the students. How accurately did you estimate their perceptions? How do they perceive your style? How helpful to their learning is your style?

Toward Facilitating Behaviors

If you have used the Scale of Priority and Spectrum of Style strategies with your class, not only should you understand the basic attitudes, teaching style, and skills that characterize a facilitator, but also as you guided the class through the strategies, you should have experienced the feelings that go along with a facilitation style. But how can you evaluate how well you did? A request for the students' judgment — "Was I a good facilitator?" — could reduce the class to collective guffaws, could produce a wall of silence, could lead to a sarcastic chorus of "you're the greatest, man." A more fruitful response, which will not destroy the open communication you established, will come from a strategy such as "Instant Replay" (without Howard Cosell, of course!).

Instant Replay

INSTRUCTION A. Gather the class into a tight semicircle close to a long chalkboard or around 10 to 12 feet of newsprint taped to a wall. (Your local newspaper often gives away roll ends.) Ask a student to record the response given by the class.

INSTRUCTION B. Give these instructions to the class: Instant Replay moves quickly. Don't raise hands. Fire answers as fast as the recorder can write. Limit each response to one or two words. Don't judge responses. No yeahs or boos from the gallery. Make your point, but don't add a long editorial.

INSTRUCTION C. In the chalkboard's upper left-hand corner, instruct the recorder to write "pictures in my mind." Ask the class to use words or phrases to describe the images they see in their minds during the Spectrum strategy discussion. Start the replay.

(Example) PICTURES IN MY MIND

Mr. John talking	big ears
big words	nodding his head
sore hands	waving arms
questions	sitting on desk
Tow Twist asleep	pointing at roof
making me think	laughing
me talking	listening

INSTRUCTION D. As the response dwindles, ask the recorder to begin a new column, "words she or he used." Repeat the procedure with other spin-off headings: "what I thought," "my feelings," "I was pleased that," "I learned."

INSTRUCTION E. Conclude the Instant Replay with a discussion. Using questions only, help the class to draw conclusions from the recorded lists. Two points are salient here: how did you act? and how did the class respond when you were "facilitating"?

Instant Replay has a magic quality to it. Used with any age group or in any subject area, it helps to involve the shyest and most reluctant contributors. A sixth-grade social studies class in Harrisburg used Instant Replay to conclude each week's study.

THIS WEEK'S REPLAY

How I teach	What I do	How I feel	I learned that	I ought to
smiles	help my friend	good	books are fun	work harder
cool breezes	feel warm	happy	I like this room	be quiet
fun	read a lot	nice	I'm not scared	share
hard worker	my best	warm	I like geography	do my job
you help me	draw	important	my teacher will help me	write better
nice words	watch movies	busy	I want to be the	finish my report
blue eyes	clown	funny	first lady President	read more books
busy as a bee	work hard	welcome		be nicer to kids
warm butter	too much	quiet		help my team
a helping hand	homework			relax
pretty teeth	feel good			keep my yap shut
organized	have fun			say thank you
a big heart	better			

After a tenth-grade biology class using Instant Replay called on its teacher to give more help with study-group organization, the class was divided into four- and five-person study groups. Group membership rotated after each unit. Before that, in a series of cell-experiments, groups had been experiencing a frustratingly high number of experiment failures.

BIOLOGY CLASS INSTANT REPLAY

What I do	What the group does	What Mr. J. does	We ought to
read instructions carefully	expects too much	dispenses equipment	spend more research time
keep equipment clean	works hard	checks the steps done	get more instructions explained
plan our objectives	dictates the dirty work to me	advises on planning	
day-dreaming		listens	read more carefully
assign jobs	very careful	keeps us busy	agree on our mutual expectations
read other books	clowns around	makes us feel important	
make decisions	shares the load	gives us	work together
cover our tracks	careful planning		form new groups
keep records	follows instructions		start over
be serious	too serious		find out what we're doing
argue	listens to Mr. J.		share responsibility
let Sue and Tom do it	Lets Tom and Sue run the show		ban dictators
			get it together

My Facilitating Behaviors

INSTRUCTION A. In the first column, traditional teaching behaviors are listed. In the seventh column, facilitating behaviors are listed. In the columns after each list, questions are asked. Check the boxes opposite each listed behavior for which you can make an *affirmative* response.

I USE THIS TECHNIQUE

traditional behaviors	Always	Regularly	Sometimes	Seldomly	Never
1. give lectures					
2. measure achievement by tests					
3. grade achievement					
4. lead all class question-answer discussions					
5. assign required readings for entire class					
6. keep physical distance from class					
7. give most assignments to entire class					
8. direct formation of groups					
9. tell students what they need					
10. plan and control curriculum					
11. impose learning style on class					
12. plan and control reading selections					
13. stress intellectual development					
14. encourage competition					
15. give subject matter top priority					
16. follow RLT model					
17. require that students stay at desks					

I USE THIS TECHNIQUE

facilitator behaviors	Always	Regularly	Sometimes	Seldomly	Never
1. permit small groups formed by students					
2. support groups					
3. assign individual learning projects during class time					
4. conduct individual needs assessment as basis of student's perceptions					
5. use clarifying strategies with small groups and/or individuals					
6. establish classroom learning stations					
7. offer nondirective guidance					
8. help students set own goals					
9. help students decide curriculum					
10. help students select own style of learning					
11. evaluate learning according to mastery					
12. help students master the processes					
13. help students see themselves as thinking, feeling, valuing persons					
14. give priority to student choice					
15. build cooperative trust atmosphere					
16. make self-concept top priority					
17. give students opportunity to use resources outside classroom					

Two Roads

The teacher can go in one of two ways: on the one hand there is the traditional teaching-learning model; on the other, the facilitating model. Both cannot be traveled. Whichever is selected, it is chosen "knowing how way leads on to way."

Advantage Spectrum

INSTRUCTION A. List the advantages and disadvantages of each style.

Traditional		Facilitating	
Advantages	Disadvantages	Advantages	Disadvantages

INSTRUCTION B. Complete this sentence in your Journal: "Having weighed the advantages and disadvantages of each style, I elect to perfect the _____ _____because . . ."

New Directions

INSTRUCTION A. Having selected a style, list in your Journal what you *need* in order to perfect that style. If you have decided, for instance, that learning is a process that involves thinking, feeling, valuing, etc., and believe that helping individual students to improve their self-image by "learning how to learn" is your primary responsibility, then you must question what process-learning skills you need to improve or what classroom procedures you must change (i.e., to help students self-evaluate, to improve my listening skills, to learn group dynamics, to furnish learning stations). It, on the other hand, you have elected to use the traditional model, list those needs (i.e., improve my tests, organize lectures, etc.).

INSTRUCTION B. Select the five most critical areas of need identified above. Place them in a rank order. Rank the "most urgent" need in space 1.

1. _____
2. _____
3. _____
4. _____
5. _____

INSTRUCTION C. Rewrite each need as a goal to accomplish. In your statement include (a) what you want to accomplish, (b) how you would like to accomplish it, (c) who can best help you, (d) the time span you will impose, and (e) how you will determine when you have reached your goal.

Processing This Chapter

PURPOSES: _____

_____

_____

_____

FEELINGS: _____

_____

_____

_____

CONCEPTS: _____

_____

_____

_____

APPLICATIONS: _____

_____

_____

_____

_____

13

He who conquers
others is strong;
He who conquers
himself is mighty.
Lao Tzu,
Tao Te Ching

Creating Personal Structures

Freedom is a frightful word. To those with power and control, it connotes anarchy, social class, and rebellion; to those who are dominated, it connotes repression, enslavement, and powerlessness. Over the centuries, the universal need for individual liberation has made people fight established structures. The Magna Charta, the Declaration of Independence, the Bill of Rights, the XIVth and XIXth amendments to the Constitution have marked the evolution of the freedom fight in this country. At each step, the individual's need to control her or his life has struggled against the shackles of ignorance — racial and ethnic bias, sex discrimination, and class repression.

But nothing dies more slowly than outdated customs and archaic social structures. Two hundred years after the Declaration of Independence denounced King George as "a tyrant, unfit to be the ruler of a free people" because he used his power to oppress the colonies, two hundred years after our Constitution created the office of the President to serve the people, those same people witnessed a nearsighted attempt to restore absolute power into a few hands. The model that the Constitution imposed upon government was a simple reversal of the traditional political-social power base. The divine right, established in Israelic tradition with the anointment of David and continued throughout the western tradition, gave the king absolute authority over his subjects. The king, or the delegated nobles, made law, enforced law, and punished transgressions.

The Constitution, however, established a model government that evolved out of the turmoil of the Protestant Reformation and the American Revolution. The average citizen, "endowed with inalienable rights" would dictate the duties and powers of the President through elected representatives.

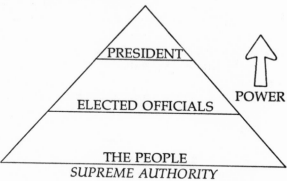

SUPREME AUTHORITY

Except when an individual becomes enamoured with the power given by the electorate, most American institutions resemble this model. There is, however, one major exception which does not: *the American school system is a divine right structure.*

AUTHORITY
AMERICAN SCHOOL SYSTEM

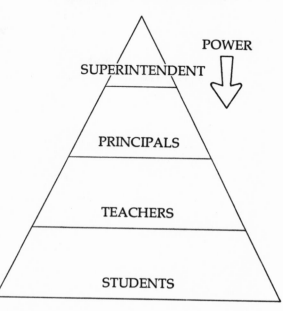

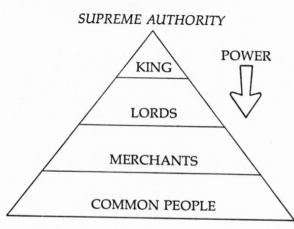

In the divine right structure, the power to control what, how, when, or where teachers teach and students learn is vested in the superintendent. Neither students nor teachers have the opportunity to make choices of real significance to the learning or teaching processes. Even if a student elects a special course, or if a teacher selects materials, approval from a higher authority is always necessary. Is it any wonder then that the dominant lesson taught by the schools and reinforced by the passivity-reinforcement of TV leads so many to refrain from getting involved — "avoid the hassle," "it's not my worry," "you can't fight city hall"? Is it any wonder that words like "freedom," "liberation," and "justice" are buried? Is it any wonder that students from high school through graduate school indulge in cribbing, cutthroat competition, and "doing my own thing"?

The more authority-bound a school is, the greater will be the resistance to an open change based on trust. A restrictive superintendent will fear giving teachers any freedom to choose; the teachers, imbued with the fear, will respond in a like manner to the students.

The 3 C's

Control-oriented educators love the 3 R's; the simpler the concept of schooling, the greater the power. For the individual teacher who wants to correct the power-flow, it is the 3 C's which are needed: Courage, Commitment, and Confidence. The battle to reverse the educational model from control to control is arduous, sometimes job-threatening, and always lonely.

Where do I start? Begin with yourself. You have already identified the skills which you have and those you need. If you seek retraining, select workshops or courses which will involve you as a participant learner. You don't need RLT courses on group dynamics or values clarification. "Learn by doing."

After you have gained the skills, make a small plan to introduce your students to experience-based learning —

____a voting strategy on contemporary social problems

____a rank order on favorite TV shows

____a reflection on the qualities of a good citizen

____Journals

____"Today, I learned . . ." completions to end a class

____small groups to role-play a historic event

____brainstorm solutions to the Civil War

____a chart of the causes of water pollution with its environmental consequences

____small groups to plan and do a social action project.

When you have tried a few strategies, begin to process the activities. Focus the students' attention not only on the content and purpose of the strategy, but also especially on the processes used (choosing, reacting, clarifying). Bring closure to each process discussion with thought-feel cards, sentence completions, or a Journal entry.

DANGER
You Are Abdicating
Your Decision-Making Authority
TO
KIDS!!
Be Wary Of Your Principal and Peers.
You Are Causing Waves.
Waves Always Have
B A C K W A S H

Words to the wise are never sufficient. If you decide to *help* students *learn* to make decisions by introducing strategies and new structures, you will discover through the grapevine that immorality, license, and chaos are running rampant in your room. Don't worry about the wild rumors and stories you hear. Do worry when the tales stop. (It's the calm before the storm.)

Once the students become involved in the introductory strategies, you will not want to turn back. Nor will they let you! If you plan to go beyond the introductory stage, you must consider three other factors:

(1) *The parents:* If the kids are "turned on," you'll have parent support. Increase that support by using the same principle which started you on the change: involvement. Bring the parents in to share their ideas and to help (making materials, tutoring, special speakers).

(2) *The principal:* Principals have an unenviable task. They walk a tightrope with dynamite in hand. If your principal is not careful, thoughtful, and able to balance on that rope, watch out. If she or he becomes a super-supporter of your idea and wants everyone else to imitate you, be wary. The person of authority who imposes something you happen to like can be just as ready to oppose. Share your plans with the principal. Get her or his help and advice, but insist that what you do is not to be imposed on other teachers, unless *they freely choose.*

(3) *The faculty:* If you stimulate an amoeba, it will draw itself in. If you threaten a person, the reaction is similar. When you begin to share control with students, the word will spread. "Miss Smith, why can't we learn like they do in Mr. Acco's room?" To avoid complications and misunderstandings, share your ideas with the other teachers. Don't be threatening. Ask their advice and help. If there are kindred spirits, give each other support. At all costs, avoid giving the impression that *you* are the savior, and *they* the dictators, chumps, anti-humanists, or whatever.

How do I focus my students' total attention on the control of their own learning? You don't. The essential difference between traditional teaching and facilitating is who *chooses* to do what. If students focus on self-direction, its because *they* choose that style. This question, although it may seem too fine a distinction, should read: *How do I help students choose the teaching-learning style most appropriate to their needs?*

Having introduced the class to process learning with introductory strategies and exercises, consider these steps:

Step 1. Give the class assessment strategies to evaluate the traditional teaching style and the facilitating style. Process the strategies by comparing (a) your skill in using each style, (b) their reactions, positive and negative, to each style, (c) the advantages and disadvantages that they perceive in each style. Allowing yourself no more than equal voice, come to a class consensus. If the consensus results in the election of the traditional style, decide with the class what improvements you and they will need. If, as is more likely, the consensus leans toward involvement-learning and shared decision-making, you will want to decide with them (a) to what extent shared decision-making is possible, (b) how individual objection to a consensus will be respected, (c) who will have what responsibilities, and (d) what are the next steps. In essence, you and the students will begin shared decision-making by consenting to realistic ground rules.

Step 2. Decision-Making Mechanism
After you and the class have clarified the ground rules, you must agree upon a decision-making mechanism that provides *the opportunity for any person in the class who wishes* to participate at any time. This group will have the task of adjudicating disputes, resolving issues which affect the class, and coordinating the curriculum and instructional program.

Step 3. Curriculum Planning
Within the parameters clearly set by state requirements or school policy, the class will begin to plan a curriculum. If they have not yet learned process strategies, and *if they request your help* (The first major test: you keep your two cents worth out! If they foul up the process, resist the urge to step in, take over, and *teach* the correct way. Stand back. Help them deal with the frustrations and conflicts that will naturally occur. Avoid judging, but help them *process* the experience. *When they ask for your help,* give it, but not before and not with an "I told you so,") give help, but give it *indirectly.* Once the students have mastered some strategies and understand the learning

process steps, the class can assess needs, set goals, and find the curricular resources.

Do not become disappointed at the degree of floundering and misdirection which your students experience. At this stage, the most crucial decisions are those which help you and the students break the bonds of mutual dependency. This may mean much effort and much frustration for all. You may feel you are in limbo, but don't despair.

(a) The more you encourage your students to feel, value, think, and relate, the more ready they will become to accept the decision-making responsibilities and master the process-learning skills. Remind yourself regularly that you are giving first priority to changing passive and dependent self-concepts to self-controlling, inner-motivated self-concepts.

Self-Concept	Self-Control
Process Skills	Self-Direction
Subject Matter	Creative Knowledge

(b) The more you involve students by using strategies, exercises, and methods that help them examine, clarify, and choose, rather than dictate to them what they *must know* and *do*, or abandon them "to do their own thing," the more likely they are to master the process skills. With the proven ability to assess needs, find resources, organize learning, and self-evaluate, they will find minimal difficulty in applying the processes to conventional learning. Many parents and teachers, raised in the traditional system, find it difficult to perceive that the lack of walls, the lack of imposed physical, curricular, and RLT instructional modes with required courses, required reading, tests, grades, class periods, Carnegie units, departmental structures, etc., can produce significant learning. "Kids need structure." "What happens when my child is placed in a structured situation?"

No matter what a person's age, structure is, of course, necessary; but there are different kinds of structures and different sources. In some cities, schools are sometimes referred to as prisons because the external control imposed upon students by "quiet and order" administrators has created a school atmosphere that seethes with hostility and discontent. In direct opposition are the schools that take a *laissez-fare* stance. A neoromantic, "do your own thing" philosophy creates the illusion that the child's natural goodness, unchecked by social institutions, will flower to a rich bloom. Between these extremes are many alternatives, 99 percent of which lie toward the control end of the spectrum. Between these extremes — the one based on the assumption that humans are basically evil and need external controls imposed by a benevolent, wise authority, the other on the assumption that humans are innately good but corruptible by malevolent society — is an alternative in which neither good nor evil is considered an essential characteristic of persons or institutions. In this alternative, it is assumed that the individual creates a self-image framed by interaction with other humans and the immediate physical environment. This self-image, a product in process, acts and reacts only to the degree that it feels capable. To the degree that it feels secure with the people in its environment, the self-image opens itself to experience. Thus, a *facilitating style*, which is based on trust, involvement, and open-ended decision-making, *works to help the individual create structures grounded in a positive self-image which will enable the individual to self-control or self-direct learning.* Thus, the structure exists, not artificially imposed without regard for individual differences, but developed by skilled help on the basis of personal choice. Once the individual has developed personal structures, she or he experiences little difficulty in adapting to situations, some of which will necessarily be highly controlled and others of which will have no controls. The results of such research as the "Eight Year Study" and the experience of humanistically based schools in the last few years demonstrate that students who have learned to build their own structures do take control of their learning, do adapt to a wide variety of imposed structures, and do succeed in mastering even the most demanding academic and artistic disciplines.

As the decision makers apply strategies to each process, both curriculum content and instructional modes will take shape within the parameters previously identified. At this point, there is one clear and present danger. Some students, caught up in the self-deluding magic of their own power, may attempt to impose controls or limits on less verbal students or less confident students. As facilitator, your responsibility is to support those less vocal opinions without creating a confrontation between groups. This is a sensitive but crucial task.

Step 3. Form Listen-Support Groups.
Given a climate of mutual trust, the capability of students to plan and use strategies for process learning, your confidence in your own abilities, as well as the students' help, the class forms listen-support groups which will meet for at least 20 minutes each week during class time.

What are the purposes of listen-support groups? In any process-learning program, be it confined to a single classroom or expanded to a school-without-walls, individual learners are scattered in many directions. For most, this experience is exhilarating at first, but after the honeymoon is over, the absence of regular, secure contact with old friends becomes disconcerting. Thus, the first purpose of LSG is to provide a home base to which one can return regularly or in a pinch for support, security, and refueling.

The second purpose of LSG is the development of those listening skills that are prerequisite to forming firm trust relationships. "When I go to LSG, I know that I will find friends who care about what I have to say. I can talk openly to people I trust and they won't jump all over me."

The third purpose, based on the first two, is to provide a climate for realistic self-evaluation based on honest feedback. "I trust my LSG friends, and I know they'll be honest with me. But I'm not afraid of what they'll say because I know it's up to me to make the changes. I get uptight when somebody tells me what I have to do, but here I'm learning to accept the picture my friends see."

How are these groups formed? LSG's evolve naturally from the strategies and small group exercises you have used. After students have had several months to form relationships, begin with some listening skills strategies.

The Listening Wheel

INSTRUCTION A. Assemble random groups with four or five students in each. Begin with a whip strategy such as "this year I am most pleased . . ." After the first round, give the second whip lead: "**This year, I am most displeased about . . ."** Instruct the class to listen carefully to each statement. When the second whip is completed, allow any student to ask any other group member a question about her or his statement.**

Allow the respondent to talk for 15 or 20 seconds; then freeze roles. From this moment on, each student in the group will have a single role.

1. *The questioner* **will maintain her/his role as listener.**
2. *The responder* **will do all talking.**
3. **The other students in the group will** *observe* **and** *record.*

The questioner will become the listener. By using eye contact, supportive body language, or clarifying questions ("Can you say more about that?" "Can you clarify that?") she or he will draw out the ideas and feelings of the respondent. (The respondent may pass on any question.) After five minutes, the questioner must repeat what she or he has heard said. In this process, the observers note how and to what extent nonverbal communication, eye contact, and questioning skills are used. As the questioner feeds back the feelings, ideas, and attitudes she or he perceived, the original speaker should use listening behaviors. When the first round is concluded, rotate the roles. Conclude the strategy with a class discussion that processes the listening skills.

Resent-Demand-Appreciate

Follow the instructions for the listening wheel. Use a triple whip that focuses on the group membership. Begin the whip by instructing the starter to make three statements to another person in the group: "I resent that you . . .," "I demand that you . . .," "I appreciate that you . . ." Assign roles for the first round of listening and for the rotation procedure. Keep attention focused on the RDA statements.

Listening Support Groups

After you recognize that students are becoming more proficient listeners who recognize and use body language, feelings, values, and attitudes to communicate, begin the support groups. Allow each student to select two persons in the room with whom a trust relationship has been established. Instruct the class to figure out the procedures that will assure that everyone is invited into a group and that conflicts are resolved with full respect for feelings. Brainstorming and other problem-solving strategies should facilitate this session.

Each LSG should determine its own procedures, goals, and strategies within the three-purpose framework.

Processing This Chapter

PURPOSES: _____

_____

_____

_____

FEELINGS: _____

_____

_____

_____

CONCEPTS: _____

_____

_____

_____

APPLICATIONS: _____

_____

_____

_____

The obligation of any-
one who thinks of him-
self as responsible is to
examine society and try
to change it and to fight
it—at no matter what
risk. This is the only
hope society has. This
is the only way societies
change.
James Baldwin,
"A Talk To Teachers"

14
Changing

The first phase of the change cycle is complete. You are ready for a new beginning. Where do you go from here? What is your action project?

Beginnings: A Final Strategy

INSTRUCTION A. This is a rank order. Three change models are described below. Each might outline a model that you could decide to use. In each case, it is assumed that you are a change agent capable of initiating and carrying through the change process. Rank according to your ability to implement successfully

_____You work in a traditional school.

_____You decide to open your classroom with student decision making, process learning, support groups, learning stations, individualized materials, and mastery evaluations. You obtain parent support for this idea.

_____You decide to plan an alternative program for 100 students, who volunteer with parent permission, and six full-time faculty. The program will combine in-building resources with beyond-the-walls learning opportunities. Students will learn the process skills and work with faculty to schedule appropriate learning experiences. The self-contained program will give priority to self-image and process skills. The students will govern the program in conjunction with the faculty. Students and faculty in the alternative program will not take courses in the traditional program, although its resource materials will remain available.

_____You decide that the entire school should be restructured. Each student will select one of 12 alternatives, each one staffed by eight faculty. Each alternative will house 150 students. Each house will focus primarily on process learning and secondarily on meeting a specific subject-matter need (classical, multicultural, fine arts, career investigation, practical arts, Chicano studies, etc.). Students will use the house as home base for process skill mastery, community decision making, etc., but may elect to use faculty resources in other alternatives or beyond the walls. Each house will plan its own budget, make curricular decisions, and maintain its operation. All houses will share centralized administrative services for records, purchases, and cross-scheduling.

The action you take must reflect what you feel is important to you. Perhaps, the three options just provided are more than you wish to tackle. More likely, you'll want to alter details and create your own plan.

My Plan For Change

INSTRUCTION: Do your best brainstorming!

1. What is needed? _____
_____
_____

2. What are the obstacles to the needs? _____
_____
_____

3. How can I overcome these obstacles? _____
_____
_____

4. What are my goals? _____
_____
_____

5. Who can help? How? _____
_____
_____

6. What materials, equipment, and space do we need? _____
_____
_____

7. Where do I get these materials or the money? _____
_____
_____

8. What is our plan? Who has responsibility for what? _____
_____
_____

9. How do we evaluate the project? Who has responsibility? _____
_____
_____

W9-COZ-699

Dionysus in 69

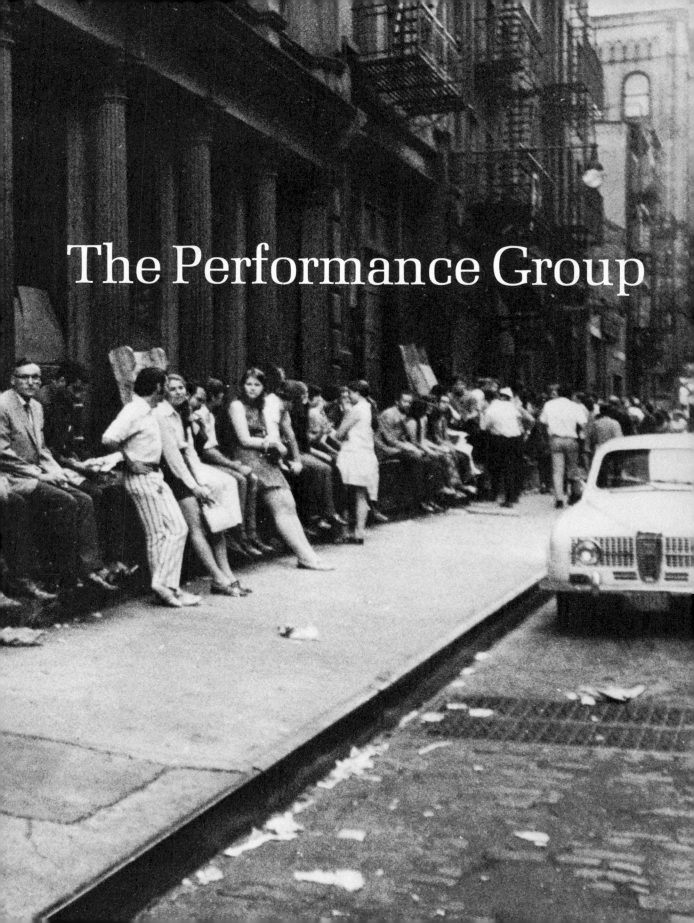

The Performance Group

FARRAR, STRAUS AND GIROUX / NEW YORK

Edited by RICHARD SCHECHNER

Designed by FRANKLIN ADAMS

Photographs by FREDERICK EBERSTADT
With additional photographs by RAEANNE RUBENSTEIN
and two folios of photographs by MAX WALDMAN

Dionysus in 69 was created by The Performance Group and played in the Group's theatre, The Performing Garage (33 Wooster Street, New York City), from June 6, 1968, until July 27, 1969. There were no performances during August and September 1968.

The production was directed by Richard Schechner. The environment was designed by Michael Kirby and Jerry Rojo and was constructed by Rojo and members of the Group.

The play text of *Dionysus in 69* is based on group improvisation, composition by members of The Performance Group, and the William Arrowsmith translation of Euripides's *The Bacchae*. Transcriptions from performance tapes were made by Charlotte Russiyan.

Some people who worked on *Dionysus in 69* did not remain with The Performance Group for the play's entire run, or never were members. Rozanne Levine performed from February until July 1968. Gwendolyn Galsworth, Ron Schenk, and Charles Strang performed during the fall of 1968. Judy Allen, Cara Crosby, and Eric Ubben helped run the business department and maintain the performing environment. Sam Blazer, a member, performed from the start until May 1969, when he left the Group.

Vicki May Strang, a member, was the stage manager of *Dionysus in 69*. She was also business manager until June 1969.

All the photographs in this book are by Frederick Eberstadt, except for about sixty taken by Raeanne Rubenstein and two six-page folios, based on the birth and death rituals, taken by Max Waldman in his studio.

The Eberstadt and Rubenstein prints were made by Image Photographic Services, New York; Mr. Waldman made the prints of his photographs.

Lines from the following translations are reprinted with the permission of the University of Chicago Press: Sophocles's *Antigone* (translated by Elizabeth Wycoff, copyright 1954 by the University of Chicago) and Euripides's *The Bacchae* (translated by William Arrowsmith, copyright 1959 by the University of Chicago), both included in *The Complete Greek Tragedies*, edited by David Grene and Richmond Lattimore, published by the University of Chicago Press.

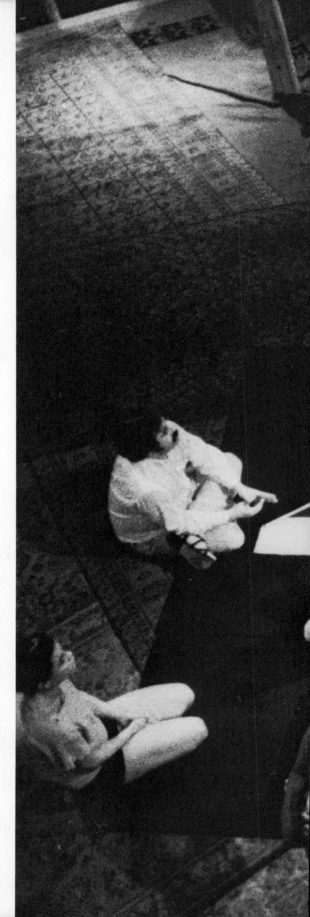

The audience begins to assemble at around 7:45 P.M. They line up on Wooster Street below Greenwich Village. Sometimes the line goes up the block almost to the corner of Broome. On rainy nights, or during the coldest parts of the winter, the audience waits upstairs over the theatre. The theatre is a large space, some 50 by 40 and 20 feet high. At 8:15 the performance begins for the audience when the stage manager, Vicki May Strang, makes the following announcement. Inside, the performers began warming up their voices and bodies at 7:45.

VICKI   Ladies and gentlemen! May I have your attention, please. We are going to start letting you in now. You will be admitted to the theatre one at a time, and if you're with someone you may be split up. But you can find each other again once you're inside. Take your time to explore the environment. It's a very interesting space, and there are all different kinds of places you can sit. We recommend going up high on the towers and platforms, or down underneath them. The password is "Go high or take cover." There is no smoking inside and no cameras. Thank you.

Work began on *Dionysus in 69* in January 1968. The Performance Group was barely two months old. We had finished the beginning. The forty-eight people who came to the first workshop on November 15, 1967, had winnowed themselves to twenty or so. (By the time the play opened, there were thirteen in the Group.) We knew something of each other and of the exercises I had taken from my work with the New Orleans Group, Grotowski, and elsewhere. The root of that work was exploration. And exploration, as we understood it then, meant exchange. We exchanged touches, places, ideas, anxieties, words, gestures, hostilities, rages, smells, glances, sounds, loves. We were working in January at the Welfare Center on the east side of Tompkins Square Park. It was a bleak walk through the winter nights to the Center. And we came there three times a week.

The room Bruce Grund arranged for us to have was spacious, perhaps 45 feet square. On one side there was a stage. We used the whole space and took no special notice of the stage. Outside the doors, the kids from the neighborhood watched us do our exercises. It was hard to keep them out, but impossible to let them in. Our work was tender and we needed privacy. Sometimes we heard the kids running away down the steps yelling, "They're fucking, they're fucking! Come! See!" Once, one of our girls was jumped in the bathroom.

One Saturday afternoon in January, we brought some copies of William Arrowsmith's translation of Euripides's *The Bacchae* to the Welfare Center. Bill Shephard wanted us to read *Peer Gynt*, but I felt strongly that Euripides was more in our way: obstacle, challenge, evocation, and initiation. We read the whole play in unison. Afterwards no one said very much. I asked people to buy scripts. The Performance Group had no money. Members paid a small amount in dues to keep us going. We had no theatre, and no prospect of finding one. But we had each other and a play we wanted to do. So our exercises found a focus and a direction. After that, we worked more and more intensely on *The Bacchae*, meeting to discuss it, to see how we would "confront it," wondering if we could do it at all. No date was set for opening. We worked in terms of a "project" not a production. Everything was tentative and dangerously close to not existing.

Such adventures always spawn nostalgia. And when the Group fights, someone invariably says, "Remember back at the Welfare Center?" Unfortunately, such educations are not so beautiful as memory makes them. The purity of the days and nights near Tompkins Square Park was also the struggle of working at two or three jobs at once, the more or less constant come and go of members, the frustration of coping with people whose determination was more than a match for their abilities, and the underlying insecurity of not having a theatre of our own.

Soon enough that became a major crisis. The community no longer was satisfied peeping under the door at us. They wanted in. We arrived one night to find that a dance was dancing in our space. Bob Collier explained to us that our time had come. We had to go.

February was spent looking for a place to work. For a few weeks we worked on the west side of Tompkins Square at the Real Great Society, but it was cold and crowded. We looked at loft after loft and tried to run some workshops. Jerald Ordover, who became our lawyer and friend, helped us to locate possible theatre spaces. One day, someone—I think it was Bill Shephard or Pat McDermott—said he had heard of a garage owned or controlled by Bob Watts, a place down "below the Village." I went with Bill and Pat to look at it. When I saw the garage, I knew we had what we needed.

It was big and high and, except for a huge green garbage truck parked dead center, it was ready for us. We negotiated and rented, the Performing Garage was ours.

We took possession March 1. It was bitter cold and there was no heating. We used electric space heaters. The floor was cement. We bought some black rubber mats. The place was filthy. The walls were light green, the floor was gray and greasy. For nearly two months we scrubbed, painted, built, and scrubbed again. We cleaned the 30 foot long, 6 foot deep grease pit again and again. Work chants rose to our throats as we hauled the buckets. It was a labor of love but we did not love it. Throughout, we met three and then four times a week to work on what had been dubbed *Dionysus in 69*. A $5,000 bank loan to me paid for the electrical work and the other necessary contracting. But most of the muscle came from the Group. We didn't know it quite, but Thebes was being built.

In many ways *Dionysus in 69* grew into a paradigm of environmental theatre. Here was no mere set construction, or even the building of an environment within an already articulated space. Rather, we found a space, made it ours through work, and slowly squeezed out the *Dionysus* environment by our labor. There is no better way to know a ceiling than to paint it, or to feel a floor than to scrub it.

In May, Bill Shephard told us of the Kelly Carpet Company on Sixth Avenue, where he had once worked. For $150 the manager agreed to let us take away all the scrap carpet we could carry. We arrived one afternoon with a flat-bed truck, loaned to us by Joe Pasquale up Wooster Street, and we hauled a tonnage of rug and carpet. Earlier I had decided to paint the garage white rather than the traditional theatre black. I wanted our audience to see one another, I wanted the space to open up and reveal itself. And the longer we worked on *Dionysus* the more clearly we knew we needed towers and places to "live," places to climb and hide. The environment developed with rehearsals.

The 4 by 8 and 4 by 4 platforms of various heights are movable modules. Each afternoon we played with them. Sometimes they were houses for the performers, sometimes the king's palace. Exercise after exercise evolved around the use of space, who was dominant, revolution and oppression. The two large towers, first designed by Michael Kirby and then redesigned by Jerry Rojo, anchor the environment. When rehearsal was over one night early in May, some people stayed late to help Jerry Rojo and Pat McDermott raise the towers into place.

By the middle of May, we were ready for "open re-hearsals." Saturday afternoons at three and Saturday nights at eight we let people in to watch what we were doing, to answer our questions sometimes, to experiment with, to test out. We ran the birth ritual, the caress, Pentheus's search for a woman in the audience, the chase and kill, and some other scenes. The audiences ranged from fifteen to—near opening—a hundred people. These open rehearsals were not previews but true rehearsals. On Thursday June 6 the performance opened.

Half an hour before the first person is let into the theatre, the performers lie in a circle in the center. They begin their breathing exercises, their relaxations, their voice warm-ups. Even before, at 7:30, silence is enforced throughout the theatre. Jason and several others like to take a few minutes for personal relaxation and meditation. Of course, some people are regularly late, and others know this pattern. Finley will come in just as the warm-ups are to begin, toting his coffee in a paper bag and smoking one of the seven brands of cigarettes he habitually carries. Ciel will be on time but not ready, usually fussing with her hair in front of a small mirror set up on one of the platforms. Pat McDermott will ask everyone to get ready, and say that he is going to begin the warm-ups. Margaret is late, and after the play she will tell people again, "It's a real hangup with me."

Schechner

The first chorus starts before any spectators are let into the theater. It is fragmented, organized randomly, and therefore is different at every performance. Each girl has a set of lines which she may say in any order and distort into pure sounds. The men repeat one line: "Good evening, sir (ma'am), may I take you to your seat?"

now I raise the old, old hymn to Dionysus

keep the rite of Cybele the mother

blessed are we for we shall know the mysteries of god, blessed are you for you shall be purified

he whom the spirit of god possesses, who is one with those who belong to the holy body of god

Dionysus is our god

so his mother bore him once in labor bitter

lightning struck forced by fire

consumed, she died

of light the son was born

Dionysus moves freely in the space, sometimes confronting spectators and speaking to them. He goes to each of the women in the chorus and "impregnates" them.

JASON AS DIONYSUS   Women waiting for god. Blessed is the mother. Blessed are you, for you can know the mysteries of god.

We let the public in one at a time. People on the queue outside the theatre ask me why. I explain that this is a rite of initiation, a chance for each person to confront the environment alone, without comparing notes with friends. People are skeptical. Some few are angry. Many think it's a put-on. I must confess to a perverse pleasure in teasing the people on line. Many will come up and ask anxiously, "Has it already begun?" "Well," I say, "it begins before we let anybody in, but it begins when everybody is in, and really it begins when you go in." True.

Vicki

The chorus continues.

when the weaving fates fulfilled the time
the bull-horned god was born of Zeus

with joy he crowned his son, set serpents
on his head

he is sweet upon the mountain

he drops to the earth with the running pack

he hunts the wild goat and kills it

he delights in raw flesh

with flying feet, she leaps

set serpents on his head

come dance the dance of god

let the dance begin

good evening, sir, may I take you to your seat

where the throngs of women wait driven from
shuttle and loom

possessed by Dionysus

he is sweet upon the mountain

The opening ceremonies—as we call that part of the
performance from the start of the performers' warm-
ups until the beginning of the scene between Tiresias
and Cadmus—are of indeterminate duration. Their
several functions overlap. The audience must be
brought into an unusual theatre and initiated into an
unusual space. A large space populated with towers
and platforms. No clearly defined stage. The spectators can sit just about anywhere. Sometimes when
they crowd into spaces that the performers need, one
of the men comes up and asks the ill-placed spectators to move. The action goes on around and among
the audience. Some people stand close to the door
and wait for their friends or spouses. Others go
swiftly into the space and seek a place, perhaps a
refuge. Still others wander, orienting themselves to
the scenic and sonic environments. Different parts
of the theatre offer radically different perspectives,
sounds and even temperatures. We made no attempt
at regularity, abandoning altogether the niceties of
linear perspective. The space, like the performance
itself, is designed toward gathering intensities, ex-
plosive release. Not a few spectators, once inside, ask
anyone who seems to know, "Where's the best place
to sit?" This question is often asked of others in the
audience, on the theory of any port in a storm. Even
if we wanted to help the spectator get settled, advice
about where to sit would be hard. It depends on what
you want: involvement, distance, a place near the
center of the holocaust, or somewhere long and dark
and quiet enough to doze.

Good evening, sir, may I take you to your seat?

One of the functions of the opening ceremonies is to bring the performers into close physical and psychic contact with one another. This is particularly a problem in a theatre with a permanent company. Arguments occur. Alliances are formed and broken. Large quantities of psychic and affective energy are stored, directed, and released. But the performance demands a unity. We must be together. And the ceremonies help us get together. Also, and more mundanely, the exercises distribute the performers throughout the space, so that they activate and control it. Their bodies and voices are loosened and better prepared to give during the night's activities.

The exercises themselves are adapted from Grotowski's. They are psychophysical, which means that they engage the imagination as well as the body. A set of head rolls, body rolls, backbends, runs, leaps, shoulder stands, head stands, looking and staring. Each exercise mobilizes and uses a part of the body. All of them relate the body to the mind in such a way that the two apparently separate systems are one.

Schechner

REMI BARCLAY

Agave, March–July 1969. Chorus, throughout.
Messenger, June–July 1969

SAMUEL BLAZER

Chorus, throughout until May 1969. Coryphaeus,
June–November 1968. Messenger, November 1968–
May 1969

ASON BOSSEAU

Chorus, throughout. Coryphaeus, January–July 1969.
Dionysus, November 1968–July 1969. Messenger,
une–October 1968, July 1969

RICHARD DIA

Cadmus, June–October 1968. Chorus, throughout.
Coryphaeus, June–July 1969. Pentheus, November
1968–April 1969

WILLIAM FINLEY

Cadmus, March–July 1969. Chorus, throughout.
Dionysus, June 1968–February 1969

JOAN MAC INTOSH

Agave, June 1968–February 1969. Chorus, throughout.
Dionysus, April–July 1969

PATRICK MC DERMOTT

Chorus, throughout. Coryphaeus, April–July 1969.
Dionysus, June–July 1969. Messenger, March–April
1969, July 1969. Tiresias, June 1968–March 1969

MARGARET RYAN

Agave, March–June 1969. Chorus, throughout until
June 1969

WILLIAM SHEPHARD

Cadmus, November 1968–April 1969. Chorus,
throughout. Pentheus, June–October 1968, April–
July 1969

CIEL SMITH

Agave, June 1968–February 1969. Chorus, throughout.
Tiresias, March–July 1969

	Agave	Cadmus	Chorus	Coryphaeus	Dionysus	Messenger	Pentheus	Tiresias
Remi Barclay	●		●			●		
Samuel Blazer			●	●		●		
Jason Bosseau			●	●	●	●		
Richard Dia		●	●	●			●	
William Finley		●	●		●			
Joan MacIntosh	●		●		●			
Patrick McDermott			●	●	●	●		●
Margaret Ryan	●		●					
William Shephard		●	●				●	
Ciel Smith	●		●					●

The chorus continues.

with milk the earth flows, it flows with wine,
it runs with the nectar of bees

flames float out

good evening, ma'am, may I take you to your
seat

hard are the labors of god

sweet to serve, sweet to cry Bacchus, evohe

bear your god in triumph home

escort your Dionysus home

attend him through the streets of Hellas

good evening, sir, may I take you to your seat

to the mountain

he delights in raw flesh

flows with wine

he runs with the nectar of bees

flames jump out from his trailing wand and
his long curls

I was very intrigued from the beginning with the idea
of "associative exercises." Physical exercises with a
direct relationship to mental processes. I've always
been athletic, interested in movement. I took four
years of ballet when I was very young. The most important thing I started out with was something
Schechner mentioned to me in one of the first workshops. He told me to resign myself to an imperfection
in form, to accept the fact that there was no perfect
headstand. Rather, he asked that I explore the relationship between the mental associations and the
physical process. In the beginning, when we were in
workshops, I found this opened new avenues of sensitivity with regard to textual work. Later, when we
began hard work on *Dionysus*, I was confused about
how the exercises fit into performance. They didn't
seem the same any more. After Grotowski's visit to
the play in November, he pointed out that it was
better to confine certain personal exercises to workshop. In performance, the variables were such that
the demands made upon the individual changed the
process of exploration, and weakened it.

Shephard

I never really liked the opening exercises because it's
not clear what's happening. It is true that this ceremony provides the occasion for some truly spontaneous interactions among ourselves. Optimally, we

should create a different psychic landscape and each night begin from a different place. However, within a structure which is, at best, loose, personal patterns develop which are solipsistic, repetitious, and enervating. Paradox: We want our performance to explode beyond the spherical container of technique. Art is a continuous process. Nothing is completely new and nothing is left completely to chance. Also, we operate at a physical level during the exercises which is not maintained throughout the show. Eventually the exercises should be so embedded in our movement that they disappear.

Ciel

The chorus continues.

he drops to the earth

and kills it

red with berries green with bryony

redden with berries green with bryony

let the dance drop to the earth

attend him to the mountain

he delights in the labors of god

flames float out in triumph

good evening, ma'am, may I take you to your

with milk the dance of god flows with the nectar of bees

the ivy of god lightning struck untimely torn

bear him down with labor bitter

keep the rite of Cybele who is one with the holy body of god

now I raise the old old hymn

with flying feet she delights in raw flesh

good evening, sir, may I take you to your seat

set serpents on his head

let the dance begin walking would be better

beeeeeeeeeeeeeeesbeeeeeeeeeeeeeeeeeeeeeees

let the dance begin

Many of the chorus lines are fragmented. Even syllables are distorted by extension, new sonic emphasis, and accent. These sounds are bounced around the room. Lines are broken, constructed, and reconstructed. Calls are given and echoed, communications started and severed. As more and more people fill the space, its interior volume is expanded, like a balloon blowing up.

An early exercise outdoors is the source of this sense of expanding space. One day, early in the spring of 1968, we decided to work outside, as much to celebrate the end of New York winter as anything else. We were working on the problem of the social organization of Thebes, and specifically the relationship between the men and the women. The time was before men had women—when men had to go out and hunt their women and bring them back home, domesticate them and make them as useful as they were wild and beautiful. We played a special variant of hide-and-go-seek. The women left the garage and the rule was that they could hide wherever they wanted on the block across from the theatre. After around ten minutes, the men pursued them. The game also included an opportunity for the women to organize themselves into a society out there, and they could, if they were able, capture and keep the men who were hunting them.

The men went after the women but couldn't find them. We heard them calling to each other from time to time, loud, high, and frighteningly strong echoes like those of the Arab women in the film *The Battle of Algiers*. Although I was supposed to be refereeing the game, I couldn't stay out of it. I had to find where the women went. After much searching and believing that they had cheated and gone to some other block, I found an open doorway and followed the stairs behind it up five flights to the roofs over Wooster Street. A new world. There in the mountains of communicating roofs, the women had established their society, complete with watches, centers of information, outposts, and headquarters. Some of the men had already been captured and I joined them. The game ended when twenty police, guns drawn, charged up the stairs. Someone had phoned in a report of a gang leaping from roof to roof, terrorizing the neighborhood.

The rooftop game multiplied our space sense, our movement feel. The call from the rooftops came into the garage. The wooden towers became mountains and outposts. The women knew who they were before they were the property of men and what they could become again if liberated.

Schechner

The chorus continues.

for Bromius we come

and kills it

with joy he crowned his son set serpents on his head

Twice during the opening ceremonies the chorus is recited/sung in sequence. Joan begins when she feels a compelling density of spectators or a proper rise in energies from the performers. The end of the second choral recitation overlaps the start of the scene between Tiresias and Cadmus.

JOAN   Out of the land of Asia, down from holy Tmolus, speeding the service of god, for Bromius we come! Sweet to serve, sweet to cry

MANY VOICES   Bacchus! Evohe! Make way! Fall back! Hush!

The core of the opening ceremonies is the first chorus, sung and said by the women, supported by the men. The men have only one line, addressed to the incoming audience, "Good evening, sir [or ma'am], may I take you to your seat?" They also sound a base line—wails, cries, moans, rhythms. The chorus is the sonic environment, and it is from this that the play precipitates as rain does from gathering clouds. The chorus is complex and ambivalent. The women are Asian bacchantes dancing behind Dionysus into Grecian Thebes. They are also Theban women driven out of their minds and homes by ecstasy. The chorus is initiation by example. And, for the Group, it is the matrix of the play. Scenes come from the chorus and dissolve back into it. Everyone is part of the chorus, emerging from it to play specific roles. Thus the chorus is the underground that gives birth to the entire play. As such, it is indestructible and, finally, joyful.

The principles controlling the selection and distribution of chorus lines reveal the precise nature of the personal element that confronts social ritual throughout our version of the play. I was influenced by what Grotowski told me in November 1967: "We eliminate those parts of the text which have no importance for us, those parts with which we can neither agree nor disagree. Within the montage one finds certain words that function vis-à-vis our own experiences." At an early rehearsal I asked the women to go over the first chorus and underline those words, phrases, sentences, or sections that got to them, either positively or negatively. This would be our chorus. There was no obligation to Euripides, or The

Performance Group, or even *Dionysus in 69*. It was an absolutely personal selection.

For most of the time during the opening ceremonies, the women recite the chorus lines they selected, in whatever order, at whatever tempo, with whatever volume or pitch they wish. Twice during the ceremonies, the chorus is done in sequence. Joan begins by saying loud enough for all to hear, "Out of the land of Asia, down from holy Tmolus, speeding the service of god, for Bromius we come." What follows varies widely in sonic density and intensity. Even when all the women have selected the same line, there is no requirement that they say the line in unison. Sometimes that happens, sometimes not. The rules of construction and recitation are strict, but the feed-out from these rules varies widely from night to night. Most of the other choruses in the play are structured in the same way.

Schechner

MARGARET AND REMI   Blessed, blessed are those who know the mysteries of god. Blessed is he who hallows his life in the worship of god, he whom the spirit of god possesses, who is one with those who belong to the holy body of god. Blessed are the dancers and those who are purified, who dance on the hill in the holy dance of god. Blessed are they who keep the rite of Cybele the Mother. Blessed are the thyrsus-bearers, those who wield in their hands the holy wand of god. Blessed are those who wear the crown of the ivy of god. Blessed, blessed are they. Dionysus is their god!

MARGARET   On Bacchae, on you Bacchae, bear your god in triumph home! Bear on the god, son of god, escort your Dionysus home! Bear him down from the Phrygian hill, attend him through the streets of Hellas

CIEL   So his mother bore him once in labor bitter, lightning struck, forced by fire that flared from Zeus. Consumed, she died, untimely torn, in childbed dead by blow of light. Of light the son was born. And when the weaving fates fulfilled the time, the bull-horned god was born of Zeus. With joy he crowned his son, set serpents on his head

JOAN AND REMI   O Thebes, nurse of Semele, crown your hair with ivy

JOAN, REMI, AND CIEL   Grow green with bryony

JOAN AND REMI   Redden with berries! O city, with boughs of oak and fir, come dance the dance of god. Fringe your skins of dappled fawn with tufts of twisted wool. Handle with holy care the violent wand of god. And let the dance begin

JOAN   He is Bromius who runs to the mountain. To the mountain where

JOAN AND CIEL   The throngs of women wait driven from shuttle and loom, possessed by Dionysus. Possessed by Dionysus!

CIEL   He is sweet upon the mountain. He drops to the earth from the running pack. He wears the holy fawn-skin

CIEL AND MARGARET   He delights in raw flesh

JOAN, REMI, AND CIEL   With milk the earth flows. It flows with wine. It runs with the nectar of bees

CIEL   Flames float out from his trailing wand and his long curls stream in the wind

JOAN AND CIEL   To the mountain!

JOAN   To the mountain!

REMI   With flying feet—she leaps!

I found that after eight months I could do the associative exercises very well in the sense that I could execute the balances, the body rolls, and the backbends, and the other things that I couldn't do before. I was dissatisfied. I took another tack. I limited my movements. For example, moving around the room in a walk, exploring the variations involved in the simple process of walking. I isolated my extremities, different parts of my body—my arms, legs, fingers. I set up obstacle courses for myself and went around these courses each night, imposing strict limitations on myself. I discovered very concrete psychic associations in relation to the audience entering the space, the other performers working in it, and my own role of Pentheus. Finally, it all cohered in a score for my performance. I felt that I was no longer doing the associative exercises. At the start of the play, when the audience first comes in, that is a great moment for me because each audience is very particular. They are not just an amorphous group of people, but persons with definite styles and movements, attitudes and reactions. During that time, the Bacchae are making sounds and doing the opening chorus. I spy and peer and run and hide. I spy on the performers and

the people who are coming in. The audience is alternately the Bacchae, the people of Thebes, the mountains. Added to that is a game. If the Bacchae see me, or if Dionysus discovers me, they chase me out from hiding. This sets up a stimulating game of hide-and-seek which is the first action of the play for me.

Shephard

Once it was clear that we were going to have a long run, I wondered how the performers could grow. I don't know who suggested role rotation, but it was the perfect answer. Each person could contribute his own interpretation of various characters to the swelling lore of the production. The chorus was at the conceptual center and from it spun out this role and that one. The goal was elegant and simple but extraordinarily difficult: everyone would perform every role. One night, there would be no role assignments. During the opening ceremonies, characters would emerge, here Tiresias and Cadmus, there Dionysus and Pentheus, and so on. The show would pass into ritual. We have not reached our goal, but we have come closer to understanding the process of exchange. We know very well that every performance is a negotiation between a person, the set of events which mark out a character, and the equally precise but more communal experience of the chorus.

Schechner

TIRESIAS   Cadmus, Agenor's son, the stranger from Sidon who built the towers of our Thebes, Tiresias wants you. Cadmus, Agenor's son, the stranger from Sidon who built the towers of our Thebes, Tiresias wants you. Cadmus, Agenor's son, the stranger from Sidon who built the towers of our Thebes, Tiresias wants you. You know what errand brings me—the agreement we made to deck our wands and dress in skins of fawn and crown our heads with ivy.

When McDermott and Shephard play Tiresias and Cadmus, Cadmus blindfolds Tiresias.

When Ciel and Finley play these roles, a game of blindman's buff begins at the start of the scene. Cadmus is seated among the audience, frequently high in a tower. Tiresias, already blindfolded, tries to find Cadmus—first by chance and then by homing in on his words. Cadmus does not allow himself to be caught until he finishes his first speech.

When McDermott and Dia play Tiresias and Cadmus, they start their scene during the opening chorus. They meet in a dark place behind a tower or under a platform. Perhaps a couple of spectators close by hear some of the lines. The

scene is played two or three times privately before it is said loud enough for all to hear. McDermott and Dia are conspiring.

CADMUS   Tiresias, my old friend, I knew it was you when I heard your voice. For there's something in the voice of wisdom that makes the man of wisdom known. Here I am. Dressed in the costume of the god. We must do honor to this god—insofar as we are able—because he was born my daughter's son and revealed to all men the god Dionysus. Where should we go? Tossing our heads and dancing to the gods. Expound to me, Tiresias, for in such matters you are wise, not me. Me, I could dance all night, tossing my white head, beating the earth with my thyrsus. And how sweet it is to forget my old age.

TIRESIAS   How old are you?

CADMUS   Twenty-seven.

TIRESIAS   I'm twenty-six. It's the same with me. I, too, feel young enough to dance.

CADMUS   Shall we take our chariots to the mountain?

TIRESIAS   No, walking would be better. It shows more honor to the god.

CADMUS   Let's go then. My old age conducting yours.

They start and then stop. Their movements are erratic and brief.

TIRESIAS   The god will guide us there with no effort on our part.

They do not move. Pause. Silence.

I'm not a seasoned actress. Agave and Tiresias are
the only two roles I've really wrestled with. It is very
much a physical battle with me. Voice and impulse
fighting free. The banners of The Performance Group
say, Muddy Evolution. My experience has been that
of groping rather than sudden enlightenment. I find
my way around the space with my tongue and finger-
tips. My feet inch along. My body hops and hesitates.
My eyes are blindfolded. These are not devices with
which to play a character. They are my condition. I
am very much as you see me.

Ciel

For me, that long moment when it gets quiet and
Ciel's out there alone with that tongue serving for
eyes is one of the great moments of the play. That
brute face and, a fine touch, those scrawny rabbini-
cal pigtails. And that nice body and the great vulgar
rasping and keening sounds she makes. I don't know
what it is, but she managed to fill up that room with
some kind of animal aura that wouldn't let me take
my eyes off her, that made me want to touch her,
hug her, hold on to her, mount her, whatever, and not
let her go.

Franklin Adams

CADMUS   Are we the only ones who are going to dance for Bacchus?

TIRESIAS   I don't know.

CADMUS   Why don't you ask them?

TIRESIAS   You want me to ask them?

CADMUS   Yes, ask them.

TIRESIAS   All right. You wait here. Don't move.

There are two versions of the following sequence. Tiresias goes into the audience to question individuals. When McDermott plays the role, he goes behind the spectators and comes upon them from the back. When Ciel plays, she is blindfolded and therefore moves slowly among the spectators, feeling them with her hands. She questions those for whom she senses a rapport. Cadmus warns her of obstacles.

MC DERMOTT AS TIRESIAS   Would you like to go through our ordeal with us?

CIEL AS TIRESIAS   Have you come to join the revels of the god or just to watch?

CADMUS   Careful, Tiresias.

Sometimes the spectator does not respond. More often, he does. Tiresias is happy when someone says that he will go through the ordeal or join the revels of the god. Cadmus keeps score. When three people in the audience say they will participate or when three say they won't the interrogation game is over.

CADMUS   Come on, Tiresias, we're wasting too much time. I don't know about them, but I'm just a man. I don't scoff at heaven.

There are two versions of the following speech.

MC DERMOTT AS TIRESIAS   Oh, no, we don't trifle with divinity. We are the heirs of customs and traditions hallowed by age and handed down by our fathers. No quibbling American mise-en-scène can topple them, whatever subtleties this clever Group invents—and people say they are very clever. People may say, "Aren't you ashamed of yourself, acting Euripides at your age?" Well, I'm not ashamed. Did the god say that just the young should dance? Or just the old? Or just the whites? Or just the blacks? Or just the Italians? Or just the Greeks? Or just James Brown? No, he wants his honor from all mankind. He wants no one excluded from his worship. Not even The Performance Group.

CIEL AS TIRESIAS   You don't? Neither do I. We don't trifle with divinity. We are the heirs of custom and tradition handed down to us by our fathers and hallowed by age. No quibbling logic can topple them, whatever subtleties this clever age invents. And it's a very subtle age. People may say, "Don't you feel ridiculous, dressed in those ragtag clothes, covered with sweat, dancing through the factories in worship of some unknown rebel god in whom no one believes?" But I don't feel ridiculous. Did the god declare that just the beautiful should dance? Or just the ugly? Just the rich or just the poor? Just those with soul or just those who plod? No, no, no. He wants no one excluded from his worship. Not even The Performance Group.

CADMUS   Are we there?

TIRESIAS   Yes, we're there.

Would you like to go through our ordeal with us?

Have you come to join the revels of the god or just to watch?

Sometimes, when whoever is playing Tiresias does not feel that the scene has taken the performers "there," Cadmus's question is answered with "It's hard to tell," or "I don't think so," or even "No." It is a very special moment in the performance, one which the audience can be quite unaware of: During the Cadmus/Tiresias scene, the other performers have moved from the periphery of the theatre to the center. Some come in swiftly, running and somersaulting. Others move in measured paces. One by one, they arrive and squat around the edges of three black rubber mats laid together to make a 12 by 8 foot rectangle, the "holy space." The noise of the opening chorus, its excitement and promise of ecstasy, subsides. The audience has been focusing on the scene between Tiresias and Cadmus. They are especially drawn to Tiresias's laying on of hands. Then suddenly spectators are aware of silence, of the meditating performers. Peripheral activity ceases, light intensifies at the center. It is as if the performance gathers itself to begin again.

Schechner

The performers rise from their meditative squat one at a time. While saying their chorus lines they undress. The men lie down and the women stand astride them. As each man takes his position for the birth ritual—adapted from the Asmats of New Guinea—he stops speaking. Soon only the women speak, very quietly, intoning the prayers that blend into the motions of birthing. The women speak/sing their lines simultaneously.

so his mother bore him once in labor bitter

there is the towering man who mocked
your mysteries

and when the weaving fates fulfilled the
time, the bull-horned god was born of

what was the name of the child you
bore that man?

good evening, sir, may I take you to
your seat?

Grotowski saw the play in November 1968. He liked the environment we had built in the garage and parts of the mise-en-scène. He felt the acting was hysterical, that we confused touching skin with psychic contact. He did not like the costumes. The red chitons and black underpants of the women and the black jockstraps of the men were too much like strip-tease, he said. He felt that one might either perform naked as a sacred act or let the nakedness come through everyday clothes. I decided a few days later that the performers would do sections of the play naked.

Schechner

JOAN   What was the name of your husband? What was the name of your child? When the weaving fates fulfilled the time, the bull-horned god was born of Zeus. With joy he crowned his son, set serpents on his head. So his mother bore him once in labor bitter.

CIEL   So his mother bore him once in labor bitter, lightning struck, forced by fire that flared from Zeus, consumed, she died, untimely torn in childbed dead by blow of light—of light the son was born. Blessed are we, for we shall know the mysteries of god. Thebes, nurse of Semele, crown your hair with ivy, redden with berries, grow green with bryony. Dionysus is our god. Hard are the labors of god but sweet to serve, sweet to cry, Bacchus, evohe. Who is one with those who belong to the holy body of god? Who keeps the rite of Cybele the mother? Bear your god in triumph. And when the weaving

fates fulfilled the time, the bull-horned god was born of Zeus. With joy he crowned his son, set serpents on his head. Where the throng of women waits possessed by Dionysus. With milk the earth flows, with wine it runs, with the nectar of bees.

MARGARET O Thebes, nurse of Semele, crown your hair with ivy, grow green with bryony, redden with berries. O city, with boughs of oak and fir, come dance the dance of god. Blessed are the thyrsus bearers.

REMI And when the weaving fates fulfilled the time, the bull-horned god was born of Zeus.

I always thought we should sing during the birth instead of groaning. The ritual is not an imitative action. The audience's attention should be forced beyond the surface of our bodies and the overt interpretation of the activity to "the form and rhythm of the gathering." Anyway, Dionysus should be born amidst a shout of joy. During the last weeks of the run we experimented with this, and also with recapitulating the birth during the ecstasy. These experiments came about because Lloyd Richards questioned the specificity of our intent in these scenes. Both seem more vital now. At every point where the basic rhythm surfaces, I feel stronger.

Ciel

Pentheus's first speech is sometimes given now. Often, however, Pentheus does not speak until after the ecstasy dance.

SHEPHARD AS PENTHEUS I am Pentheus, son of Echion and Agave and King of Thebes. I was away from the city when reports of strange disorders reached me. Stories of our women leaving home to frisk among the thickets on the mountains, dancing in honor of the latest divinity, a certain Dionysus, whoever that may be. In their midst stand bowls brimming with wine, while one by one the women wander off to secret nooks to satisfy the lusts of men. Priestesses of Bacchus they claim they are. But it's really Aphrodite they adore. My jailers have some of them safely in prison and the others will be hunted down off the mountain like the animals they are. Even my own mother, Agave, and Ino and Autonoë, Acteon's mother. Well, the steel-net trap is closing and I will soon stop this obscene disorder. Stories have also come to me of a stranger here in Thebes from Lydia.

His days and nights he spends with women and girls, dangling before them the joys of initiation in his mysteries. Well, let me get him under this roof and I'll stop the bouncing of his head and the throbbing of his wand. I'll have his head, and his wand, cut off.

Dionysus undresses as the other performers do, and he lays down as all the men do. The motion of the birth ritual begins. In one version, as Pentheus says "Stories have also come to me," he begins to push Dionysus out of the line of men forming the bottom of the birth-ritual canal, replacing him himself. Or, while Pentheus watches the birth ritual, either openly or secretly, the thrusting rhythm of the men's bodies forces Dionysus out. There are four versions of Dionysus's first speech. The speech is always spoken directly to the audience, after Dionysus emerges from the line of men and just before he enters the birth canal to be born.

FINLEY AS DIONYSUS   Good evening, I see you found your seats. My name is William Finley, son of William Finley. I was born twenty-seven years ago and two months after my birth the hospital in which I was born burned to the ground. I've come here tonight for three important reasons. The first and most important of these is to announce my divinity. The second

is to establish my rites and my rituals. And the
third is to be born, if you'll excuse me.

I do not want to approach Yellow Eyes again. *And here I
stand.* The god lives down the block.
Took off his yellow god glasses.
   in my bones   a god incognito   don't know what to do
   the sun goes through barechested man embracing holes
. . . . "have stung them with frenzy" . . . .

Stand here
Stare at you
at myself like
   Greased Narcissus.

tiger-dived into the thigh of Z

Lightning boltballsblew me out of my mind all the time in
the dark lumber yard with three-gallon tin blood tank with
"BACCHIC PISS" in MAGIC MARKER.
                Put on old man Cadmus specs
                the only character in slow-motion
                somewhat dishonest, genial
                who wore my face
He went away and Cadmus, carrying a styrofoam cup of diner
coffee, bumped into his going off.
                (He wheels and calls offstage.)
up to the mountains decode the mysteries lying position
stretched be gone beyond the shadow untimely ripped kitchen
dead Bobby.

BIG D EATS THE LITTLE P ( ) boogaloo jelly shit ( )
   PA OOO MAOW MAOW
                (He flails clouds and exits on.)

Then you regard me as a fiction? It's no fiction that you
run around the garage using my mask. When you're that way
I'm dangerous. Fuck off.
Finley

To be born, if you'll excuse me.

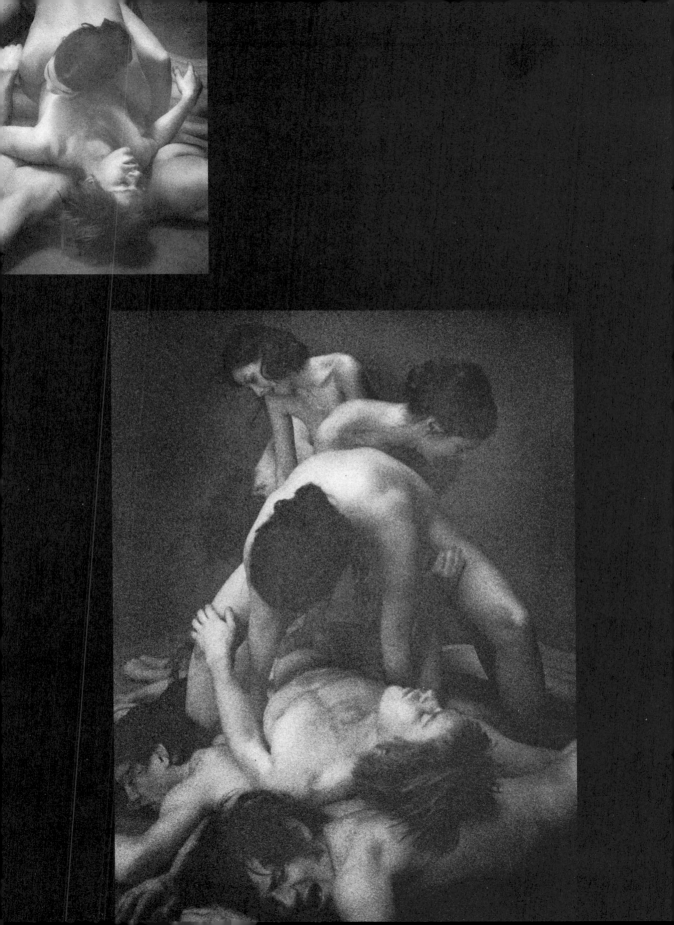

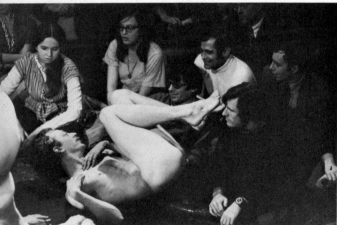

Finley my first child
Was an easy exciting birth
A long slick eel
Flopping over the rocks to shore
Mischievous merman—bespectacled and
        bemustached
Eyes open all the way.

Blue Shephard
Was as firm and full a child
As any Mother could wish to hold between her legs
A tribute to the possibilities of healthy children
A chunk of a child
Unaware of the mysteries of his birth.

Jason my red love
Was most painful of them all.
Then I grew accustomed
      to the smug in his eyes
      and the pulsing of his body
Until I'd swing down lower than usual
To touch him as he glided through
Cheek to belly
Hair to hair.

Joan was a gentle surge
Quiet sleeping child
Breasts spreading over heart
Lifting, swaying, shaken
Into cries of birth
That touched the Real.

Pat the naked ape
To birth a man is difficult
But important
The effort in each move
Shows progress
But frustration
The Earth groans
Crash—a man is born
God save the King.

Remi

JASON AS DIONYSUS   Mother! Mother! Mother!

He pulls himself from the row of men, rolls, and
ends in a girl's lap.

You're not my mother. My name is Jason
Bosseau. I am the son of Damar Bosseau and
Jessie Bartoletti. I was born twenty-seven years
ago in a small, boring, typical Midwestern town
in southeastern Kansas called Pittsburgh. Now
this town has 18,000 people in it and it's just
forty miles down the road from where last year's
Miss America was born. I've come here tonight

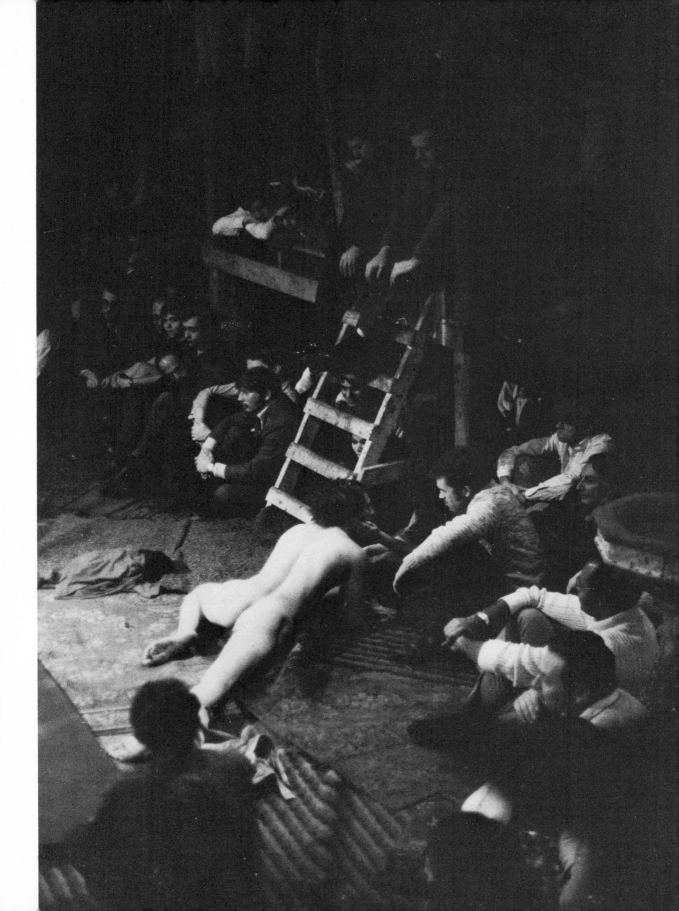

for three very important reasons. Number one is to announce my divinity. I mean: I am a god. Number two is to establish my rites and my rituals. As you can see, they are already in progress. And number three is to be born—in this, my birth ritual, if you'll excuse me.

JOAN AS DIONYSUS   Good evening. I see you found your seats. My name is Joan MacIntosh, daughter of Walter MacIntosh and June Wyatt. I was born twenty-three years ago in a hospital in Newark, New Jersey. I have come here tonight for three very important reasons. The first and most important of these reasons is to announce my divinity. I am a god. The second of these reasons is to establish my rites and rituals. As you can see, they are already in progress. And the third is to be born, if you'll excuse me.

The first speech as Dionysus is the hardest part of the play for me. To emerge vulnerable and naked and address the audience and say I am a god. Absurd and untrue. I didn't believe and therefore the audience didn't believe. Eyes glazed, body mobilized and defensive. Rehearsed with RS. Told him I felt like a fraud, doing that. He said expose that, deal with that anguish and fraud—don't cover it up and be phony. Very hard to do. I am always afraid that something will happen that I can't control. But I've found that when I'm honest, laughter and joy are liberated in me. The absurdity of telling 250 people that I am a god makes me laugh and the audience laughs with me and gradually the strength comes and the self-mockery fades away. Trusting my impulses. Starting from where I'm at. My whole performance hinges on this scene. If I am honest with myself and make contact with the audience, the performance is strong. In this scene I am totally Joan MacIntosh. I have not begun to become the god. The play is a series of revealments in which I find out that I am the god. By the time of the curse I am totally transformed.

The first transformation, going through the birth canal, is very important. It is a rite of passage toward godhead. All through the opening exercises I have been traveling to the mountain, exciting the Bacchae, being the god and then a bacchante. But the birth is my own specific ordeal. I enter the birth canal Joan MacIntosh and emerge invested with god-power. There has been an infusion. This is not to say that coming out of the birth ritual I am a character in the traditional sense. Throughout the play I am both

Joan in the garage and Dionysus in Thebes. But the birth ritual is a giving over of myself, totally, to the bodies of the men and women of the Group. It is remaining passive and yet open and receptive, like the womb, to their backs and their hands, their sweat and their sounds. These fill me and when I emerge I am more than when I went in. Once inside the ritual, the experience is polymorphous. It is flesh with no distinction of sex. It is before there are differences. It is being encased in a soft fleshy place and being moved along to the light on the other side. One night I remembered my own birth. I was me and I was being born from my own mother's womb. It was hard and painful. I screamed.

Joan

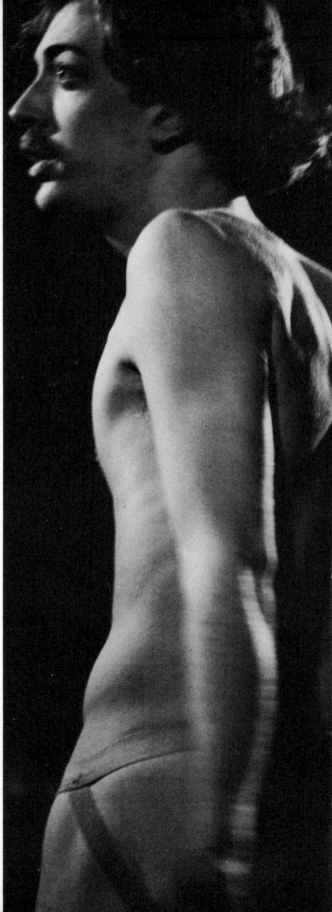

MC DERMOTT AS DIONYSUS   Good evening, my name is Pat McDermott. I was born on August 12 about a generation ago in the state of Nebraska. My mother's name is Ada Belle. Ada Belle was born in Eades, Colorado. That was a town in the shadow of the Rocky Mountains. Ada Belle used to tell me that on a clear day you could see Pike's Peak. But Ada Belle might've been lying, because the town's not there any more. Some folks say I'm a bastard. Ada Belle says different. Ada Belle says I'm the son of god. I've come here tonight for three very important reasons. The first of these reasons is to announce my divinity. I am a god. The second of these reasons is to establish my rites and my rituals. As you can see, they've already started, and they're coming along just fine. And the third reason is to be born, if you'll excuse me.

From the time the play opened until December 1968, Dionysus spoke a version of the following speech as he was being born.

FINLEY AS DIONYSUS   Now I noticed some untoward snickering when I announced the fact that I was a god. I realize that in 1968 it is hard to fathom the idea that gods walk the earth again. However, to say that I am not a god would be the same as saying that this is not a theatre, or that I am not in some way being born, if only metaphorically.

JASON AS DIONYSUS   Now I noticed when I went around tonight, before we got deeply into my mysteries, that there were a lot of snickering faces. The kind of faces that doubt that I am a god. That shouldn't be. To say that I am not a god is the same as saying that my name is not

Jason Bosseau, or that I am not twenty-seven years old, or that my parents' names are not Bosseau and Bartoletti. To say that I am not a god is like saying that my name is not Dionysus or that I am not in fact being born right here before your eyes in a garage at 33 Wooster Street.

There are two versions by Finley and one each by Jason, Joan, and McDermott of the speech introducing the ecstasy dance. Finley's first version is for a dressed, free-style ecstasy; his second, for a naked, free-style ecstasy. Jason's version is for both the naked free-style ecstasy and the dressed circle dance. Joan's and McDermott's versions are for the dressed circle dance.

FINLEY AS DIONYSUS   I was brought up a Roman Catholic. So for kicks I would go to a place on 42nd Street called the Laff Movie. They played Bugs Bunny cartoons and Laurel and Hardy shorts and lots of other stuff. I loved it. One day, when I was about twelve years old, I was in the Laff Movie and this big fat guy with a big mustache sits next to me eating a felafel sandwich. He stunk. He turned and looked at me and said, "Hey, kid, you know what? You remind me of Dionysus. I like that." I moved three seats away and called the manager. But when they came to get him he was gone. And you know what? He was right. I mean, I'm it!

FINLEY AS DIONYSUS   Here I am. Dionysus once again. Now for those of you who believe what I just told you, that I am a god, you are going to have a terrific evening. The rest of you are in trouble. It's going to be an hour and a half of being up against the wall. Those of you who do believe can join us in what we do next. It's a celebration, a ritual, an ordeal, an ecstasy. An ordeal is something you go through. An ecstasy is what happens to you when you get there.

When the birth ritual is followed by the circle dance, the ritual ends with a two-beat freeze. Then the performers break, go back to the edge of the mats, dress while repeating the same lines they said while undressing, and squat again. This time they face out toward the audience rather than in toward the center of the mats. Dionysus speaks when everyone is squatting.

JASON AS DIONYSUS   Here I am. Once again born the god Dionysus. Those of you who believe, who are willing to let yourselves go and admit the possibility of believing that I am a god, you're going to be part of a genuinely holy experience. But those of you who do not

believe, I must warn you that you are flirting with cataclysm. Our ordeal brings a lot of pain. But it leads to an ecstasy. It's a celebration of me, of my nativity. And if anyone tries to stop it, I'll kill him.

Our first experiment with nakedness was in a workshop in February 1968. It was a phallic dance in which the woman celebrated the maleness of the men. Nudity was voluntary, but by the end of the exercise all but two people were naked. The Welfare Center was not our space, kids kept peeking in under the doors, and we didn't do more naked work until we got the garage. There, before *Dionysus* opened, we rehearsed the ecstasy dance naked. We started to sense to what degree clothes were a social mask and how that mask could be worn even while naked.

One Monday night in March we worked at the Electric Circus. The place was closed to the public and Morton Subotnick and Tony Martin ran a sound-and-light environment on us as we unfolded an improvisation. The Group was divided into "clothes city" and "love city." Clothes city was freezing and wanted to wear more and more clothing. Love city was naked and wanted only to be close to each other and touch. It was an epic struggle when war broke out between them, a blowup of a child's game. I don't remember who won, but I do recall the strange, almost monstrous confrontations between people wrapped in layer after layer of winter clothes and naked people.

In the fall, we probed the relationship between nakedness and psychic vulnerability, eroticism, functional nudity, and private communication. Among the exercises was one in which everyone squatted or faced the wall so that no one could see anyone else. Then one person went to another and did something to or with that second person. This act could be strictly private or the doer could select any number of witnesses, one person or more or even the whole Group, arrange them in whatever configuration he wished, and then do his action. Another exercise combined the "transformation-circle" exercise with psychophysical vulnerability. As each person in the circle related an event or action to his neighbor, he took off clothing as part of the telling. Again, nakedness was voluntary, so by the end of the exercise some people were naked and some were not.

When we brought nakedness into the performance in November 1968, we tried to make it functional. We didn't want to look pretty or act erotically. We

. . . join us in what we do next

wanted to show birthing, killing, and dying. I wanted
to establish nakedness not as part of aesthetics but as
a way of doing something. The public performances
were traumatic for many Group members. Our naked
workshops were never voyeuristic. On the rare occasions when visitors saw us work naked, they too had
to be naked. Thus the experience of being the object
of so much looking on the part of the audience
numbed us, and brought to a halt the difficult but
rich workshops.

Schechner

JOAN AS DIONYSUS   Here I am. Dionysus this
time. Now I noticed that there were some
disbelievers among you when I announced my
divinity. If you deny me and my mysteries, if
you deny that I was born a god before your very
eyes, then you deny truth and you shall suffer
for it. If, however, you believe what I tell you,
you shall have an extraordinary experience
tonight. Something you won't forget. Together
we can make one community. We can celebrate
together. Be joyous together. Reach ecstasy
together. So join us in what we do next. It's a
circle dance around the sacred spot of my birth.
It's a celebration of me, of my nativity.

MC DERMOTT AS DIONYSUS   Now I noticed
some of you were slapping bugs when I was
telling you I was a god. Well, I tell you, if you
don't believe me, it's going to be a couple of
hours of being up against the wall. On the other
hand, if you believe what I say, we can shake
this tin roof and get the blood running low.
Later on, it'll go up to your eyes and you'll see
clearer. What we do next is called an ecstasy.
It's a circle dance around the spot of my birth,
and the more people that join, the bigger the
circle gets. Oh, yes, it's a ritual. If you don't
know what a ritual is, a ritual is an intrauterine
device that is not prophylactic. It's a celebration
of me, a celebration of my nativity.

The ecstasy dance has had several shapes and tones,
almost an index of the development of the Group.
Certain performance elements are live measures of
our intensity, mood, and growth.

The ecstasy originated in experiments with music
and movement, the relationships between the two,
and probes into our own feelings. From the start, our
goal was to express ourselves directly and metaphorically at the same time. Early on, while we were still
working in the Welfare Center, I would stop the associative exercises, isolate small groups of performers on mats, and distribute among them a drum, a
tambourine, a flute, and a bugle. "Let these instruments play you," I instructed. "Don't try to 'do' anything with them. Think of them as extensions of
yourselves, your feelings, your situation, and your
action." Then I would describe a situation, the circumstances for an improvisation in which music, or
rather sound, was very important. People learned to
play with instruments more than to play them in the
usual way. The bugle became a sharp scream or
sometimes a thing to pound percussively on the
mat. Battles were fought, ritual battles that took
several hours. And after an encounter between two
hostile forces, dances arose to celebrate victory or
to commemorate defeat.

From this early work we gained a sense of sonic environment, of "articulating a space" through sound.
We began to feel music as an extension of our bodies
and to recognize sound as something to give and
take.

The first time we did the birth ritual—before it
was part of *Dionysus*—everyone in the Group went
through the canal. We were born to each other. In
imitating the Asmat ceremony, we found a connec-

tion not only between them and us but among ourselves. It is this connection we celebrate in the ecstasy dance. It is in honor of Dionysus, but the Dionysus who is of The Performance Group. This god is our creation, and his terror and beauty extensions of our own possibilities. No abstract deity handed down through literature, Dionysus in the garage is the energy of all focused through one.

This energy changes as we change. At first we played instruments and asked the audience to join us. It was like a discothèque that deepened in intensity until it transcended its promises and became perilous. Joan played the flute, Remi and Jason tambourines, Ciel temple bells. Richard Dia or Bill Shephard beat rhythms on a big conga drum—later stolen from the theatre by someone from the audience. When the music was right, performers and spectators stripped. The dance ended abruptly when Pentheus interrupted it. He stood high on a tower and shouted through a bullhorn or he moved from dancer to dancer, dragging them from their revelry.

After nakedness, the scene changed entirely. In my notes to the Group on December 8, 1968, I said: "I notice a 'blindness' in our nudity. We do not want to see ourselves naked. The numbness that

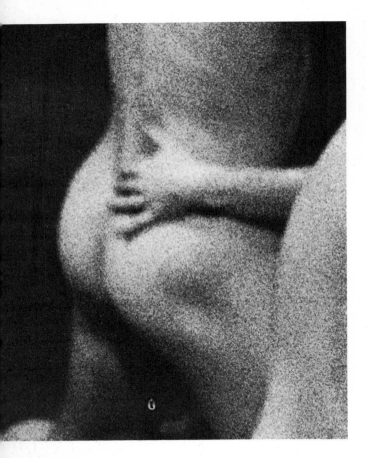

some people say they feel is a severe form of this blindness. More moderate forms are people keeping their eyes closed, people relating to others through touch and sound but not through sight. The exercise we did on Wednesday, though not the end of our explorations into nudity, did clarify certain things: (1) The birth ritual is a birthing not only of Dionysus but of each of us through him. (2) Undressing before the birth ritual is a sacred and surgical preparation. At once potent and sterile. It is a way of clearing the way. (3) The fetal meditation, in the squat, is a way of clearing and purifying the mind. The associative opening ceremonies are a foretaste of the actualization of the performance. The meditation is the beginning of 'this night's performance.' We rise, one at a time, as each finds either peace or balance. (4) We leave the fetal position to birth ourselves. (5) The ecstasy is an ordeal/celebration. It is the 'all-night dance.' The mats are the sacred place. To leave the mats is to leave that place and negotiate with the profane world. Leaving takes courage and incorporates the knowledge that life must be lived and that life is not pure. The audience may participate, clothed, off the mats. But they must not come on the mats unless they are as we are. The use of musical instruments is optional. The perfect ceremony uses no instruments. But, as we know, most ceremonies are not perfect—props are part of the human condition.

"The second phase of the nudity—the death ritual and body pile—is more clearly defined. It is the second half of the birth ritual. It is the result of profanation and at the same time a sacred act. To die is natural—to kill is both obscene and sacred. For birth, the audience is invited or at least permitted to participate. For death, the audience is challenged. 'Are you people proud of this?' Remi asks."

In April 1969 the ecstasy dance changed again. The ordeal had become routine. We returned to an earlier idea of the ecstasy but, because we had changed, our return was on a further curve of a spiral. We wanted the audience to participate, but we didn't want a discothèque anymore. In my Performance Theory class at NYU (four members of the Group were in that class), we staged for ourselves an "all-night dance," modeled on non-literate ritual. Jason was the "shaman" for the all-night dance. He made the arrangements and was master of ceremonies. The rhythm was slow, relentless, continuing for more than four hours, from 2 A.M. until dawn. Several people felt literally ex-static, standing outside themselves,

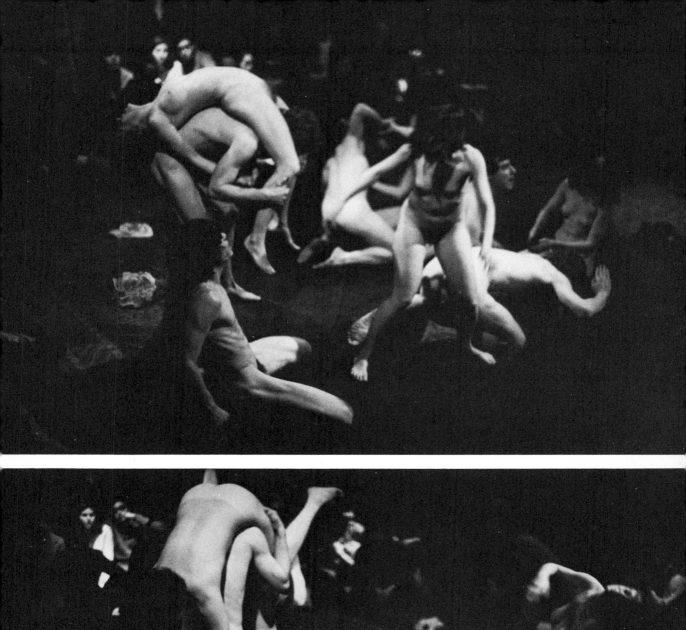

beyond being still. When we discussed the dance a few weeks later, the words "abandon," "arise," "within," "without (self)," and "inner movement" struck true. It was this kind of self-emerging movement we all wanted to bring again to the ecstasy.

In my notes of March 30, 1969, I said to the Group: "Ecstasy—gone as far as we can go now. Next spiral step, to involve the audience again." On April 3, I wrote down the basic rules for the new ecstasy dance. "Living tension between personal style and social tradition. Not individual—that is, no liberty to do simply what one likes. But an over-all pattern within which variations are possible. Circle movement. Song. Encompassing. Slowly increasing tempo and intensity. Receptive to others."

Schechner

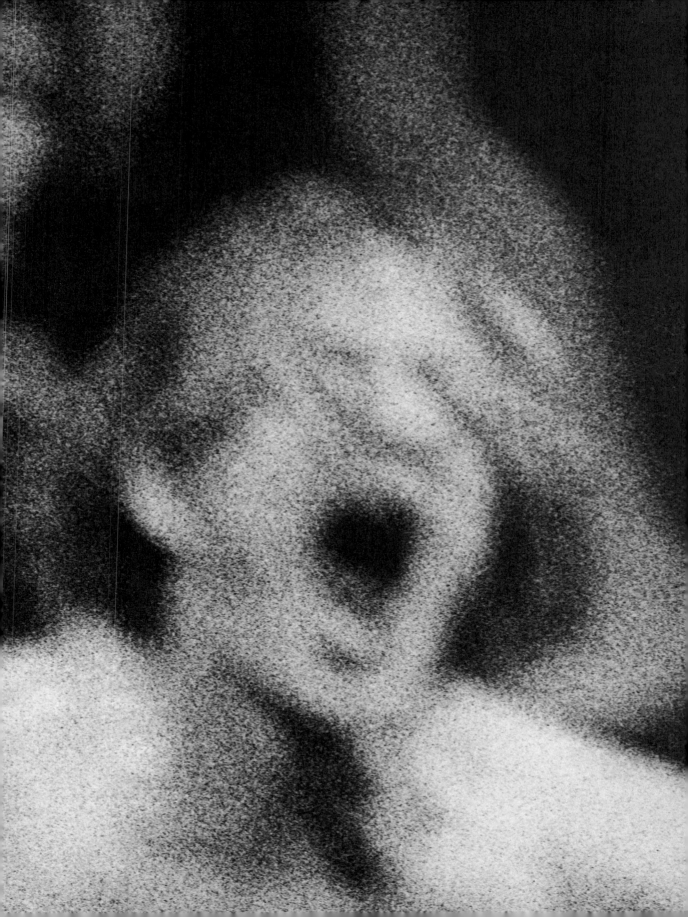

The circle dance begins when everyone is squatting around the mats. Anyone may begin the "OM" sound, which slowly swells and opens, taking on a slow, driving rhythm. Anyone may be the first to add words to that rhythm: "On Bacchae, on you Bacchae, bear your god in triumph home." These words are sung in unison, in syncopation, and in counterpoint. Variations on the basic chorus text are frequent: "So his mother bore him once," "Come dance the dance of god," "Of light the son was born." The dance moves slowly to the right around the mats. People from the audience join, either on their own or when invited. If enough people join, the dance goes around the towers and fills nearly the whole floor of the theatre. Its pace accelerates slowly. The dance continues until Pentheus stops it by forcibly pulling the performers out of the circle, one by one. When a performer leaves the ecstasy, he sits in a newly formed circle on the mats and chants, "Pen—thee—oos, Pen—thee—oos." Soon the ecstasy song and rhythm are counteracted by the long, wailing "Pen-thee-oos" chant. When everyone is in the circle, Pentheus steps to the center and speaks.

When Dia plays Pentheus and the ecstasy is performed naked, the dance ends differently. Dia goes upstairs during the opening ceremonies. He waits there until he hears the ecstasy reach a climax. Then he comes down and goes outside and pounds on the large, metal garage doors. He opens the smaller door and enters the theatre from the street. As soon as the performers hear him, they grab their clothes and run to corners of the space to dress and hide. Only Tiresias and Cadmus are left in the center. Pentheus enters and approaches them.

The first night I entered, there were people from the audience blocking my way. As Pentheus, I must include the audience in my reality. I am the dictator-king whose word is law. I couldn't say things like "Excuse me" or "Would you please move?" And I couldn't start crawling and stumbling my way to the mats. Clearly they had to make way for me, their king. I could have said "Move!" but that would have sounded more like a longshoreman than like the King of Thebes. Finally I said simply, "Clear a space," and they did. When they do not, I call for the "men of Thebes," who carry the offending spectators away. If they struggle or return to block my way, I throw them in "prison," that is, have them put down in the pit. If the disturbance continues, I, Pentheus/Richard Dia, King of Thebes/performer, banish/kick out a citizen/audience member from Thebes/the garage. My response to audience participation or disruption depends on many variables: what's happened, who made it happen, how many are involved, where we are in the play. I keep one goal top in my mind: I want to keep the action going.

Dia

I am Pentheus, son of Echion and Agave, and King of Thebes.

DIA AS PENTHEUS   Tiresias the seer tricked out in a dapple fawn skin and you, my own grandfather, playing at the bacchante with a wand. Sir, I shrink to see your old age so foolish. Shake off that ivy, Grandfather, shake it off.

When Pentheus speaks from the center of the circle where people are chanting his name, he begins without the direct address to Tiresias and Cadmus.

PENTHEUS   I was away from the city when reports reached me of these strange disorders here. Stories of our women leaving home to frisk in mock ecstasy among the thickets on the mountain. My own mother, Agave, dancing in honor of the latest god, a certain Dionysus, whoever that may be. And Ino, and Autonoë, Acteon's mother. In your midst stand bowls brimming with wine, while one by one you wander off to secret nooks to serve the lusts of men. Priestesses of Bacchus you call yourselves, but it's really Aphrodite you adore. Well, I've captured some of you and the rest will be hunted down out of that mountain like the animals you are. I will not tolerate these rancid, obscene mockeries of piety. Stories have also reached me of a stranger here in Thebes from Lydia. One of those charlatan magicians with long, yellow curls and the spells of Aphrodite in his eyes. His days and nights he spends with our women, dangling before them the joys of initiation in his mysteries.

Only Dia says the following sentences.

DIA AS PENTHEUS   And this is the man who claims that Dionysus is a god and was sewn into the thigh of Zeus. When in point of fact we know that is a lie.

PENTHEUS   Whoever this stranger is, let me bring him under this roof and I'll stop the tossing of his head and the throbbing of his wand. I'll have his head and his wand cut off. You can go now.

The performers dissolve the circle and disperse to various parts of the theatre. Spectators who have danced and sat with the performers also go back to their places. Pentheus, Tiresias, and Cadmus are alone in the center.

Sometimes when Shephard plays Pentheus he speaks before the birth ritual. He does not repeat the speech beginning "I am Pentheus, son of Echion and Agave, and King of Thebes" at this time. When he has spoken earlier, he dances with the revelers and during the dance discovers and

reviles his own nakedness. Ashamed and enraged, he dresses, pulls each performer individually out of the ecstasy, waits for the formation of the "Pen—thee—oos" circle, and then begins to talk. Or he climbs one of the high towers during the ecstasy and speaks through a bullhorn. At the sound of his amplified voice all the stage and house lights come up full. Everyone in the theatre is caught in the midst of their bacchanal.

SHEPHARD AS PENTHEUS   If I allow disorder in my house, I'd surely have to license it abroad. A man who deals fairly with his own, he can make manifest justice in the state. But he who crosses the law, or tries to bring the rulers under him, shall never have a word of praise from me. The man the state has put in place must have obedient hearing to his least command when it is right and even when it is not. He who accepts this teaching I can trust, ruler or ruled, to function in his place, to stand his own even in a storm of spears. A mate to trust in battle at one's side. There is no greater wrong than disobedience. This ruins cities, tears down homes, and breaks the battle front in panic. If men live decently, it is because discipline saves their very lives for them. Should I then yield this city to one man? Better I should be beaten by a women. I will not yield this city to one man. Go back to your homes.

As in the first version of this scene, at the close of Pentheus's speech everyone leaves the center except Pentheus, Tiresias, and Cadmus.

CADMUS   Pentheus, you are a reckless boy. You don't understand the consequences of your words. You may be talking madness.

TIRESIAS   You give a wise man an honest brief to plead and his eloquence is no remarkable achievement. But you're glib. Your words come rolling out smoothly on your tongue as if you were wise instead of foolish. The man whose glibness flows from his conceit of speech declares the thing he is: a worthless and a stupid citizen.

CADMUS   Tiresias advises well, my boy. This god whom you ridicule may some day possess enormous power and prestige throughout Hellas.

TIRESIAS   Mankind, young man, possesses two supreme blessings. The first of these is the goddess Demeter or Earth, whichever name you choose to call her by. It was she who gave to man his nourishment of grain. But after her

there came the son of Semele, who matched her present by inventing liquid wine as his gift to mankind. For, filled with that good gift, suffering mankind forgets its grief. From it comes sleep and with it oblivion to the troubles of the day. There is no other medicine for misery.

As Tiresias speaks, a high open sound swells from different parts of the room, until it seems to fill the whole theatre. This sound ends abruptly with Tiresias's phrase, "favor of heaven."

TIRESIAS   And when we pour the shining wine, we pour the god of wine himself, that through his intercession we may win the favor of heaven.

PENTHEUS   This is your doing, Tiresias.

CADMUS   Grandson, your home is here with us, with our customs and traditions, not outside, alone.

PENTHEUS   You want still another god revealed so you can pocket the profits from burnt offerings and bird watching.

CADMUS   You sneer, do you, at that story that Dionysus was sewn into the thigh of Zeus? Let Tiresias teach you what that really means.

TIRESIAS   When Zeus rescued from the thunderbolt his infant son and brought him to Olympus, Hera plotted to hurl the child from heaven. But Zeus, like the god he is, countered her. Breaking off a tiny fragment of that ether that surrounds the world, he molded from it a dummy Dionysus and this he showed to Hera. But, with time, men garbled the word and said that Dionysus was sewed into the thigh of Zeus. That was their story, when, in fact, Zeus showed the dummy to Hera and gave it as a hostage for his son.

In this scene, Tiresias is a messenger before the event. The dramatic function of the scene is clear. The prophecy charges the air with suspense. Theologically, however, the reason in Tiresias's words is harder to decipher. I almost gave up on it. At first it seemed double-talk. This excited that part of me which wanted to play Tiresias as half seer, half jester. Another part of me felt Tiresias as a serious figure.

        Mark my words,
Pentheus. Do not be so sure that power
is what matters in the life of man; do not mistake
for wisdom the fantasies of your sick mind.

When I spoke these words I enacted Beck, Chomsky, Arden, Laing, Brown, even Faulkner—and all the modern prophets who have seen that slave revolts are rational acts but wars of nationhood are not, who have called for new definitions of madness and sanity, and who have not been afraid to diagnose the insanity of those most rational of men, the managerial warmakers. Especially I enacted the Harvard biologist George Wald, who said: "That was a United States Senator holding [sic] a patriotic speech. Well, here is a Nobel laureate who thinks that those words are criminally insane." This kind of defiance was mixing in my blood and prevented me from accepting the "showed/sewed" story as something that turns on a pun. Tiresias is expounding arcane matters.

Eventually I came to see in this passage a parable of the theme of *The Bacchae*. The story is about a scarecrow god which Zeus creates in order to protect his real son from Hera's wrath. I took the parable this way. Hera is the people. She professes to love the child but only wants to kill it. Dionysus is the real

god incarnate. But the people cannot bear the sight of the human form divine. Thus, out of self-interest, the deity must be concealed. He has two choices, aborted incarnation or crucifixion. Crucifixion: fixion, fixation, putting the god in a box, prostitutional deity, genies in lamps. If the god were revealed straight out, men would make of him what he is not. To the extent that they misunderstand him, they require him to be what he is not. Mankind requires the god to be the god incognito.

At the end Cadmus tells Agave that she, like Pentheus, denied the god. How? Euripides only hints. Agave uses the appearance of the god as an excuse to enact what Pentheus outlaws. Pentheus becomes her voyeur. She denies the god in the way she receives him.

Illuminated by this parable, the tragic outcome of the play is not the result of wrath and revenge but of misunderstanding and weakness on the part of the people. The people include Agave and the revelers. They have not allowed god his true form. Euripides gives a unique twist to the Dionysus legends. He makes Dionysus a self-serving god. It is Pentheus who dies as a sacrificial victim. Dionysus's wrath is his mask, his mortal integument. If men know that gods hide, they will be slow to attack.

Euripides's play is an insult to the people. The world is going downhill at the end of *The Bacchae*. There is not, as there is in Shakespeare, a return to normalcy.

McDermott

CADMUS   Even if Dionysus is no god, as you assert, persuade yourself that he is. The fiction's a noble one. Aunt Semele will seem the mother of a god and that bestows no small honor on this house. It's good politics.

TIRESIAS   Moreover, this is a god of prophecy. His worshippers, like madmen, are endowed with mantic powers.

CADMUS   Once the god enters the body of a man, he fills it with the breath of prophecy.

Led by Tiresias, but coming from all over the theatre, is the sound of rapid, shallow, and accelerating panting. It crescendoes and stops suddenly as Tiresias continues speaking.

TIRESIAS   He has usurped the function of warlike Ares. Thus, at times, you see an army, mustered under arms, stricken with panic before it even lifts a spear. That is the work of

Dionysus. Some day you will see him among the crags at Delphi, twirling and waving his wand, leaping the pastures that stretch between the peaks, great throughout the Hellas that once was yours.

PENTHEUS   Tiresias, if it weren't for your old age, I'd have you imprisoned with these Bacchic women for importing here to Thebes these filthy mysteries.

TIRESIAS   Mark my words, Pentheus. Do not be so sure that power is what matters in the life of man. Do not mistake for wisdom the fantasies of your sick mind.

Only Ciel's Tiresias has the following line, said as she takes off her blindfold and throws it at Pentheus.

CIEL AS TIRESIAS   Listen to me! Change your course or you will die a bloody death.

CADMUS   Think, Grandson, you are pleased when men stand outside your door and the whole city glorifies the name of Pentheus. So, too, the god. He delights in glory. Crown your head, pour him libations, welcome the god to Thebes.

As Cadmus says "glorifies the name of Pentheus," a faint echo of the "Pen—thee—oos" chant emanates from corners of the room. Pentheus's name is chanted three times.

PENTHEUS   Once you see wine shining at the feasts of women, you may be sure that the festival is rotten.

CADMUS   Your mind is distracted now. What you're thinking is sheer delirium.

TIRESIAS   Dionysus, I admit, does not compel a woman to be chaste. Always, and in every case, it is a woman's character and nature that keeps her chaste. And so, therefore, even in the rites of Dionysus, the unchaste woman will be unchaste.

In the version of Ciel and Finley, Tiresias and Cadmus roll on the floor in imitation of a sexual orgy. They laugh and touch each other. Pentheus looks on, unable to express his shock and rage. Tiresias and Cadmus end abruptly.

TIRESIAS   But Cadmus and I, whom you ridicule, will join the dances of the god and crown our heads with ivy. An old and foolish pair, perhaps. But dance we must.

CADMUS   Come with us. The revels have begun.

PENTHEUS   Go worship your Dionysus if you want to. But don't wipe your madness off on me.

TIRESIAS   You're mad, beyond the power of any drug to cure, for you're drugged with madness.

PENTHEUS   You're going to regret this folly of yours.

There are two versions of the end of the scene.

MC DERMOTT AS TIRESIAS   The words of fools finish in folly.

The word "folly" is trilled and echoed in decrescendo throughout the theatre. Tiresias somersaults around Pentheus and ends near the blood fountain.

CIEL AS TIRESIAS   I speak not prophecy but fact. The words of fools finish in folly.

Tiresias and Cadmus join hands, scream, and then somersault over Pentheus. The screams are taken up by the other performers. The "tag chorus" overlaps the end of the Tiresias, Cadmus, Pentheus scene. The decrescendo "folly" or the screams cover the first words of the chorus. The performers speak the chorus simultaneously, each performer addressing a particular segment of the audience. Only Tiresias is free to move. The others have a precinct and they try to convince spectators that the bacchantes are right and Pentheus is wrong. Pentheus silences the performers by running to them and putting his hand over each of their mouths. They are stopped, often in mid-sentence, their bodies frozen. The first part of the chorus ends when all the performers are silent and Pentheus returns to the center of the mats.

MC DERMOTT   Let me come to Cyprus, island of Aphrodite, home of the loves that cast their spells on the hearts of men. Or Paphos, where the hundred-mouthed barbarian river brings ripeness without rain. To Pieria, haunt of the Muses. And there desire, and there the right is mine to worship as I please

SHEPHARD   A tongue without reins, defiance, unwisdom, their end is disaster. But the life of quiet good, the wisdom that accepts, these

SAM   These blessings he gave: laughter to the flute, and the loosing of cares when the shining wine is spilled at the feast of the gods. Far in the air of heaven the gods of heaven live. But they watch the lives of men. Briefly we live, briefly, then die. And what passes for wisdom is not wisdom. Oh, let me come to Cyprus, island of Aphrodite, or Paphos, where the hundred-mouthed barbarian river brings ripeness without rain. To Pieria, haunt of the Muses, and the holy hill of Olympus. There the lovely graces

JOAN   Holiness, queen of heaven, holiness on golden wing, who hovers over earth, do you hear what Pentheus says? Do you hear his blasphemies

MARGARET   Holiness, queen of heaven, holiness on golden wing who hovers over earth, do you hear what Pentheus says? Do you hear his blasphemy against the prince of the blessed, the god of garlands and banquets, Bromius, Semele's son

JASON   Do you hear what Pentheus says? Do you hear his stupid blasphemies? Dionysus gave us the simple gift of wine, the gladness of the grape. Briefly we live, briefly, then die.

Wherefore I say he who hunts a glory, he who tracks some boundless, superhuman dream may lose his harvest here and now and garner death. Such men are mad and their counsels evil. Let me go to Cyprus, island of

CIEL   The deity, the son of Zeus, in feast, in festival delights. He loves the goddess Peace, generous of good, preserver of the young. To rich and poor

REMI   These blessings he gave: laughter to the flute and the loosing of cares when the shining wine is spilled at the feast of the gods. The life of quiet good, the wisdom that accepts, these abide unshaken, preserving, sustaining the houses of men. Oh, let me come to

After a brief silence, the chorus begins again, each performer starting where he left off. The mix of sound each night is different. Spectators close to a performer hear that person and overhear the sonic mélange. There is a building of energy and a reaching toward climax as Pentheus moves more and more swiftly through the crowded space trying to reach and quiet each performer. The first time a performer is silenced by Pentheus, he must stay quiet for a count of one hundred. The second time, for a count of fifty. The third time, for a count of ten. After that, he can begin again as soon as Pentheus leaves his vicinity. Pentheus's attempts to keep the place quiet grow more and more frantic. Spectators frequently add their voices to those of the performers. It is not unusual for spectators to physically try and stop Pentheus. As the scene builds, songs begin in different parts of the room. They are simple nursery rhymes or popular melodies. The songs spread infectiously. One dominates, and soon the performers and the audience are singing and clapping together. Pentheus finally collapses with exhaustion and frustration.

CIEL   He gives the simple gift of wine, the gladness of the grape, the laughter of the flute. But him who scoffs he hates, and him who mocks his life

MC DERMOTT   Far in the air of heaven the sons of heaven live, but they watch the lives of men and what passes for wisdom ain't. The deity, the son of god, in feast, in festival delights. He loves the goddess Peace, preserver of the good, keeper of the young. But him who scoffs he hates and him who mocks his

SAM   Go and there desire and there he loves the goddess Peace, he loves the goddess briefly

JOAN   These blessings he gave: laughter to the flute, and the loosing of cares when the

shining wine is spilled at the feast of the gods,
and the wine bowl casts its sleep on feasters
crowned with ivy. A tongue without

To the tune of *Hi-Ho the Derry-O*.

Laughter to the flute, laughter to the flute,
Hi-Ho the Derry-O laughter to the flute!

DIA   A tongue without reins, defiance,
unwisdom, their end is disaster. But the life of
quiet good, the wisdom that accepts, these abide
unshaken, preserving, sustaining the houses of

During the later part of the chorus, Dionysus acknowledges all the performers except Pentheus.
Dionysus does not participate in the chorus. He
finds a place among the audience and watches.
He may chat with members of the audience.

MARGARET   These blessings he gave: laughter
to the flute and the loosing of cares when the
shining wine is spilled at the feast of the gods,
and the wine bowl casts its sleep on feasters
crowned with ivy. Far in the air of heaven the
sons of heaven live. But they watch the lives of
men. And what passes for wisdom

CIEL   Let us go to Cyprus, island of

REMI   Cyprus, island of Aphrodite, homes of
the loves that

JASON   Home of the loves that cast their
spells on the hearts of men. And there desire,
and there the right is ours to worship and do
as we

DIA   Men. Far in the air the sons of heaven
live. But they watch the lives of men. And
what

JOAN   Reins, defiance, unwisdom, their end is
disaster. But the life of quiet good, the wisdom
that accepts, these abide unshaken, preserving

To the tune of *Yankee Doodle*.

Dionysus god of wine, god of joy and laughter!
Dionysus god of wine, god of joy and laughter!
Dionysus god of wine, god of joy and laughter!
Dionysus god of wine, god of joy and laughter!

MC DERMOTT   Happy are those for whom the
day is blessed, and doubly blessed the night

SAM   These blessings he gave: laughter

REMI   Cast their spells on the hearts of men.
Or Paphos, where the hundred-mouthed
barbarian

SHEPHARD   Abide, unshaken, preserving, sustaining the houses

To the tune of *Clementine*.

Lovely graces, lovely graces, where the lovely
    graces go!
There the right is mine to worship, where the
    lovely graces go!

Each night a different song dominates and becomes the only one. The repertory is extensive.

To the tune of *Row, Row, Row Your Boat*.

Laughter to the flute, laughter to the flute,
La, la, la, la, la, la, la,
Laughter to the flute!

To the tune of *Mary Had a Little Lamb*.

What the simple people do, people do, people
    do,
What the simple people do, I too believe and
    do.

To the tune of *Auld Lang Syne*.

The things that simple people do,
I too believe and do.
The things that common men believe,
I too believe and do.

To the tune of *Jingle Bells*.

Shining wine, shining wine, shining wine is
    spilled,
When we pour the shining wine, we pour the
    the god himself!

To the tune of *The Battle Hymn of the Republic*.

Far in the air of heaven, the sons of heaven live!
Far in the air of heaven, the sons of heaven live!
Far in the air of heaven, the sons of heaven live!
And they watch the lives of men!

To the tune of *Here We Go Round the Mulberry Bush*.

Let us go to Pieria, Pieria, Pieria!
Let us go to Pieria to worship as we please!

To the tune of *London Bridge Is Falling Down*.

Dionysus, god of joy, god of joy, god of joy!
Dionysus, god of joy!
Di-o-nysus!

What the common people do, people do, people do!
What the common people do!
I too believe and do!

During the tag chorus I am physically exhausting myself in silencing the Bacchae and trying to avoid obstacles, people in my way, climbing towers without slipping, literally going as fast as I can, surpassing myself, pursuing an action to its very end, so that my life mask cracks and falls away and I am revealed in my vulnerability. The audience is very amused. But I don't feel their amusement. To me it is derision, mockery. They are mocking me personally. And I feel it very deeply and personally.

Shephard

Of all the parts of the play, the tag chorus has changed the least. Even the birth and death rituals have had some evolution. But the tag chorus has been the same since we first did it in an open rehearsal in May 1968. This is because the tag chorus is a perfect physical expression of a psychic reality. Pentheus wants silence and the chance to sit still. The Bacchae want to dance and stir up all the people. Pentheus responds to every sound, running a gauntlet of noisy derision, utterly exhausting himself. The audience sees, and participates in, the dismantling of Pentheus's patience, authority, dignity, and stamina.

Schechner

When Pentheus is too exhausted to run or stand, he falls. With his first shout, the bedlam of the chorus ends.

PENTHEUS   Go! Someone! To the place where this prophet prophesies. Tear it up! Pry it up with crowbars. Demolish everything you see. Throw his fillets to the wind and weather. That will make him mad enough. And then go and scour the city for that effeminate stranger. The man who infects our women with this strange disease. And pollutes our beds. When you find him, I want him brought here to me in chains.

There are two versions of the following line.

SHEPHARD AS PENTHEUS   He shall die the death he deserves by being stoned to death in Thebes.

DIA AS PENTHEUS   He shall come to rue his drunken merrymaking here in Thebes.

PENTHEUS   Well! Where is he?

Dionysus is sitting among the audience.

DIONYSUS   Here I am.

CORYPHAEUS   O greatest light of our holy revels, how glad I am to see your face.

DIONYSUS   Thanks.

There are many variations of the first encounter between Pentheus and Dionysus.

Of the more than 1300 lines in Arrowsmith's translation of *The Bacchae*, we use nearly 600, some more than once. We also use sixteen lines from Elizabeth Wycoff's translation of *Antigone* and six lines from David Grene's translation of *Hippolytus*. The rest of our text we made ourselves—some of it written at home, some worked out in workshops. The textual montage, the arrangements and variations, developed organically during rehearsals and throughout the run. The performers wrote their own dialogue. I wanted as much personal expression as possible in a play that deals so effectively with the liberation of personal energy. There is a formal pattern to the text's construction, however. It is not improvised. Pentheus has to stick very close to Euripides until the time when he is so deeply threatened by Dionysus that the performance mask falls away and the person playing the role is revealed. Dionysus, from the very start of the play, says his own text, but as the play goes on, he moves closer and closer to the Euripides text. It is as if Pentheus starts out as a character and learns about the person underneath, while Dionysus starts out as one of us and elevates himself to the rigidity of godhood. In practice, it did not work out so simply.

The first person to play a role establishes its over-all

textual shape. Therefore, Finley and Shephard had a great deal to do with the words of Dionysus and Pentheus. The greatest textual liberties were taken for the role of Dionysus. In other parts we did as much with displacement, montage, and split emphasis of the Euripides/Arrowsmith text as we did with direct rewriting or new writing. But in every case the creative energies of individual Group members were put to work. When a text was brought into rehearsal, I did not try to revise it, even when I felt it lacking. I wanted to work with the material at hand. I made suggestions but did not insist on them. In the end we came up with a script that does, I think, make sense, incorporate conceptual as well as affective diversity, reflect the complicated internal dynamics of the Group, and do justice to the implications of Euripides's genius.

Schechner

PENTHEUS   Well, stranger, you are attractive, at least to women, which explains, I think, your presence here in Thebes.

SHEPHARD AS PENTHEUS   Where did you get that lousy haircut?

MC DERMOTT AS DIONYSUS   I told Ada Belle: It's time for me to be about my father's business. And she said to me: Son, you ain't goin' nowhere till you cut your hair.

PENTHEUS   You don't wrestle, do you? Your curls are long. And what fair skin you have. It's not a daylight complexion. No, it comes from the night, when you hunt Aphrodite with your beauty. Now then, who are you and from where?

DIONYSUS   That's a simple question.

There are four versions of the following speech.

FINLEY AS DIONYSUS   My name is William Finley and you've heard no doubt of the flowering slums to the east on Sixth Street?

JASON AS DIONYSUS   My name's Jason Bosseau and you've probably heard of the flowering slums to the east of here over on Fifth Street?

JOAN AS DIONYSUS   My name is Joan MacIntosh. And you've heard no doubt of the flowering slums to the east on Seventh Street?

MC DERMOTT AS DIONYSUS   My name's Pat McDermott. You've heard no doubt of the circus at Bleecker Street and Macdougal?

PENTHEUS   I know the place. It rings the city
of Sardis.

There are four versions of the following speech.

FINLEY AS DIONYSUS   Well, I don't live there.
I used to dance there, until they closed the Circus
down. I live to the west, on Christopher Street,
at 91. That's 69 plus 22.

used to get these strange notes stuffed into the mailbox at 91 from faggots and teenieboppers: "dear god, I'd love to take some super-eight movies . . ."

    compelled to wear with rips in the neck seams   drum and mine
    changes of green, blue, brown go disguised as man wet orgy

He went away wanting them to know he never went. Yes, but who noticed it.

I am the phantom of Wooster Street.

He went to be revealed in other men in other lands, a popular, all-around buffoon of self-rapture. He folded his deity well, after removing with spot-lifter all spilled coffee, wine, and blood. Never leaves a ring. Good fellow.

I am the hardon that won't go down.

    then Margaret said, "You're a wet fetus Finley, Jesus!" . . . so I think about the 100 trillion microbes we're all supposed to sweat a day and figure I'm slipping too much 7-Up during the crucifixion.

Finley

JASON AS DIONYSUS   I don't come from there. I come from Kansas. But I live there now, on Fifth, between Second and Third.

JOAN AS DIONYSUS   Well, I don't come from there. I used to go to school there. I live to the west. 29 Washington Square West, 16B.

MC DERMOTT AS DIONYSUS   I don't come from there. I come from the state of Nebraska. But I can be found up there.

PENTHEUS   Who is this new god whose worship you have imported into Thebes?

Each Dionysus uses his or her own name. When a woman plays Dionysus, she does not masquerade as a man. All references to "him" or "his" become "her" and "hers." However, Pentheus sees only a man and continues to refer to "him." There are four versions of the following speech.

FINLEY AS DIONYSUS   A god descended on William Finley, Dionysus, son of Zeus, son of William Finley, and instructed me.

JASON AS DIONYSUS   A god descended on Jason Bosseau, son of Zeus, son of Damar Bosseau. He instructed me.

JOAN AS DIONYSUS   A god descended upon Joan MacIntosh, daughter of Zeus, daughter of Walter MacIntosh. She instructed me.

MC DERMOTT AS DIONYSUS   A god descended on Pat McDermott, son of Zeus and son of Ada Belle. He instructed me.

PENTHEUS   You have some local Zeus that spawns new gods?

There are four versions of the following speech.

FINLEY AS DIONYSUS   No local Zeus. I speak of
your Zeus, the same Zeus we were just talking
about. You know, Zeus.

JASON AS DIONYSUS   No local Zeus. I speak of
the express Zeus. The same Zeus we were just
talking about. Zeus.

JOAN AS DIONYSUS   No local Zeus. I speak
of your Zeus, the same Zeus we were just talking
about. You know, Zeus.

MC DERMOTT AS DIONYSUS   No, no local Zeus. The express Zeus, your Zeus, the almighty Zeus, the omniscient Zeus. The same Zeus we were just talking about. Zeus.

PENTHEUS   How did you see him? In a dream, or face to face?

There are two versions of the following speech.

DIONYSUS   Well, first he saw me and then I saw him. It was sort of like now. Face to face. As proof, he gave me his mysteries.

MC DERMOTT AS DIONYSUS   Well, I saw him in a dream. It was sort of like now. It was face to face. It was a face-to-face dream. As proof, he gave me his mysteries.

PENTHEUS   What form do they take, these mysteries of yours?

DIONYSUS   Oh, my mysteries are very difficult to describe. But they're out of sight.

PENTHEUS   Tell me then the benefits those who know your mysteries enjoy.

DIONYSUS   Well, I can't speak for them and they can't hear you right now. But it's worth hearing about soon.

PENTHEUS   Your answers are designed to make me curious.

DIONYSUS   Curiosity is useless with my mysteries. You just have to accept them the way I am.

PENTHEUS   You say you saw a god. What form did he assume?

DIONYSUS   He assumed the form he had to take at the time. The choice was his, not mine. Or mine, not his. Or whatever you say.

PENTHEUS   You're evading the question. That's what I say.

DIONYSUS   Ask me some more. I'll do better.

PENTHEUS   Have you introduced your rites to other cities, or is Thebes the first?

DIONYSUS   No, Thebes isn't the first. Foreigners everywhere dance the way I dance.

PENTHEUS   They are more ignorant than Greeks.

There are two versions of the following speech.

DIONYSUS   No they're not. They're just quicker than Greeks.

MC DERMOTT AS DIONYSUS   No, no, they're more limber than Greeks.

PENTHEUS   Do you hold your rites during the day or at night?

DIONYSUS   Mostly at night. You see, darkness is better.

PENTHEUS   Better suited to lechery and seducing women and rape.

DIONYSUS   Yeah. If that's your thing. Daylight's nice. Anytime's good, if you like it.

Dionysus begins to approach Pentheus. When McDermott plays Dionysus, he sings, "Honey in the morning, honey in the evening, jelly at suppertime." When Dia plays Pentheus, he approaches Dionysus. There are two versions of the following speech.

SHEPHARD AS PENTHEUS   You're going to regret all this pernicious sophistry.

DIA AS PENTHEUS   You're going to regret all of your clever answers.

DIONYSUS   You're beautiful.

Dionysus you are my lover,
Deep inside me you flow.
You are my Hopi chant,
My prayer for wholeness.
Slowly, unmistakably, the might
      of the god moves on.

                                        Jason

When Shephard plays Pentheus, Dionysus embraces him or offers his hand. Pentheus throws Dionysus to the ground. When Dia plays Pentheus, he strikes Dionysus in slow motion, punching and kicking him. The chorus begins a slowly accelerating drumming that grows during the scene.

PENTHEUS   What a bold bacchante. You wrestle well, when it comes to words.

DIONYSUS   Okay, what are you going to do with me now?

There are several versions of the following exchange. First, a "standard" version.

PENTHEUS   First, I am going to cut off your hair.

DIONYSUS   Now wait a minute. My hair is god's hair. If you touch my hair, you touch god. Respect my hair.

PENTHEUS   Then I'm going to have you castrated and thrown in prison.

Next, a version between Shephard and Finley.

SHEPHARD AS PENTHEUS   First, I'm going to cut off your hair.

FINLEY AS DIONYSUS   Now wait a minute. My hair is god's hair. If you touch my hair, you touch god. Please respect my hair.

SHEPHARD AS PENTHEUS   Next I'm going to take away those glasses.

FINLEY AS DIONYSUS   Oh, these? Here. You can have them. They belong to William Finley. They're Dionysus's. I was just wearing them for him.

SHEPHARD   Finally, I'm going to imprison you along with your women.

Third, a version between Shephard and Jason.

SHEPHARD AS PENTHEUS   First, I am going to cut off your hair.

JASON AS DIONYSUS   Hold on. My hair is god's hair. If you touch my hair, you touch god. Touch my hair and I'll kill you.

SHEPHARD AS PENTHEUS   Then I'm going to take away that button.

He is referring to a *Dionysus in 69* button, in red and blue, designed yin-yang style, that is sometimes given out by Dionysus to the audience at the end of the play, Jason wears one of these.

JASON AS DIONYSUS   Oh, this? Here, you can have it. It belongs to Dionysus. I have hundreds more back there by the light board. I was just holding it for him.

SHEPHARD AS PENTHEUS   Then I'm going to have you castrated and thrown in prison with your women.

Finally, a version between Shephard and McDermott.

SHEPHARD AS PENTHEUS   First I'm going to shave you bald.

MC DERMOTT AS DIONYSUS   No you're not. Only god touches my hair.

SHEPHARD AS PENTHEUS   I'm going to cut off your balls and stick them in your mouth and put you down in that hole. I'm going to put you in prison.

The standard text continues.

DIONYSUS   Shit. Here I stand. One man under guard. But guard will set me free. He hears you. He sees what you're doing.

PENTHEUS   You'll be with your women in prison when you call on your god for help.

From this point on, Dionysus often refers to Pentheus by his "real" name. For convenience, the "standard" first name in this text will be "Bill." However, when Richard Dia is specifically alluded to, "Richard" will be used.

DIONYSUS   Look. You don't understand, Bill. He's here with us. He sees you right now. He knows what you're doing.

PENTHEUS   Where is he? I don't see him.

DIONYSUS   If you don't see him, you're blind.

PENTHEUS   Seize him. He is mocking me and Thebes.

DIONYSUS   I warn you, place no chains on me.

PENTHEUS   I said to take him away. And I'm the stronger here.

DIONYSUS   Bill, you're beautiful, but you're crazy. Now, look, I'll count to three. Someone take him away. One. Two.

PENTHEUS   Take him away!

DIONYSUS   One. You don't know the limits of

your strength. Two. You're acting as if you don't know what you're doing. Three. You don't know who you are.

PENTHEUS   I am Pentheus. Son of Echion and Agave. And King of Thebes.

There are several versions of the following exchange.

DIONYSUS TO SHEPHARD   Pentheus? Son of Echion and Agave and King of Thebes? Bullshit. You're Bill Shephard. You're in the Group. You're no god, but you are in the Group. Pentheus? Echion? You're coo-coo. Take him away.

Whenever Pentheus says anything to me, I receive energy, so that no matter what he says—putdown, anger—it makes me stronger. We dealt several times in rehearsal with my feelings of fradulence. I was a little girl dressed in mommy's clothes and digging it. I was putting one over on everyone. I giggled. Then I became a woman seducing Pentheus. And finally a god, secure in that, believing in that, able to follow through on my impulses because the action was securely inside me.

Joan

What I discovered when we started our improvisational workshops with the city of Thebes was that being the king was not merely playing a role. It was defining very clearly my relationship to the rest of the people in the Group. I felt very guarded. I felt superior to some, maybe even arrogant. Armed with these feelings, I stepped into the situation. I felt that the Bacchae, the people on the other side, were content with being winners. The stark dichotomy between good and bad—that was the way I first felt it. I sensed I was not really a king. I didn't know what I was. Later I discovered I was a scapegoat. It certainly was no longer just a play.

Shephard

MC DERMOTT AS DIONYSUS TO SHEPHARD   Pentheus? Son of Echion and Agave and King of Thebes? Bullshit. You were a little man with a big dream. And now you're a big man in trouble. That's who you are.

DIONYSUS TO DIA   Pentheus, son of Echion and Agave and King of Thebes? Bullshit. You're Richard Dia. You were born in New York City. Your father makes mandolins. You're a nice guy. Sometimes we have coffee together. You're in

the Group. You're no god, but you're in the Group. When you get like this, you're impossible. Will someone please take him away?

There are two versions of the following speech.

SHEPHARD AS PENTHEUS   Throw him into the stud stalls where the beasts copulate.

DIA AS PENTHEUS   Throw him into the stables under the palace.

PENTHEUS   Since he enjoys darkness so much, give him all he wants. Let him dance down there in the dark. As for these women of yours, I'm going to have them sold as slaves or put to work at my looms. That will silence the beating of their drums.

There are two versions of the following speech.

DIONYSUS   Okay, okay, I'll go. But I won't suffer. That's not what happens. We've been playing your game long enough. I'm getting bored with it. So now we're going to play my game. The Dionysus Game. It's much more fun. If you say I'm not the god, I say you're not the king. And you're not the king. When you chain me, you chain the god. See you in 69!

MC DERMOTT AS DIONYSUS   Okay, I'll go. But I won't suffer. That's not what happens. You see, if you say I'm not the god, then I say you're not the king. And if I say you're not the king, you won't be the king. We've been playing your game long enough. Now we're going to play my game. It's much more fun. It's called the Dionysus Game.

Dionysus goes into the pit. The drumming stops. Out of the silence, from the periphery of the theatre, the chorus comes, one by one. Pentheus is encircled and trapped. All face in, looking at him or beyond him at each other. Each says something joyful or eventful that happened to him that day. Or, if nothing comes to mind, a performer simply says his name. As each person speaks, he turns his back on Pentheus. Some sample remarks.

CIEL   I said to Pat, "Tell me five things your hands do." And he answered, "They write, they rest, they smoke, they wash, they die."

REMI   We painted another room in our apartment today, adding a red room to the blue room and the yellow room.

JASON   I had a parakeet when I was twelve years old. And the parakeet's name was Chico. And one day he flew away.

MC DERMOTT   For a long time I tried to think of who Sam Yorty reminded me of. And finally it hit me. Ozzie Nelson.

FINLEY   My name is William Finley.

DIA   Joan, on my way up Broadway today I was stopped by two men and one woman. One of the men said, "We are three witches."

SHEPHARD   Today I wrote one of the most important letters of my life.

MARGARET   There is a cop in Central Park who rides a big bay horse and carries a parrot on his shoulder.

JOAN   Today I was seduced by Sydney the Giant Far Eastern Slithery, tickled by Morris the Midget Mauler, and raped by Sigmund the Sadist.

Watching the performance night after night, I am aware of the subtle changes taking place in the actors themselves, in the play's score, and in the interaction with the audience. My favorite segment, I suppose, is the Pentheus circle. I never know what anyone is going to say. I enjoy being surprised. Also, it is the one place in the play where the individual, often wry humor of the performers shines through.

Vicki

During the transformation-circle sentences, Dionysus comes out of the pit and sits among the audience. When the last performer speaks, Dionysus asks a question of one of them.

DIONYSUS   Pat, who does Ozzie Nelson remind you of?

PENTHEUS   How did you escape?

DIONYSUS   How did I escape? How did you escape?

PENTHEUS   How did you escape!

DIONYSUS   Okay. You asked first. I escaped with someone's help.

PENTHEUS   Who is this mysterious someone?

There are several answers to this question.

FINLEY AS DIONYSUS   Eight androgynous hermaphrodites. They who make my cock grow for mankind.

JASON AS DIONYSUS   Dionysus, the god who has enough power to turn on all mankind.

JOAN AS DIONYSUS   Dionysus. She who turns on all mankind.

MC DERMOTT AS DIONYSUS   An androgynous, philanthropic hermaphrodite. He who lets his balls hang down like grapes on the vine.

PENTHEUS   Splendid contribution, that.

DIONYSUS   Don't knock the gift that is my biggest glory.

PENTHEUS   Oh, you're very clever, but not where it counts.

DIONYSUS   That's where you're wrong. Where it counts most, there I am clever most.

Dionysus gestures and the chorus sings the tag-chorus song for that night. As they sing, they dance around Pentheus, moving more and more swiftly. They continue until Pentheus screams and Dionysus gestures the chorus to be silent. During the next dialogue between Dionysus and Pentheus, the chorus is standing very close to Pentheus, pressing in around him. Also, the performers are making and passing faces among themselves. Surrounded by ridicule, Pentheus is fueled by rage and frustration.

PENTHEUS   Like a blazing fire, your Bacchic ecstasy spreads. But it comes too close. We are disgraced, humiliated in the eyes of Hellas. You there, go down to the Electran Gates and order out all the heavy-armored infantry. Call up the fastest troops among our cavalry. The mobile squadrons and the archers. We march against the Bacchae! Affairs are out of hand when we tamely endure such conduct in our women.

There are two versions of the response to Pentheus.

FINLEY OR JASON AS DIONYSUS   Oh, Bill, you're too much. Always ranting and screaming to people who aren't there. Talking about armies and cavalry. Making long speeches of bad poetry. You know you've got to learn to give. You can't always command.

JOAN OR MC DERMOTT AS DIONYSUS   Bill, you're too much. Who are you talking to? There's no army in this room. You know, Bill, if I were you I'd stop giving so many orders. I'd learn to take orders.

PENTHEUS   Don't you lecture me. I put you in that pit once and I can put you down there again.

DIONYSUS   Bill, you don't understand. You're a man. I'm a god. This is a tragedy. The odds are against you. If I were you, I'd give me a present. A sacrifice. Gods don't have everything, you know.

PENTHEUS   I'll give you—your god—the sacrifice you deserve. Your victims will be your women. I'm going to make a great slaughter in the woods of Cithaeron.

There are three versions of Dionysus's response.

FINLEY AS DIONYSUS   You'll be destroyed. Their yes will flood your no. Our ecstasy will eat up your hate and shit it out again. You don't have a chance.

JASON OR JOAN AS DIONYSUS   You'll be destroyed. Our collective yes will take your uptight little no and laugh it out of here. You don't have a chance.

MC DERMOTT AS DIONYSUS   Their bouncing breasts will turn back your spears. You don't have a chance.

No portion of the production gave us more trouble than the Dionysus Game. In the Euripides text, the action at this point is improbable for a modern audience. Thunder and lightning shake the city. Dionysus appears from prison just as an earthquake utterly destroys Pentheus's palace. Fire leaps up from Semele's tomb. Dionysus says, "I humiliated him, outrage for outrage." Then he describes how Pentheus assaults a bull, thinking it is Dionysus, and how the fire and earthquake reduce Pentheus to rage and panic. Finally Dionysus describes how Pentheus attacks "a phantom which resembles" Dionysus. In short, Pentheus is mortified. Our problem was to translate this into actions viable both for us and for our audiences.

We turned to exercises from workshop. We had been playing an encounter game in which one performer challenges another. A question or statement is made which, according to the rules of the exercise, must "cost something." An answer is given that is equally revealing and difficult. And so on, until everyone has contributed at least once. When we did this exercise during the performance, I added the stipulation that the exchange must be meaningful, no coded communications. After everyone in the Group had participated in the encounter, people could turn on Shephard, who was playing Pentheus at this time. Shephard had to answer the questions, but could not ask any. The game continued until Shephard's opacity was sufficiently pierced so that he could not respond to a question. Then he said, "This is mortifying," and the scene was over. Once the questioning went on for more than an hour.

It was this "mortification scene" that gave the production its reputation for psychodrama. By October 1968, it became clear that the Group had hardened to the encounters. Questions bounced off toughened surfaces. A game that had honesty as its most moving quality became dishonest. So we turned to new explorations from workshop and began to use the "transformation circle."

In the transformation exercise, a description of an event or an action is passed around a circle, each person taking a word, image, association, or tone from the person talking to him, transforming that into something of his own, and passing it on to the person next to him. It is a fine exercise for contact and relating. The events and actions spoken of are actual and drawn from the immediate experience of

the performer. Using this exercise in performance is simple. Immediately after the tag chorus, the performers come down from the towers and make a circle around Pentheus. As they speak their transformations, they turn their backs on Pentheus, so that in a few minutes he is isolated in the center of a circle made up of his fellow performers. Pentheus is left alone in the midst of a project that everyone else has temporarily abandoned. Their laughter about everyday happenings is in stark contrast to his rage about Dionysus. Their personalizing points up more clearly his fierce commitment to the theatrical situation. The transformation circle is, in one way, the opposite of the mortification encounters. In the encounters, the attention focuses on Pentheus. In the circle, Pentheus is abandoned.

For reasons that were never very clear to me, the performers were dissatisfied with the transformation circle. Around December 1968, we tried another version of this scene, again based on exercises taken from workshop. After the tag chorus, Pentheus remains in the center while the other performers somersault around him, saying, as they tumble, derisive things about Pentheus. The somersaulting begins in slow motion and steadily accelerates until it is very fast. At the same time, Dionysus comes from the pit and engages Pentheus in "ritual combat." In ritual combat, two people face each other in a clearly delimited space. The combatants mobilize their bodies and an attack is launched, first by one, then by the other. No physical contact is allowed. The attack may be a thrust, a sound, a continuous action. Once a move is made, it cannot be withdrawn. So, for example, if a fist shoots out, it must be kept out. Or if someone begins a sharp hissing sound, it must continue until the end of the struggle. Given these rules, ritual combat is all-consuming. It usually lasts less than forty-five seconds. What was wrong with ritual combat in this scene was that Dionysus had to win each time. The game was rigged and impossible to play with conviction.

Ultimately, in February 1969, we went back to a modified version of the transformation circle that worked very well. The performers in the circle say something to each other or to the audience that gave them pleasure during the day of the performance. As each performer speaks he turns his back on Pentheus. If a performer can think of nothing to say, or does not wish to relate an event or action, he simply says his name. When everyone has turned around, performers begin to make faces at each other, passing these funny faces around the transformation circle. These faces grow more bizarre and finally precipitate into silent, convulsive laughter.

Why has this part of the play been so hard to settle? Because it is an abrupt change in tone, a disruption of the play's structure. We cannot show palaces crumbling and fires burning. We have no cattle, no mysterious god, no earthquake. Most of all, we do not have an audience that believes in the old myths. What we have is an audience that wants to believe in our performance and knows the power of modern ecstasy. We show a performance breaking down. Our private lives fill the breach, and we display ourselves shamelessly. A psychic space opens between those performers who are free to show themselves and the man playing Pentheus, tied to the text as to a stake. This indulgence of the many at the expense of one, this eruption and disruption, is the heart of the fantasy Dionysus offers. From this moment it is clear that Pentheus is doomed. He alone cannot turn free from his own tragedy.

Schechner

The action becomes very personal at this point. The performer playing Dionysus has to understand and offer to the performer playing Pentheus something Pentheus wants very much. Each pair of performers has worked out the problem for themselves. In all the versions, when Dionysus says, "Try it yourself," or "You can't get it from anyone else," or "I'm the one. You'll see," the chorus runs away from Pentheus, leaving him alone in the center of the room.

First, a version between Finley and Shephard.

SHEPHARD AS PENTHEUS   Finley, it's hopeless talking to you and you never would wrestle me.

FINLEY AS DIONYSUS   I don't wrestle, Bill. But I can tell you how to end this hassle.

SHEPHARD AS PENTHEUS   How? By taking orders from my own slaves?

FINLEY AS DIONYSUS   No, look. I'll bring them down without force. You don't need the heat.

SHEPHARD AS PENTHEUS   This is some kind of trap.

FINLEY AS DIONYSUS   A trap? A trap? A trapity-trapity-trapity-trap-trap-trap. Paranoia! Paranoia! Why is it a trap if I use my powers to help you?

SHEPHARD AS PENTHEUS   You stand to lose too much if I win. And I know that you and Remi and Ciel and McDermott are out to get me.

FINLEY AS DIONYSUS   You're right. We've been rehearsing secretly for months. We've been conspiring against you. Fool.

Shephard takes Finley's glasses off, gives them to someone in the audience to hold. He puts Finley in the starting position for Olympic wrestling, Finley kneeling on all fours, and Shephard on his knees, with his arms around Finley. Shephard throws Finley. Finley does not resist.

FINLEY AS DIONYSUS   Why did you do that?

SHEPHARD AS PENTHEUS   Because I had to.

FINLEY AS DIONYSUS   What can I give you?

SHEPHARD AS PENTHEUS   I have this energy inside here, like a little animal. It's gnawing, eating me from the inside, trying to get out.

FINLEY AS DIONYSUS   I can give you any woman in this room.

SHEPHARD AS PENTHEUS   I don't need you.

FINLEY AS DIONYSUS   Then try it yourself.

There is another, much shorter, version between Finley and Shephard.

SHEPHARD AS PENTHEUS   It's hopeless talking to you and you won't wrestle me.

FINLEY AS DIONYSUS   I don't wrestle, but I can help you end this hassle.

SHEPHARD AS PENTHEUS   I want to go to the mountain. I want to set the hounds on, shouting. And poise the Thessalian javelin, drawing it back here, where my fair hair hangs above my ear. I would hold in my hand a spear with a steel point.

FINLEY AS DIONYSUS   I can give you any woman in this room.

SHEPHARD AS PENTHEUS   I don't need you.

FINLEY AS DIONYSUS   Then try it yourself.

Shephard then goes into the audience, seeks a woman, and touches her, kisses her, tries to make love with her.

The Finley and Dia version.

DIA AS PENTHEUS   It's hopeless talking to you. I just want to obliterate you.

FINLEY AS DIONYSUS   Richard, I can't be touched. I can't be touched. Can't be touched, can't be touched, can't be touched.

DIA AS PENTHEUS   All the love that I bare in these private hours of dying plunges me into stillness and vacancy where a muddy cloud hovers about my head and feet stagger lost in the swamp, ankle deep, stagnant. I, I crucified, laid bare to stumble.

FINLEY AS DIONYSUS   I reject that. It sucks.

DIA AS PENTHEUS   I need someone to accept that.

FINLEY AS DIONYSUS   I can give you someone to accept that.

DIA AS PENTHEUS   No, you can't.

FINLEY AS DIONYSUS   Yes, I can. Any woman in the audience. Anyone you want. Look around, Richard. Her? Or her? I can give her to you, Richard.

DIA AS PENTHEUS   I don't need you.

FINLEY AS DIONYSUS   You don't need me? Well, then, try it yourself.

Dia does not go into the audience seeking a woman. He recites some of his own poetry, asking for someone to come and help him.

DIA AS PENTHEUS   Come to me, someone. I need someone to be a mother to me, to be an angel to my needs. My needs are great. Sound the alarm, my need is great. Put up a wall if you're a mason. But if you're not, don't worry about walls. Come to me, someone. Put up a wall if you're a mason. But if you're not, don't worry about walls. Come to me, someone. One, two, buckle your shoe, forget you're sad, forget you're blue. Every shadow is a cloud and every tear is only water. And remember this. Wherever there are shadows, there must be light nearby. And sorrow is a stepping stone to joy. Am I to become only my own echo, reflecting off stone walls? Why are there no shadows here? Where is the key to unlock the misery I abound in?

The Jason and Dia version.

DIA AS PENTHEUS   It's no use talking to you because you always felt that your life style was so much better than my life style.

JASON AS DIONYSUS   Hey, Richard, my life style is better than yours. You know it. I mean, I've traveled to many places, many countries, and I've given to more than one hundred women. I've known many ecstasies.

DIA AS PENTHEUS   And that makes you a god?

JASON AS DIONYSUS   That's part of it. Another part is that I could go out into this audience right now and select a woman of my choice and achieve ecstasy here and now. We'd make love and it would be good. I could do that.

DIA AS PENTHEUS   So could I.

JASON AS DIONYSUS   You don't believe that, Richard. Those are just lines. You can barely say them. You'd need my help, Richard, to get anywhere at all.

DIA AS PENTHEUS   I don't need you for anything.

JASON AS DIONYSUS   You don't need me for anything?

DIA AS PENTHEUS   Nothing.

JASON AS DIONYSUS   Not even this?

DIA AS PENTHEUS   Not even this.

JASON AS DIONYSUS   Okay, Richard, okay. Try it yourself.

Here, as in the version with Finley, Dia recites his poem.

The Jason and Shephard version.

SHEPHARD AS PENTHEUS   It's hopeless talking with you, Bosseau, and you never would wrestle me.

JASON AS DIONYSUS   I don't wrestle, Bill, but I can give you what you need.

SHEPHARD AS PENTHEUS   I don't need anything from you.

JASON AS DIONYSUS   Bill, I can give you compassion. I can even give you ecstasy.

SHEPHARD AS PENTHEUS   I don't believe you. I don't believe anything about you.

JASON AS DIONYSUS   Well, you won't get it from anybody else.

In this version, as in those with Joan or McDermott as Dionysus and Shephard as Pentheus, Shephard remains in the center and slowly, silently, and seemingly from within, crumbles.

The Joan and Shephard version.

SHEPHARD AS PENTHEUS   It's hopeless talking to you. And you can't wrestle.

JOAN AS DIONYSUS   I don't wrestle. But I can give you what you want.

SHEPHARD AS PENTHEUS   I don't want anything from you.

JOAN AS DIONYSUS   I can give you compassion.

SHEPHARD AS PENTHEUS   I don't believe you. I don't believe anything about you.

JOAN AS DIONYSUS   You can't get it from anyone else.

I escape from the pit and Pentheus is surrounded. I humiliate him. I grow in power, he shrinks in power. The problems of other scenes become more transparent here. To live through the scene beat by beat and not charge ahead to the end to get it over with. When I tell Bill that I can give him compassion, I mean it. I can help him, no one else can. I alone can complete the play. The stakes are very high.

Joan

The McDermott and Shephard version.

SHEPHARD AS PENTHEUS   It's hopeless talking to you. And you won't fight.

MC DERMOTT AS DIONYSUS   No, I don't fight. But I can give you what you want.

SHEPHARD AS PENTHEUS   I don't want anything from you.

MC DERMOTT AS DIONYSUS   I can put you out of your misery.

SHEPHARD AS PENTHEUS   I'm not miserable.

MC DERMOTT AS DIONYSUS   Sure you are.
That's why you want to fight me.

SHEPHARD AS PENTHEUS   I don't need you.

MC DERMOTT AS DIONYSUS   Nobody else can do
it for you. You'll see. I'm the one.

As in the version with Joan, Pentheus remains in
the center saying nothing. He looks at various
people in the audience. Sometimes a person will
come to him. More often, no one will.

While Pentheus is in the center, the chorus and Dionysus move through the theatre. They meet in small groups, talk, laugh, point at Pentheus, split, and meet again somewhere else. They talk quietly to the audience. The focus is divided between Pentheus in the center and the furtive chorus all around. Dionysus is the ever shifting nucleus of the chorus.

CHORUS, BUT NOT IN UNISON   When shall I dance once more with bare feet the all-night dances? Tossing my head for joy in the damp air, in the dew, as a running fawn might frisk for the green joy of the wide fields. Free from fear of the hunt. Free from the circling beaters and the nets of woven mesh. And the hunters hallooing on their yelping packs. And then, hard pressed, she sprints with the quickness of wind. Bounding over the marsh, leaping to frisk, leaping for joy, gay with the green of the leaves. To dance for joy in the forest. To dance where the darkness is deepest. Where no man is.

DIONYSUS   What time is it?

MC DERMOTT   Slow, but unmistakable, the might of the gods moves on. It punishes that man infatuate of soul and hardened in his pride who disregards the gods. The gods are crafty. They lie in wait a long step of time to hunt the unholy.

MARGARET   Small is the cost to believe in this: Whatever is god is strong.

I thought for a long time about what Pentheus wanted. Compassion—because compassion is more than sympathy, it is understanding. Some people have come to me at that moment and said, "What can I give you?" My answer is, "But you must know."

The one time the sequence was completed was when Katherine Turner came out into the room. It was a unique experience. I was ready for it because earlier in the run when I sought a woman in the audience and tried to make love to her, I acted with restraint. I was afraid of what might happen. But when Katherine came to me, in May 1968, my score for the role was concrete. The confrontation between us was irrational. Her concern for me was not based on the play, my playing a role, whether or not I was going to die, or any of that. What happened was that I recognized in one moment that the emotional energy Katherine was spending on me lifted me out of the play, as though someone had grabbed me by the hair and pulled me up to the ceiling. I looked

around and I saw the garage and the other actors and I said, "It finally happened." The play fell away, like shackles being struck from my hands. The way the play is set up, Pentheus is trapped inside its structure. But on that night it all seemed to fall away and I walked out the door.

Shephard

One Sunday night when I was playing Dionysus, a woman came out to Bill Shephard and satisfied him. I went to break it up and get on with the play. Bill said, "I'm sorry, Joan, you lose." I answered, "Well, what are you going to do now?" And Bill got up and left the theatre with the woman. I announced that the play was over. "Ladies and gentlemen, tonight for the first time since the play has been running, Pentheus, a man, has won over Dionysus, the god. The play is over." Cheers and cries and celebrations. Objectively, I cheered too. Subjectively, I had lost. I felt betrayed. I was hurt and angry at Shephard. I had invested so much of myself in the performance that it became real. I had lost a lover. Amazed both at the commitment I had and at the relationship with Bill, I learned something corny but true: that if you invest all of yourself in the work, the risks are very great. Since then, I have had to fight against subtle defenses that creep in—defenses against feeling betrayed.

Joan

On one other occasion people have planned and successfully changed the ending of the play. In June 1969, a small group of young people, led by some who had seen the play before, dragged Pentheus from the theatre. McDermott was playing Dionysus; and Shephard, Pentheus. It was not as clear cut as the time when Katherine took Bill away. This time Bill was comatose and a fist-fight almost broke out between Jason, acting on Dionysus's behalf, and several of the kids taking Pentheus out. After Shephard was dragged from the theatre, he came back but did not want to continue performing. Jason was very upset and went upstairs. Other performers were confused, blaming both McDermott and Shephard for an unresolved situation. I was not there at the start of the performance and walked into the theatre as Shephard was being dragged out. I sensed a bad scene developing and, perhaps unwisely, spoke to both performers and audience. I explained what had happened, how rare it was, and asked for a volunteer Pentheus from the audience. A young man who had seen the play five times volunteered. We asked him a few questions, explained what was expected of him, put in an improvised scene in which the performers, instead of reciting the death speeches, voiced their reactions to the night's occurrences and went on with the play. I participated in the death dance, kill, and clean up. Later I argued with the kids about what they had done. And to this day I do not know whether my intrusion was correct or not.

Schechner

DIONYSUS   We're going to kill him in twenty minutes. At 10:15. Pass it on.

SAM   Wisdom. Honor. Victorious. The gods are crafty. They lie in ambush a long step of time to hunt the unholy. Beyond the old beliefs no thought, no act, shall go. Whatever is god is strong. Wisdom. Honor. Victorious. Honor is precious forever.

REMI   Small, small is the cost to believe in this. Honor is precious forever.

JOAN   Honor is precious forever. Slow but unmistakable the might of the gods moves on. In various ways one man outraces another.

MARGARET   Dislocate his elbow. We're going to kill him in twenty minutes.

JOAN   In twenty minutes we're going to kill him. At 10:15 we're going to kill him. Will you help us kill Pentheus?

CIEL   The gods are crafty. They lie in ambush a long step of time to hunt the unholy. Slow but unmistakable the might of the gods moves on and it punishes that man infatuate of soul. What is wisdom? What gift of the gods is held in honor like this: to hold your hand victorious over the heads of those you hate. Honor is precious forever. Small is the cost to believe in this: whatever is god is strong. We're going to kill him in twenty minutes, okay?

Some of the best moments of Dionysus, and some of the worst, have been created by individual spectators who sought to participate tangibly. Tangible participation, spontaneous or invited, does not necessarily mean deeper audience involvement. Involvement depends on the symbolic consciousness, or creativity, of the spectator. Involvement may or may not become tangible. If it does, the spectator pulls

himself, along with actors and other spectators, out of the show; or he may plunge himself, and them too, deeper into it. Participation is a challenge to the ability of both actors and audience to create symbols. Rituals can be created and the scope of symbolism expanded. Ritual involvement reveals the audience. The reciprocal privacy of stage and auditorium is not maintained. Ritual assembles; it dispels the illusions of routinization and privacy. It does not pretend to the public performance of private acts.

McDermott

Pentheus is almost always rejected by the woman he tries to make love with. Or he collapses in the center because no one comes to help him. During the run of 163 performances, someone effectively aided Pentheus on two occasions. (These extraordinary variations are discussed in the commentary.) People frequently try to help him, offering comfort or routes of escape. Most of this is futile. When Pentheus gives up, Dionysus approaches him once again. Because of the intimate nature of this scene, there are many versions. The tone of the scene changes sharply from night to night.

Early in rehearsals with Bill Shephard and Bill Finley we had to find an equivalent for dressing in women's clothes. In Euripides, Pentheus is possessed and humiliated, rewarded and destroyed. Shephard suggested homosexuality as the counterpart. It was the most difficult thing he could think of doing in public. The homosexual kiss is supreme revealment and concealment at the same time. Dionysus's purpose works through Pentheus's submission. And both performers taste something that attracts and repels them. Neither is homosexual. To many homosexuals in the audience the scene is titillating. Sometimes, as much from anxiety as from amusement, spectators shout encouragement to Pentheus. Unwittingly, they mortify him as Euripides intended: "I want him made the laughingstock of Thebes."

When Joan plays Dionysus, the dynamics of the scene are reversed. She says what few women say aloud, in words that few men have heard spoken to them in earnest. Pentheus is afraid. He is terrified at giving himself over so totally to a woman. In both cases, Dionysus is revealed as wanting completion. The personal stakes are highest here. The scene is not between Dionysus and Pentheus. It is between Finley, McDermott, Jason, or Joan and Shephard or Dia. These people work out themes articulated by Euripides, but wholly in their own terms. Afterwards, the play begins to surface back toward fiction.

Schechner

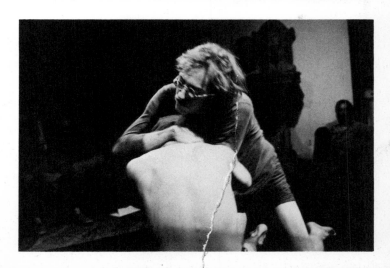

First, a "standard" version, used most of the
time by Finley or Jason playing with Shephard or
Dia.

DIONYSUS   Bill, I can give you what you want.
I can give it to you, Bill. But first you have to
do something for me. I can give you someone
to accept you. But you have to do something
for me.

PENTHEUS   What do you want me to do?

DIONYSUS   First I want you to relax. To be
open. To be open to me. I want you to be
vulnerable. To be very loving and very relaxed.
Bill, I want you to be a woman for me.

PENTHEUS   What does that mean?

DIONYSUS   Ecstasy doesn't come cheap. If you
give me what I want, I'll give you what you
want. I'll give you any woman in this room. But
first you have to make love to me.

PENTHEUS   You're an old hand at cunning.

DIONYSUS   Dionysus taught me everything I
know.

PENTHEUS   What specifically do you want me
to do?

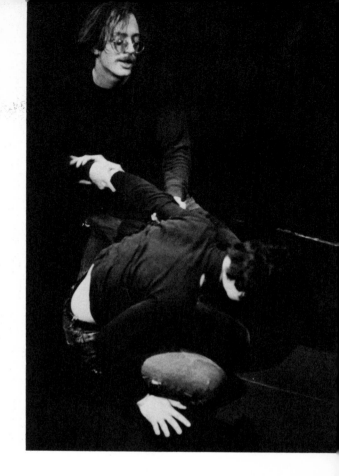

DIONYSUS   Specifically, I want you to take off
my shirt and my pants and my underwear.
Then I want you to caress my body all over. I
want you to caress it very slowly and carefully.
And then I want you to caress my cock until it
gets hard. And then I want you to take my cock
in your mouth and caress it with your lips and
your tongue and your teeth. I want you to suck
on my cock. Bill, I want you to suck my cock.

PENTHEUS   What?

DIONYSUS   I want you to suck my cock.

PENTHEUS   Are you out of your mind?

DIONYSUS   If you don't do what I want, you'll
have to confront the Bacchae and that means
violence and rejection. Do you want everyone in
this room to reject you, one after another? Is
that what you want?

PENTHEUS   No. No. No.

DIONYSUS   Then try what I ask. It's not so
hard. Try it.

They kiss.

PENTHEUS   I can't do it here.

DIONYSUS   Who said you had to do it here?
We can go upstairs, or in the toilet, or behind
the dimmer board, or down in the pit. Why not
down in the pit, Bill? No one will see us there.
It will be very private.

Pentheus goes to the pit, opens the door. Just before he goes down, he says:

PENTHEUS   Either I'll do what you want or
I'll tear you limb from limb.

I come to the temple to worship. I come to the temple to become more whole. I am acting out my disease,
the disease that plagues my inner being, that stops up
the flow, the flow that gives to all those who see. Dionysus is not a play to me. I do not act in Dionysus.
Dionysus is my ritual.

                                          Jason

There are variations. When Finley is playing with
Dia, Dionysus's speech after "I want you to suck
my cock" goes:

FINLEY AS DIONYSUS   If you don't do what I
want, you'll have to confront the Bacchae, and
that means violence and rejection. Do you want
to go out in the middle of the room and recite
your silly poems again?

DIA AS PENTHEUS   No.

FINLEY AS DIONYSUS   Do you want to have
them rejected by everyone in this room, one
person after another?

DIA AS PENTHEUS   No.

When Jason is playing with Dia, the sequence
goes:

JASON AS DIONYSUS   Richard, if I am out of my
mind, you will have to confront the Bacchae,
and that means violence and rejection and
bloodshed. And that means you will be killed.
Now is that what you want?

DIA AS PENTHEUS   No.

JASON AS DIONYSUS   Do you want to be
rejected by every woman in this room, one
after another? Do you! Do you!

DIA AS PENTHEUS   No! No! No!

JASON AS DIONYSUS   Well, then, Richard, why
don't you try it? It's not so hard.

The scene is different when Dionysus is a
woman. The version between Joan and Shephard.

Here the exchange of power takes place in a very concrete way. He submits to me and is mine. The scene allows me to confront the terrific sexual power that is potentially mine. It frightens me. At the same time, sexually and psychically to want Bill, to expose my anguish and my fear, makes me very alive. Every word he says is important to my life. I anticipate nothing.

Joan

JOAN AS DIONYSUS   Bill, I was right, wasn't I? I am the only person in this room who cares enough about you. I am the only one who can give you compassion. I can give you compassion and ecstasy, Bill. But first you have to do something for me.

SHEPHARD AS PENTHEUS   What do you want me to do?

JOAN AS DIONYSUS   I want you to do exactly what I tell you to do.

SHEPHARD AS PENTHEUS   What do you mean?

JOAN AS DIONYSUS   Ecstasy doesn't come cheap.

SHEPHARD AS PENTHEUS   You're an old hand at cunning.

JOAN AS DIONYSUS   Dionysus taught me everything I know.

SHEPHARD AS PENTHEUS   What specifically do you want me to do?

JOAN AS DIONYSUS   First I want you to relax. Then I want you to take off your clothes. I want you to be vulnerable and open to me. Then I want you to take off my shirt and pants and caress my body. I want you to kiss me full on the mouth. I want you to caress my face and hair with your fingers. I want you to blow into my ears and bite them with your teeth and lick them with your tongue. I want you to rub and scratch my back, my arms, and my legs. I want you to suck on my breasts. I want you to lick and tickle my belly. I want you to spread my legs and caress the insides of my thighs. I want you to put your mouth inside my cunt and bite it gently with your teeth and lick it with your tongue. I want you to eat me around the folds of skin and way deep inside.

SHEPHARD AS PENTHEUS   I can't do what you want.

JOAN AS DIONYSUS   You can't do what I want?
Well, if you can't do what I want, then you'll
have to confront the Bacchae and that means
violence and rejection. I'll have every person in
this room reject you, one right after the other.
Is that what you want?

SHEPHARD AS PENTHEUS   No.

JOAN AS DIONYSUS   Then try what I ask.

Pentheus begins to undress.

SHEPHARD AS PENTHEUS   I can't do it here.

JOAN AS DIONYSUS   You don't have to do it
here. We can go into the pit. Why don't you go
into the pit and wait for me there? We can be
alone there. No one will see us.

The version between McDermott and Shephard.

MC DERMOTT AS DIONYSUS   I told you, Bill. It's
hard to find a friend, Bill. It's hard not to be
lonely, Bill. It's hard to leave your misery
behind, Bill. I told you. I'm the only one. I can
do it for you. I can put you out of your misery.
But first you have to do something for me. Oh,
please do something for me.

SHEPHARD AS PENTHEUS   What do I have to
do for you?

MC DERMOTT AS DIONYSUS   It's simple, Bill. It's
not hard. Ecstasy doesn't come cheap, you
know.

SHEPHARD AS PENTHEUS   You're an old hand at
cunning, aren't you?

MC DERMOTT AS DIONYSUS   You've got your problems, I got mine.

SHEPHARD AS PENTHEUS   What do you want from me?

MC DERMOTT AS DIONYSUS   I want you to take your clothes off, Bill. I want you take your clothes off and lie down next to me. And then take mine off, Bill. And then caress me, Bill. And then kiss me. And lick my eyes. Put your tongue in my ears. Way down deep. Put your tongue in my nose, Bill. And then I want you to lick my legs. And eat my hair. And I want you to bite my ass. And then I want you to put your tongue in my crotch and lick my crotch and hold my balls in your hand and make me feel good and send me up, man, send me up! And put my cock in your mouth! Bill, put my cock in your mouth! Take it away! Take it away from me, Bill! Drink it! Drink it! Drink it!

SHEPHARD AS PENTHEUS   I can't do what you want!

MC DERMOTT AS DIONYSUS   What! You can't do what I want? You know what I'm going to do about that? I'm going to tell people you were not nice to me! And they'll rip you to pieces! They will rip you to pieces! You want that?

SHEPHARD AS PENTHEUS   No.

MC DERMOTT AS DIONYSUS   Then you try.

They kiss.

SHEPHARD AS PENTHEUS   I can't do it here.

MC DERMOTT AS DIONYSUS   You don't have to do it here, Bill. Do it down there. Go on down there and wait for me.

After Pentheus goes into the pit, Dionysus addresses the audience. The names used change depending upon who is performing the roles. Finley, Jason, and Joan use the same speech. McDermott's version is somewhat different.

DIONYSUS   Friends, skeptics, fellow Bacchae. That man is ours. To be more precise, he's mine. To quote Euripides: "For sane of mind that man would never wear a woman's dress, but obsess his soul and he cannot refuse." Now what that means is this: Bill Shephard has to know me. He has to submit to me. I am his only reward. He has to know me, William Finley, Dionysus, god most terrible and yet most gentle to mankind.

---

smiling no objection   volume on low   clapped in chains
oblong white plastic water jug   awaiting the wanted
shock underworld
        arms and hands and fingers stretch the rest of me.
        My head is warm. Stomach shivers jumping fishes.
        Head falls back. Sound spumes up to that red gel
        "I am it! I'm coming back here, dig it dudes"
grease pit mustard   picnic with Blue   red night light
come release me   unlock my terror   spin around fiend
He went down after nights of Wainwright births and hospital
fires. Nights of being born on flat tar-baby square. Grapes
become raisins.
Sugar god
Demand us all
My need to have it all
Give me to me like
        Bitch dogs in heat

(He comes on.)

I haven't left you

(He rubs him up and down.)

Written 'FINLEY GOD LIVES' in fingerpaints over the font. Ciel said, 'Paint it out before they come in.' Schechner tells her to leave it but Vicki covers the scribble with white latex. 'It's neater . . .'

Finley

MC DERMOTT AS DIONYSUS   He's mine. He's all mine. He's mine, he's all mine! Thousands of years ago Euripides said, "Sane of mind that man would never wear a woman's dress, but obsess his soul and he cannot refuse." Now what that means is this: he's got to know me, Dionysus, Patrick McZeus, god most terrible and yet most gentle to mankind.

CORYPHAEUS   Let the truth be told, there is no god greater than William Finley. Reveal yourself a bull.

Or:

CORYPHAEUS   Let the truth be told, there is no god greater than Jason Bosseau. Reveal yourself a bull.

Or:

CORYPHAEUS   Let the truth be told, there is no god greater than Joan MacIntosh. Reveal yourself a bull.

Or:

CORYPHAEUS   Let the truth be told, there is no god greater than Patrick McDermott. Reveal yourself a bull.

The part of the play we now (July 1969) call the "moiety dance" used to be the "caress." The difference between dancing and caressing is absolute and the change in the action reflects a change in our attitudes and abilities to accept the consequences of our doings. The caress was a reduction and extension of the ecstasy dance. When Dionysus followed Pentheus into the pit, the performers moved slowly into the audience either individually or, usually, in groups of two, three, or four. Members of the audience were selected at random within the framework of simple rules: no one anyone knew; someone who seemed responsive.

The caress began with touching, erotic but not passionate. It came from one of our exercises in workshop in which five or six of us gently massage, kiss, stroke, push, and pull a person laying on the ground. It is an exquisitely polymorphous experience, full of smells and difficult sensations. But soon resistances fall away, a basic animal-comfort trust arises, and one flows with the touching. A low hum usually accompanies the caressing. Possibly because relaxation of the vocal apparatus naturally goes with such a full sensual experience. We brought this exercise into the performance because it suited Pentheus's fantasies of his "reward" and Euripides's description of what the first or second phase of the Dionysian revels was like.

Friends, skeptics, fellow Bacchae . . .

After people were into the caress, Dionysus and Pentheus emerged from the pit, spied on the body piles. Then Dionysus pulled the Agaves from the piles—Joan and Ciel—and turned Pentheus over to them. They stripped and kissed and handled him. But their caressing became more and more violent, transforming into animal cries and clawing. Pentheus, frightened, pulled himself free from his mother/lover. Meanwhile, in the body piles, each of the performers had transformed the caress into wild animal biting and scratching and the room filled with fierce cries.

We worked in rehearsal for many weeks on the "animal chase," learning how to make our bodies into those of animals, especially big cats (though we had, at one time, a gorilla, a strange huge bird, and a rabbit in our menagerie; imagine, if you can, a killer rabbit—it is frightening).

The people in the audience, experiencing a total sensory immersion, were surprised by loud screams and bites and scratches. This transformation was not altogether sudden, but passed through a phase familiar to lovers when the stimulation intensifies and strokes become clawings and nibbles bites. Often, pandemonium filled the room, with the screams of the audience joining our own. Pentheus was tracked down, mortally wounded by being gouged in the gut. He dragged himself back to the death ritual.

But these events, effective as they were, could not be maintained. With increasing frequency, audiences gawked, talked, or wanted to make out with the performers. Sometimes this was pleasant, but on more than one occasion a nasty situation unfolded in the darkened room. The performers refused to continue with the caress. One girl put it very bluntly: "I didn't join the Group to fuck some old man under a tower."

Ironically, the caress liberated the energies Euripides describes in the play. And I don't doubt that the old Greek knew of the endless subversions these energies undergo. As an experiment, the caress was fine. As part of a well-known play that attracted the culture tourists and not a few skin freaks, it was dangerous and self-defeating.

The substitute for the caress is the moiety dance, drawn from the same source as the ecstasy. We first used the moiety dance in December 1968. The Group divides into two parts, each dancing behind one of the large towers. The moiety near the light board invites the audience to join; the one near the exit dances alone. The dance is more limited than the

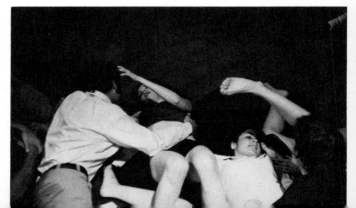

caress. In the caress, focus was diffuse and intense at the same time. For those in the caress nothing else mattered. For those not in, there was little to do but watch, if you were close enough, or talk, doze, or walk out.

The dance offers something that everyone can see. And as soon as the Messenger is finished, Dionysus and Pentheus come from the pit, make their tour, and start the erotic love-death.

Doubtlessly, the caress was the more radical doing. It was also more dangerous and more difficult to maintain. It depended on an innocence that a long-run play cannot have. And a willingness to participate within the terms of the production that audiences do not have.

Schechner

Dionysus follows Pentheus into the pit. There are two versions of the following scene. In one of them, members of the chorus, moving alone or in groups of two and three, seek individuals in the audience and gently caress them with their hands. Sometimes the caressing is erotic and includes full body touching and kissing. A low hum undertones the caress. In the second version, members of the chorus speak lines in different parts of the darkened theatre, one after the other. As each finishes, he moves behind one of the two central towers. There, two slow dances begin. The rhythm is that of the ecstasy. The words are, "We dance to the glory of Bacchus. We dance to the death of Pentheus. What is the name of your husband? What is the name of your child?"

JASON   Spinning out of control, the unbeliever marches blindly to his own death. He spits at the god and the god turns that spit into blood. Blood and more, life. Life is the price this unholy beast must pay as a sacrifice to the god. O Dionysus! Leader! Let us go. Please let your Bacchae go. Let us know ecstasy. Let us know freedom. Let us kill this man who hunts our freedom. Let us kill! Let us kill! Let us kill!

SAM   The unbeliever uncontrolled assaults the mysteries and rages to the death that gods exact to humble and insult us. We men who are not gods, who run to death. Smile, Bacchus, and bring him down, this unbeliever. Trample underfoot his madness and his mystery.

CIEL   Bending, twisting, in grief, in rage we go. The unbelievers. The incomplete. Assaulting the mystery of who we are. Profaning the beauty of why we are. Headlong we rush from birth to death. Seeking, weeping, alone. But this we exact: we humble ourselves with pain, never remembering who we are, that are men, that are men, that are men. Bacchus, come with your smile, cast your net around me, bring me down, trample me underfoot. I am running headlong. You can never go back to where you started from.

We created our individual versions of this chorus one night last spring. Richard asked us to write our sense of this chorus, any way we wanted to, with no more than five minutes' thinking. The words emerged in that moment. The substance harks back to something I wrote in the fall. Grotowski uses these words: "To be oneself, to be whole, to be complete." This is a sequence of development and discovery. Completeness is the total act, the transcendence of solitude, the self-in-other, the sacrifice. When Pentheus emerges from the pit, he is led to his completion:

death. If Dionysus loses him, we lose too. The final line, "You can never go back to where you started from," was added later, by chance. A boy asked me, in that darkened lull before the run to death, "If I get up and dance now, will I be able to get back to where I started from, or will I have to stay involved right up to the end?"

Ciel

FINLEY   Head-long. Head-less. Head-long. Head-less. Head-long. Head-less. Head-long. Head-less. Headlong he runs. From life to death. Headlong we run. From gods who smile. On him headless. Headlong no rest. No help. No breath. Head-less. He runs. Him-self. To death. Head-long. Head-less. Head-long. Head-less.

REMI   Furiously stupid, the little man stumbles around at the party of the gods. Cursing the mother of a god who once betrayed her promise to serve men. On hands and knees he butts the wall, shrieking injustice. A bloody head for a bloody life. The gods shriek back, with laughter. He staggers. O Bacchus, come! Come laughing! Cast your noose around this

man who hunts your revelers. Torture him.
Make him die forever.

MC DERMOTT   Blessed is the man who can say
of that which he gives, "This is mine." Damned
be the traitors. Head in his pocket, the
unbeliever denies the mysteries of god if he
forgets god's mother here. Against the
unassailable he rages headlong to his death.
Death the gods exact, make death our humble
style. That we remember who we are who are
not gods but men. Get him! Come with your
smile. Get him! Hunt the man who hunts the
Bacchae. Get him!

Bill is naked by the time I get down into the pit. We
are usually silent. Sometimes I hold him. Sometimes
we talk, touch each other, drink water. Meditation.
I listen to the Bacchae's speeches up above and wait
for the door to open. We are Bill and Joan down
there. Each time I know he won't satisfy me.

Joan

SHEPHARD   Inaccessible, the unbeliever goes
in spitting rage, madly assaulting the mysteries
of god, profaning the rites of the mother of god.

Against the unassailable he runs with rage. Headlong he runs to death. For death is the price. We are humbled by death that we remember who we are who are not gods but men.

MARGARET   He blasphemed the god. He profaned the rights of the mother of god. He runs against the unassailable. He runs to death. Yes, Bacchus, come with your smile. Catch the man who hates the Bacchae. We don't care whose little boy he is. Bring him down!

JOAN   Uncontrollable the unbeliever goes in spitting rage, madly assaulting the mysteries of god. Profaning the rites of the mother of god. Profaning the rites of his mother. Against the unassailable he runs with rage. Headlong he runs to death. For death the gods exact. Come, Bacchus, come with your smile. Cast your noose around this man who hunts your Bacchae. Bring him down. Trample him underfoot. Run to death. We run to death.

DIA   We are but men. We die. That is our proof, our justice. Who are we to try and overleap this humble circumscription, assaulting and profaning what we are who are not god but men. Come, Bacchus, bring on the man obsessed. In tune, in measured pace, bring on the man. He's doomed. He's going to die. Let the truth be told.

The Messenger goes to the pit cover and, standing over it, delivers his speech. There are four versions of the speech.

SAM AS MESSENGER   Yes, it's a death struggle. Dionysus versus Pentheus. The organism versus the law. I'm a messenger. But even if I stick to the text, it won't change a thing. I could tell you what I saw outside this garage. I could tell you how Dionysus led Pentheus into a trap on a mountain called Cithaeron. How he tantalized hundreds of women into frenzy, released their energies so they could kill a man for their sport. For a god's sport. What I can't tell you is the reason why anyone, god or candidate, can promise a man joy, freedom, ecstasy. And then make him settle for a bloodbath. I don't mind preparing you for a bloodbath. Then Dionysus and Pentheus will rise from the pit, we'll get on with the action, and you can have a kind of mute catharsis. But there is chance to consider. Each of you is chance. And most of you are passive. Night after night you go along

with Dionysus, just as we do. And night after
night you confirm the need for a Pentheus.
Look, if Dionysus could lead you into the
promised land, Dionysus or someone else could
lead you right out again. Dig? Most of us have a
pretty cheap fantasy of self-liberation. So before
I open the pit door and set your catharsis
in motion, consider this. It's harder to be a
man than to be a god. And tragedy leaves
behind no morals because it consumes them. So
don't understand us too quickly. Dig?

The song at the start of McDermott's Messenger
speech is to the tune of *The Seventh Son*.

MC DERMOTT AS MESSENGER
Get the man, get the man,
Get the man who gets the Bacchae down.
Get the man, get the man,
Get the man who gets the Bacchae down.

Wear your smile, wear your smile,
Wear your smile to the great bloodbath.
Wear your smile, wear your smile,
Wear your smile to the great bloodbath.

Hunt the man, hunt the man,
Hunt the man who hunts the Bacchae down.
Hunt the man, hunt the man,
Hunt the man who hunts the Bacchae down.

Yes, it's a death struggle. Dionysus against
Pentheus. An organism against the law. I'm the
messenger. I don't mind preparing you for a
bloodbath. Then we can get on with the action.
And you can have some kind of mute catharsis.
I don't mind that. It's the pornography of death
that I mind. The pornography starts now. So,
if there are any persons of principle in the
audience, they should leave now. It's not too
late. We're just now getting to the obscenities.
What happens is this. There are certain pig-like
features about a policeman. So someone beats
up an oink-pig, a thing alive, a thing with sense
and feeling, in order to express his sentiments.
What happens is someone rapes a girl in
Central Park to get that warm, wet, wild, free
feeling inside. What happens is, at a theatre or a
football game, someone starts up something like
this.

Snaps fingers.

And then because no one hears the silences, it
wants to go like this.

Faster.

And then it wants to keep right on going till there's nowhere else to go.

Fibrillations.

And it's this.

Stop. Silence.

Nothing. Because who knows the beat of liberation? Who knows the pulse of his own life? What happens is that Dionysus, according to his convenience and popular demand, becomes another Pentheus. Most of us have a pretty cheap fantasy of self-liberation. And if Dionysus, or someone else, could lead us into the Promised Land, then Dionysus, or someone else, could lead us right out again. Don't bother to get The Man unless you plan to close his office down, permanently. The first rule of the revolution is: Dig yourself. Dig yourself. So don't understand too much too quick. Okay?

I'm the messenger.

Let the message be ancient, relevant but classic. In Euripides, Pentheus is hunted down and killed off-stage. We act out that death so our messenger does not have to narrate the event.

Let the Messenger speak poetry; let him be an honest man. Every honest man is a prophet. Without explanations, let the message take the form of a moral. The moral will not dull the play.

Let the play become the war in the heart of every man. Let the play be revolution in the heart of William Blake. The inciting incident of Euripides's play is belief and disbelief. The inciting incident is divinity. Can god be in us, do we have it in us? Can Aunt Semele have (a) god? If so, there is no need for political powers. If so, the concept of political control is called into question. Divinity will set you free. The man in god does not need the President and patriotism. Let only servants rule; let all be servants. No man can serve two masters.

Dig yourself. To act out the prevailing taboos is not to be free, no more than to act out the prevailing totems. To destroy property, to get women, will not set you free. Property and women are totems. Do not do The Man the service of acting out his guilts and fears. Make the revolution. Do your thing. Turn god on. Fuck power.

The law cannot proscribe what it cannot formulate. The law proscribes The Man's taboos. The law cannot proscribe the healing up of the need for bondage in the hearts of men. When they question you or arrest you, speak in tongues. It is tactically good for the revolution to speak in tongues.

In practice, the Messenger speech has functioned as a rebuke. But it is not reactionary. It is reactionary in reference to what is reactionary in the revolution. Often, audiences swing with me up to "policeman." Then they become quiet. I want them to laugh with me in the first part of the speech. Sometimes they swing with me up to "nothing." There are usually some who snap their fingers with me. Some nights, in the ecstasy, the audience demonstrates what I metaphorize with the finger-snapping. They join in and build the pace until it cannot be sustained. Then we have to re-establish the pace. The slow, steady pace of the dervish. The demonstration: joining, for the hell of it, a movement of the lonesome and the desperate. Like the inhabitants of any ghetto, playgoers are mostly lonesome and desperate.

McDermott

REMI AS MESSENGER   This is a power play, a death struggle. Dionysus against Pentheus, an organism against the law. I'm the messenger. I've come to prepare you for a bloodbath. Nothing unusual. It happens everyday. Someone has to get the knife, the bullet, the bomb so the man behind the weapon can be free. Free. A man like Pentheus has everything set up to protect his comfortable position. We all know his rules. So along comes Dionysus, living by impulse, a tempter who points out the planned obsolescence of our lives. He promises a trade-in. Our rigid structure for his expanding one. But he doesn't say where his stops. Just the promise of freedom. To walk down the street the way a surfer rides a wave. To go naked before a congressional hearing. To drop acid in the water supply of New York City. To bomb Chicago and dance in the rubble. Free. We all want to believe and go with it. But you know what it's like? It's like at a convention or a football game, somebody starts a sound, then another joins, and another and another, until the sound is lost in a roar, and the roar goes on until there's nothing left. Don't understand too much here too quickly.

JASON AS MESSENGER   Ladies and gentlemen! The allied forces of Dionysus have just issued the following official statement to the diverse good people assembled here: Pentheus is going to die. Repeat. Pentheus is going to die. Members of the Bacchae have agreed to the

terms of a ritual death, which will take place in the center area of this temple in five minutes. With the downfall of Pentheus, Dionysus will assume complete control of this space. And this theatre will be liberated. Repeat. This theatre will be liberated. The allied forces of Dionysus further declare that Dionysus, in his position as god and leader, will for the good of all people assume absolute ownership of the collective will of the people. Therefore, a state of emergency will be declared while Dionysus decides exactly what the will of the people will be. Further statements on the plans of the god's new order will come directly from Dionysus himself in about ten minutes.

The Messenger opens the pit cover. Dionysus and Pentheus emerge. Pentheus is naked.

DIONYSUS   Come out. Come on. You can see them dancing.

PENTHEUS   You're my best friend now.

DIONYSUS   Would you like to see them dancing?

PENTHEUS   Yes, I'd pay anything to see that sight.

DIONYSUS   Why are you so curious?

PENTHEUS   Of course, I'd be sorry to see them drunk.

DIONYSUS   But for all your sorrow, you'd still like to see them?

PENTHEUS   Yes, very much. I can climb the tower here and hide.

DIONYSUS   Be careful. If you hide, they may find you and kill you.

PENTHEUS   Right. I'll go openly.

DIONYSUS   That's dangerous too.

PENTHEUS   What can I do? I can't wait another minute.

DIONYSUS   Come with me. I won't let them hurt you.

PENTHEUS   Do I look like any of them? Like Ciel, or Finley or Margaret?

DIONYSUS   You look like all of them. Like any one of them.

PENTHEUS   To be a real bacchante, how should I dance?

Dionysus teaches Pentheus how to dance. Then he leads him to where the others are dancing.

DIONYSUS   Watch. Like this. You raise up one foot and one arm. Then you raise up the other foot and the other arm. And then you give it a little kick. And you go like this. And like this, Bill. And you kick your foot out.

PENTHEUS   I feel like I could put my shoulders against these towers and push them over, Bacchae and all.

DIONYSUS   You used to be crazy, but I like you now.

PENTHEUS   Should we take crowbars, or should I put my shoulders against them and push them over?

DIONYSUS   No, don't destroy this place. It's holy.

PENTHEUS   You're right. Women shouldn't be mastered by brute force.

DIONYSUS   Am I your best friend now?

PENTHEUS   I trust you completely. Come on.

DIONYSUS   Would you like to get closer?

PENTHEUS   Yes, yes. I am the one. I am the one. I am the one. I am the one. I am the one.

DIONYSUS   You are the one.

PENTHEUS   No one else in this city dared to go.

DIONYSUS   A great ecstasy awaits you. But you are worthy of it. You and you alone will suffer for your city. I am taking you there. But someone else will bring you back.

PENTHEUS   You mean my mother?

DIONYSUS   Yes. You'll be carried high.

PENTHEUS   The higher the better. I've no fear of heights.

DIONYSUS   A sight for all men to see. Cradled in your mother's arms.

PENTHEUS   I want my reward. I want my reward.

DIONYSUS   You're going to have an extraordinary experience. You're an extraordinary young man. Everyone will be jealous of you and your ecstasy.

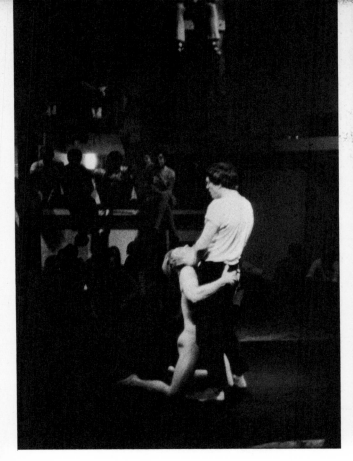

Dionysus leaves Pentheus in the center. Dionysus goes to the fountain and dips his hands in the blood. He returns to Pentheus and stands over him, both arms extended.

PENTHEUS   I seem to see two suns blazing in the heavens. And two cities, each with seven gates. And you're a bull! Horns have sprouted from your head. Have you always been a beast?

There are two versions of Dionysus's reply.

DIONYSUS   It's the god you see. And you are soft and vulnerable now. I like you.

MC DERMOTT AS DIONYSUS   Oh, I've always been a beast!

Dionysus caresses, perhaps kisses, Pentheus, marking him with blood. Then he calls for Agave, using both the character's name and the performer's name. There are two versions of the following speech.

DIONYSUS   Agave! Margaret! There's a boy in the woods. A young boy. I've marked him for you. I want you to find him, and caress him, and kiss him, and love him, and kill him for me!

MC DERMOTT AS DIONYSUS   Agave! Agave! Agave, there's a beautiful young animal in the

woods. And I want you to find him for me. And caress him. And make him happy. And then I want you to kill him as a sacrifice for me.

Dionysus starts to climb the tower that has the bullhorn on it. When McDermott plays Dionysus, he wipes the blood off his hands with a towel before he climbs.

There are four versions of the following speech.

FINLEY AS DIONYSUS   Who gave him to you? Who? Who? I did. I gave him to you. Me, Dionysus, William Finley, I gave him to you. The rest the event shall show.

JASON AS DIONYSUS   Who gave him to you? Who? Who? Me, Dionysus, Jason Bosseau, I did, I gave him to you. The rest the event shall show.

JOAN AS DIONYSUS   Who gave him to you? Who? Who? I gave him to you! Me, Dionysus, Joan MacIntosh gave him to you. The rest the event shall show.

MC DERMOTT AS DIONYSUS   And remember who gave him to you! I did! Dionysus! Patrick McZeus. The rest the event will show.

As Agave comes to the center the dance ends.
First Agave and then the other women come to
the center and caress Pentheus. They fondle and
kiss him. They sing to him. They play with him
sexually. Slowly they become more threatening.
Their caresses transform into tugs, their kisses
into bites. They start clawing and tearing at Pentheus. They begin to pull him apart.

Pentheus breaks free of the women. He runs. In one version, all the performers turn into animals and chase Pentheus through the theatre, finally catching and wounding him. He drags himself to the death ritual. In another version, the performers are the "circling beaters" and Pentheus the hunted prey. Wherever he goes, someone confronts him. He is maneuvered into a corner, against a wall. When he is trapped, the moiety-dance song begins again and Pentheus willingly accompanies two of the men to where the death ritual is to be acted out.

We were within two weeks of opening and I had no idea how to stage the death of Pentheus. I wanted him chased and killed, but I didn't know how to have his body brought back or how to suggest dismemberment. We tried several things. First, all the men came in and lay down, as if they were parts of the body. It was not convincing. Then we had the men carry Pentheus in and lay him down and take positions around him. Pretty, but dull and not in keeping with the rest of the play. I talked the problem over with Pat McDermott one afternoon outside the theatre before an open rehearsal. He suggested we try reversing the birth ritual. Instead of facing away from Pentheus, the women face toward him; instead of helping him through, they raise their bloody hands over their heads. Pentheus crawls through looking for aid and comfort. But this womb has become a vagina dentata and those teeth tear him to pieces. Repeating the birth ritual is to build the performance the way suspension bridges are built. The play's major events are carried between two opposed identical posts, although there are things which lead up to and away from these posts. Furthermore, the negative symmetry of the birth and death rituals expresses in action the two towers facing each other across the room which are the major architectural events of the space.

Schechner

When there is the caress of the audience instead of the dancing behind the towers, the Messenger speech comes after Dionysus gives Pentheus to Agave.

JASON AS MESSENGER   There were three of us. Pentheus, me, and the tall, slinky stranger, the man with the long blond hair. He was our guide, he took us there. To the mountain, to Cithaeron, far beyond our homes in Thebes. When we got there, we were like spies, trying to see the action without being seen. And there they were, all of them. Joan, Ciel, Remi, Margaret, and even Pat, Sam, and Richard. They had organized themselves into two

pleasure units, and each bacchante was deeply
into his own pleasure thing. But Pentheus,
unhappy man, was frustrated, and he wanted to
get closer to his fellow performers. "Stranger,"
he said, "from where I stand I cannot sense
what is really going on. But if I climbed higher,
then I could see their shameless orgies better."
And then the stranger performed a miracle.
Reaching for the highest branch of a great fir,
he bent it down, down, down to the dark earth,
till it was curved the way a taut bow bends.
Like that he forced that mighty mountain fir to
the ground. No mortal could have done it.
Then he seated Pentheus at the highest tip and
with his bare hands let the trunk of the tree rise
straight up, up, up, slowly and gently, so as not
to throw its rider. And the tree rose, towering
to heaven, with Pentheus at the top. Now
Pentheus was a completely different man. His
eyes looked drugged. He was totally in the
hands of his god, totally exposed to pleasure.
But hardly had the caressing begun when a
voice over the loudspeaker cried out: "Sisters,
this man is our enemy. He refused to believe
that I am a god. So as fellow worshippers of
me, your god, I command you to kill him."
Those were his orders. And even as he spoke,
a flash of awful fire bound heaven and earth.
Suddenly all hell broke loose. And the gentle
humming sounds of the Bacchae disappeared,
and in their place were the cries and the screams
and the moans of wild animals. They were no
longer individuals, or even two separate pleasure
units. They became one angry mob, one single
mindless body gone mad. Their victim was still
alive but trapped and doomed. The women
surrounded him, but they did not attack until
his own mother, Agave, cried out: "We must
kill this animal. Remember, violence is as
American as cherry pie." And, with that, Agave
struck first, and then the rest joined in and the
rout was on. The pitiful remains lie scattered
on the mountain. His mother, picking up his
head, impaled it on her wand. She seems to
think it is some mountain lion's head which
she carries in triumph through the thick of
Cithaeron. Leaving her sisters at the dances, she
is coming here, gloating over her grisly prize.
She calls upon Bacchus. He is her "fellow
huntsman," "comrade of the chase, crowned
with victory." But all the victory she really
carries home is her own grief.

The death ritual is the reverse of the birth ritual. Pentheus, already naked, waits. The other performers undress. The men look up at Dionysus. The women move slowly to the blood fountain and dip their hands in, deep.

CIEL To hold your child.

JASON Good evening, sir, may I take you to your death?

REMI Streaming with his blood.

MC DERMOTT   I'm ready, sir, I want to die, sir.

DIONYSUS   Go on, Sam, get down, Sam, die, Sam, die!

One by one the men dive down on the mats. The women straddle them, as in the birth ritual, except that this time the women face the opposite direction, so they can see Pentheus as he enters the death canal. The women repeat over and over the line, or fragments of it, "To hold your child in your arms, streaming with his blood."

MARGARET   To hold your child in your arms, streaming with his blood!

DIA   Yes, sir, it's my turn now, sir, can I go now, sir?

The men salute Dionysus. Their going down on the mats is a military ceremony.

DIONYSUS   Yes, Dia, for me, Dia, you can go now, Dia.

JOAN   Streaming with his blood.

FINLEY   Please, god, let me go now, god, I want to go now, god.

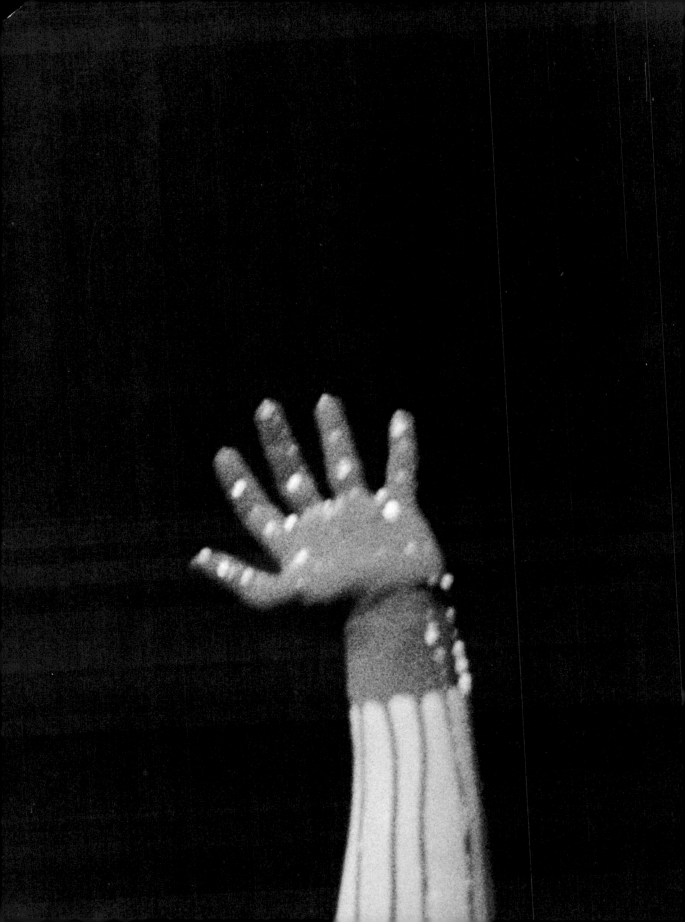

DIONYSUS   Down, Finley, down, quick, quick, die.

SHEPHARD   I'm ready, sir. Yes, sir.

DIONYSUS   Die, Shephard.

CIEL   In your arms, streaming with his blood.

To Pentheus.

DIONYSUS   It's your turn. You go. You die now. You die.

I watch the kill, participate sympathetically in it. I want the women to kill the men. Sexual climax. But I do not reach climax because I do not physically kill. I have gone up and away from human needs. I am no longer Joan MacIntosh but totally Dionysus. I feel supreme joy with myself and hatred for everyone in the room. They betrayed me. They didn't give me enough. I was not satisfied.

Joan

Pentheus crawls into the death canal.

PENTHEUS   Mama, mama, it's me, Pentheus, your little boy. Don't kill your little boy for what I did wrong.

The women kill the men.

A life wager lies dormant in the middle of our play. Every night Pentheus is left alone in the center, weighing the balance between self and actor. He tries to peel away the actor until the person stands exposed. There is a chance that the wager will be won and the play end then. To a less obvious extent, this risk is a subtext for each of us throughout the play. One night, months before Bill was "rescued," I refused to kill Pentheus. I felt, somehow, that I, like Bill, should have an opportunity to save myself from the inevitability of my role and my action. I was also trying to save myself from a terrible suspicion that the wager was a lie: we were acting a play like everyone else. The play continued and concluded without my killing, leaving me to try my reality in my own way. (One thing about improvising on your personal sense of truth is that your fellow actors often don't know what the hell you're doing.) Although I underwent an emotional experience and an exposure, the personal truth eluded me. I found that I could not shed the actor, that no matter how you try to escape the bounds of the theatrical you find yourself inside one or another succession of symbolic acts.

Ciel

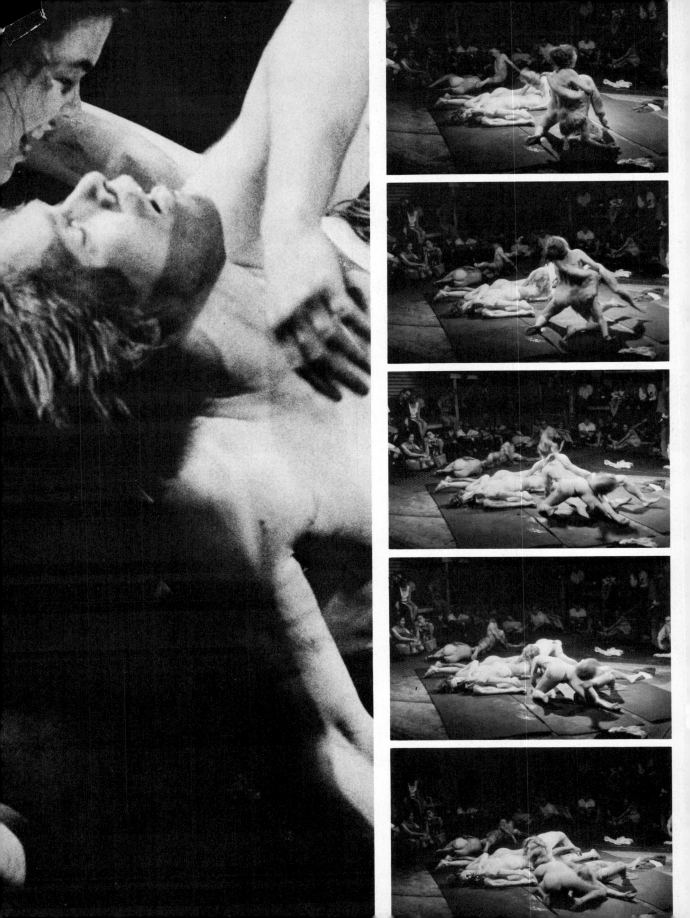

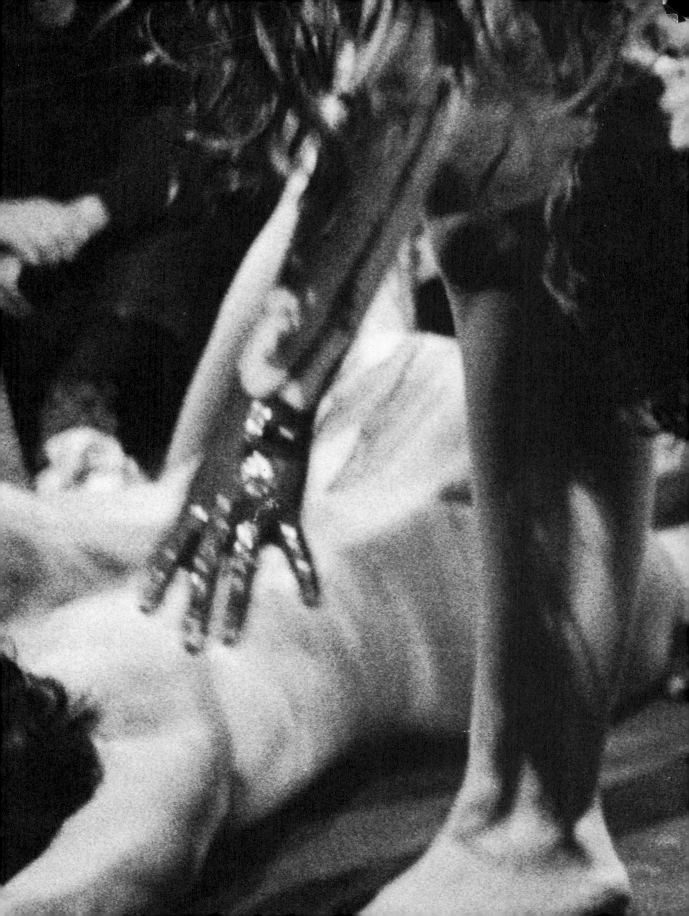

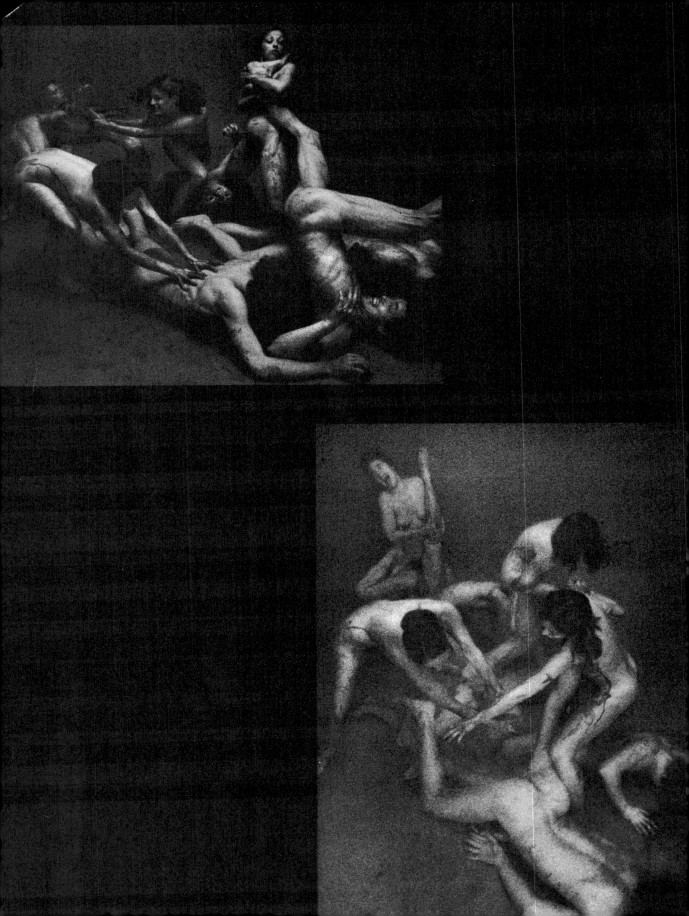

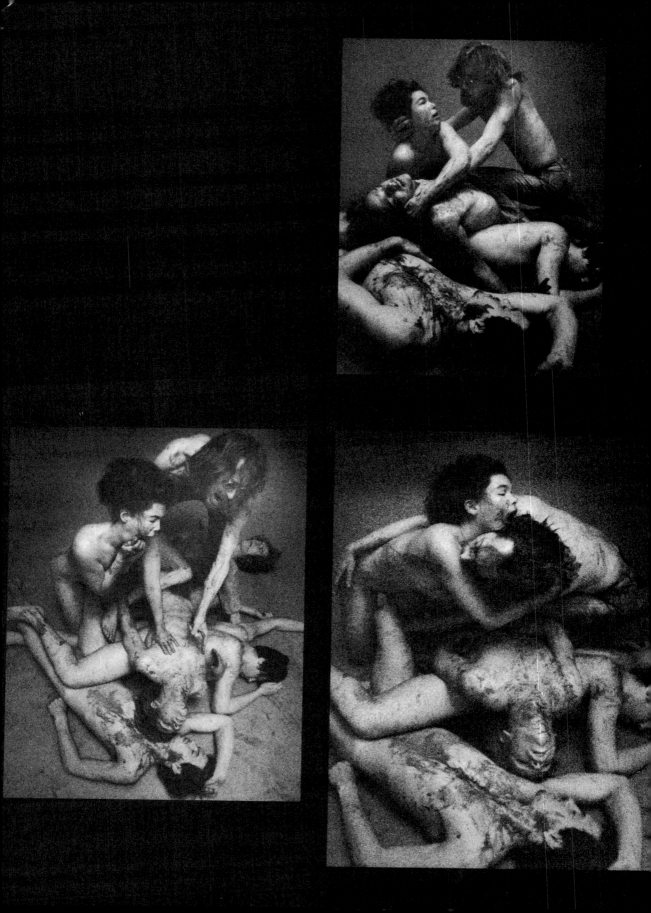

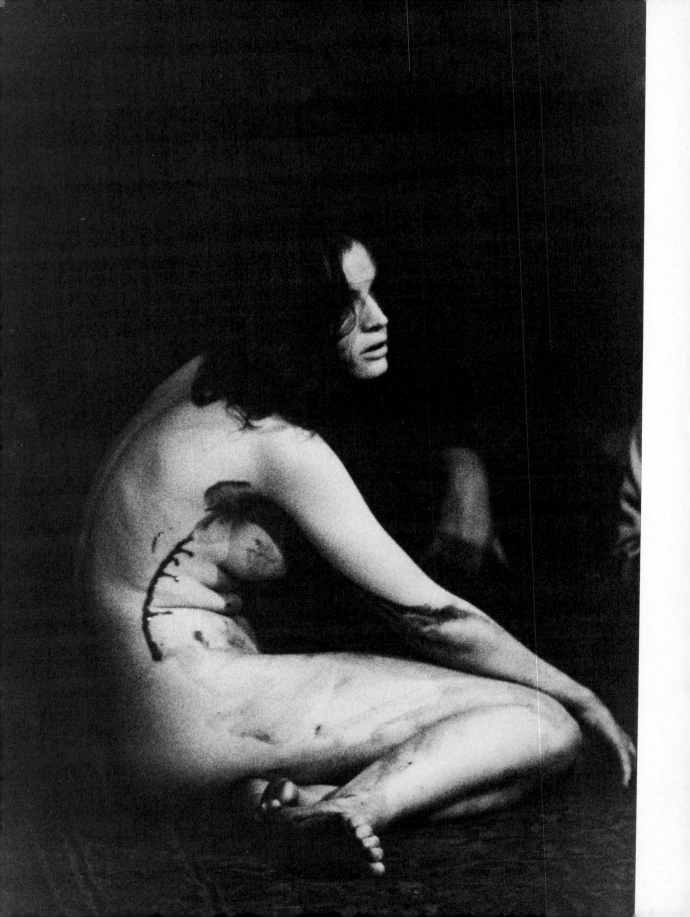

There are two versions to the scene in which Agave discovers that she has killed her son, Pentheus. All the women have killed. They are each Agave. In the first version, as soon as the killing is over, the women rush into the audience and confront one or several spectators.

AGAVES   Bacchae of Asia! I bring this branch to the palace, this fresh-cut spray from the mountains. Happy was my hunting. The whelp of a wild mountain lion and snared by me without a noose. Look, look at the prize I bring. I caught him, my prize, on Cithaeron. I struck him first. The Maenads call me Agave the blest. After me Cadmus's daughters reached the prey. After me. Happy was my hunting. Share my glory. Share my feast. See, the whelp is young and tender. Beneath the soft mane of his hair the down is blooming on his cheeks. Our god is wise. Cunningly, cleverly, Bacchus the hunter lashed the Maenads against his prey. Praise me. Do you praise me now? And Pentheus. He will be proud. He will praise his mother. I have caught a great quarry, this lion's cub. I have won the trophy of the chase. A great prize that everyone can see!

Then one of the women, usually Margaret, speaks directly to Dionysus.

MARGARET   Dionysus! Finley!

DIONYSUS   Speak.

MARGARET   I come from the mountain with this fresh-cut spray. Happy was my hunting.

DIONYSUS   I see. I welcome a fellow reveler of god.

MARGARET   The whelp of a wild mountain lion and snared by me without a noose. Look. Look at the prize I bring.

DIONYSUS   Where did you catch him?

MARGARET   On Cithaeron. There my prize was killed.

DIONYSUS   Who killed him?

MARGARET   I did. I struck him first. The Maenads call me Agave the blest.

DIONYSUS   Was anyone with you?

MARGARET   Cadmus's daughters.

DIONYSUS   Ah.

MARGARET   But after me they reached this catch. After me. Our hunting was happy.

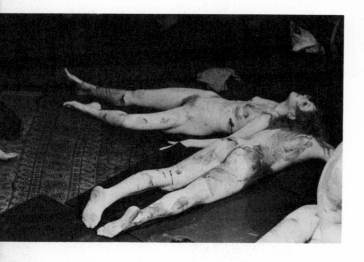

DIONYSUS   Happy indeed.

MARGARET   Then share my glory. We're going to have a feast and eat this cat.

DIONYSUS   Share what?

MARGARET   Look, the whelp is tender. Beneath the soft mane of his hair the down is blooming on his cheeks.

DIONYSUS   With that mane he looks a beast.

MARGARET   Oh, you're clever. Cunningly you lashed the Maenads against your prey.

DIONYSUS   Our god is a hunter.

MARGARET   Do you praise me?

DIONYSUS   Yes.

MARGARET   And the men of Thebes?

DIONYSUS   And Pentheus?

MARGARET   Pentheus will love it. We've caught a great quarry, this lion's cub.

DIONYSUS   Extraordinary catch.

MARGARET   Extraordinary skill.

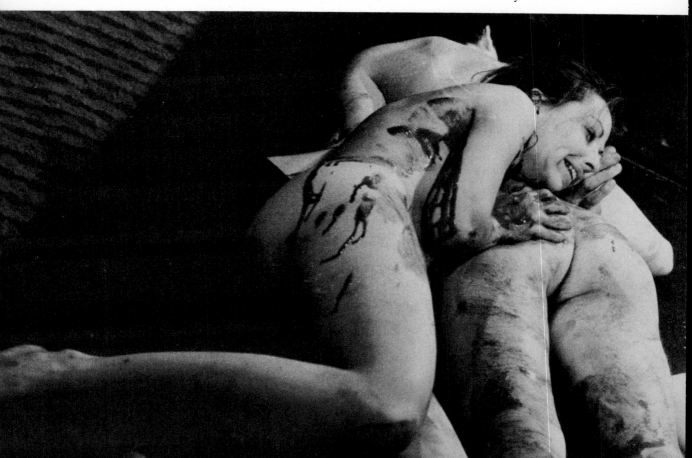

DIONYSUS   And you're proud?

MARGARET   Of course I'm proud. I killed this animal for you!

Joan and Ciel speak. As they do, Cadmus pulls himself from the body pile.

JOAN   You, citizens of this towered city, men of Thebes, behold the trophy of your women's hunting.

CIEL   This is the quarry of our chase, taken not with nets or spears of bronze, but by the white and delicate hands of women.

JOAN   What are they worth, all your boastings now and all that uselessness your armor is, since we, with our bare hands, captured this quarry and tore his bleeding body limb from limb?

JOAN AND CIEL   But where is my father, Cadmus? He should come.

JOAN   And my son.

CIEL   Where is Pentheus?

JOAN AND CIEL   I'll have him set his ladder up against that wall and there, on the beam, nail the head of this wild lion

JOAN   I have killed.

CIEL   I have killed.

JOAN   I have killed.

CIEL   I have killed.

JOAN AND CIEL   As a trophy of my hunt. Now, Father, yours can be the proudest boast of living men. For you are now the father of the bravest daughters in the world. All your daughters are brave.

CIEL   But I above the rest.

JOAN   I left my shuttle at the loom.

CIEL   And raised my sight to higher things.

JOAN   To hunting animals with my bare hands.

JOAN AND CIEL   You see? Here in my hands I hold the quarry of my chase. A trophy for our house.

JOAN   Take it, Father.

CIEL   Take it.

JOAN AND CIEL   Glory in my kill and invite your friends to share the feast of triumph. For you are blest, Father

CIEL   By this great deed I have done.

JOAN   I have done.

CIEL   I have done.

JOAN   I have done.

CIEL   I have done.

Ciel and I played the "double Agave" for the first half of the run. We both wanted the role and we were both promised the role. Because of internal reasons of Group dynamics, we were both given the role. The score of the recognition and grief is particularly difficult. I still don't feel I accomplished what I wanted. Confused. We were to relate to each other as who we were—Ciel, Richard Dia [as Cadmus], Joan—and at the same time as our characters in the play. Aside from the difficulties of dealing with Ciel as Ciel and Richard as Richard, the scene itself for Agave travels from supreme joy to profound grief and guilt. Technically I didn't know enough about performing to trust that to happen to me or to know how to make it happen. I anticipated the grief. Playing the scene was a great learning experience in dealing concretely with other actors who seemed at times to impede rather than assist me. I experienced silence, anger, guilt, rage, frozen denial. But, for all its frustrations, the scene had a security to it. There was not the aloneness of having committed such a murder. Having an accomplice was a comfort.

Joan

In Euripides's text Agave first appears when she rushes onstage with her son's head impaled on a pole. Within the space of five minutes she expresses the most profound joy and grief. The sounds and gestures of everyday life are not strong enough to convey the absolute force and speed of this centripetal movement toward self-recognition. It needs orchestration. If the god of wine himself is downright human (I speak here of Euripides's child and not Mrs. Finley's), Agave is positively Wagnerian. She could be played by a cast of thousands, with full orchestra plus Martha Graham. She feels an absolute joy which cannot be translated into the competitive, romantic, or childlike terms of my experience. Her grief is huge. It is a public act. Mine is private sorrow, depression, anxiety. The extent of my vocabulary at that time and the circumstances of the production, which asked

that we each maintain several levels of consciousness and action and that Joan and I play the scene together, all tended to mitigate the intensity and precision of feeling.

Ciel

CADMUS   This is a grief so great it knows no size. This is the awful murder your hands have done. This is the noble victim you've slaughtered to the gods, and to a feast like this you now invite all Thebes and me?

JOAN   Why do you reproach me?

CIEL   Is there something wrong?

CADMUS   What was the name of your husband?

JOAN   Echion, a man.

CIEL   A man, they say, born of the dragon's teeth.

CADMUS   And what was the name of the child you bore that man?

CIEL   Pentheus.

JOAN   William.

CIEL   William.

JOAN   Pentheus.

CADMUS   And what is this?

JOAN   A mountain lion.

CIEL   The hunters told me.

CADMUS   Look more closely.

JOAN AND CIEL   Oh, God, what am I holding in my hands?

CADMUS   Study it.

JOAN AND CIEL   What is it?

CADMUS   Study it.

JOAN   It's Pentheus.

CIEL   It's William.

CADMUS   Mourned by me before you ever knew.

JOAN   But who killed him?

CIEL   Why am I holding him?

CADMUS   You killed him. You and your sisters killed him.

JOAN AND CIEL   Where was he killed?

JOAN   Here at home?

CIEL   Where?

CADMUS   He was killed on Cithaeron.

JOAN AND CIEL   But what was Pentheus doing on Cithaeron?

CADMUS   He went there to mock the revels of your god.

JOAN AND CIEL   We didn't go to Cithaeron.

CADMUS   You were there. I was there. Everyone was there. The whole city was there. We were possessed. Possessed by Dionysus.

JOAN AND CIEL   Dionysus has destroyed us all.

CADMUS   You denied that he was truly a god.

JOAN   Where is my poor boy's body now?

CADMUS   There. This is your poor boy's body now.

CIEL   Is it all there? Is it whole?

CADMUS   I gathered the pieces with great difficulty. He has no head.

JOAN AND CIEL   My joy. My famous prize of grief.

CADMUS   He, like you, blasphemed William Finley.

JOAN AND CIEL   Dearest, dearest face. Pretty, boyish mouth.

A hand emerges from the body pile. It points down at the pile.

CORYPHAEUS   Let this scene teach those who see these things: Dionysus is the son of Zeus.

Anyone who has worked in the theatre, or on any project in which a small group uses feelings as raw material, knows the intensity and bitterness, the devotion and love that characterize such enterprises. The Performance Group has its share of conflicts, shifting alliances, explosions. From week to week one member or another is dissatisfied about something, and possibly to a degree that makes him feel that the whole project is unsupportable. Notices appear on the bulletin board; meetings are called. But the Group is unusual in several ways. First, there has been very little come and go. Everyone who worked on Dionysus throughout its run has been in the

Group since the first month, November 1967. Those who left the Group were asked to leave, for one reason or another. The couples in the Group have been reasonably stable and, to the best of my knowing, there has been no sleeping around within the Group. From November 1968 until July 1969, weekly encounter meetings (therapy) were led by Larry Sacharow and other former members of the Daytop community. These were voluntary, but by April everyone in the Group attended regularly. Most important by far is our struggle to expose our feelings, to reveal ourselves, to be open, receptive, vulnerable; to give and take hard and deeply; to use impulse and feelings in our work. And to believe that excellence in art is, ultimately, a function of wholeness as a human being.

Schechner

The second version of the scene has three parts. First, immediately after the kill, a woman goes into the audience and speaks directly to the spectators. Second, with Ciel playing Tiresias, there is a short dialogue between Tiresias and Dionysus. Third, Agave discovers it is Pentheus she has killed. This Agave is played either by Margaret or by Remi.

REMI   I danced. I made music here to free myself. But there's always someone who wants to put down my freedom. Always someone who resents my power. Pentheus put me down until I wanted to rip him apart, gouge out his eyes, murder him. So I killed him. Because nobody is going to put me down. If I have to murder every person in this goddamn room, nobody is going to keep me from being free. Nobody.

This was improvised one night. When I hurtled from the ritual murder toward a sympathetic face, my memorized lines were like marbles in my mouth. I felt ludicrous as I spouted the first words. My help-lessness became amusement at myself, which the audience instantly picked up from my tone of voice. A ripple of anxious laughter went through the room. The laughter like a whip went deep to a source of pain, and a ferocity flared out of me so unexpected that the tiny scene ended with me trembling at the release of great energy and the audience in stunned silence. All that in the space of a minute.

Remi

Or:

JOAN   Look! Look what I've done! I've killed Pentheus! I killed him! I loved him more than anything else in the world. I gave myself to him. But he never loved me. He used me. He took my love and then he betrayed me. He destroyed me and then abandoned me. So I had to kill him. I ripped his flesh from his bones. I tore his legs off. I tasted his blood. I had to kill him so I could live. I had to get rid of him so I could be free. And now I'm free!

Or:

MARGARET   Did you see that? Did you see what I did? That was no accident. Look at Pat McDermott. I told him: Don't wrench my arm. Don't stomp on a toe that's already strained. Don't threaten me! Don't bother me in the subway when I'm twelve years old. So I got to the bloodbath last. I got extra blood. I killed him! That was no accident.

CIEL AS TIRESIAS   Dionysus. Joan.

DIONYSUS   Yes?

CIEL AS TIRESIAS   Here we are. And not empty-handed. We captured the quarry you sent us to catch.

DIONYSUS   I see. I welcome a fellow reveler of god.

CIEL AS TIRESIAS   Our prey was tame.

DIONYSUS   Where did you catch him?

CIEL AS TIRESIAS   We tracked him down on Cithaeron. On Cithaeron he was killed.

DIONYSUS   Who killed him?

CIEL AS TIRESIAS   His mother, Agave, the women of Thebes, and I.

DIONYSUS   Ah.

CIEL AS TIRESIAS   Your victory is fair, fair the prize, this famous prize of grief. Glorious the game.

DIONYSUS   Glorious indeed.

CIEL AS TIRESIAS   You walk among the ruins you have made.

DIONYSUS   I proved to him and every man in Thebes that I am a god.

CIEL AS TIRESIAS   Yes. You're clever. Cunningly you lashed the Maenads against your prey.

DIONYSUS   Our god is a hunter.

CIEL AS TIRESIAS   Do you praise me now?

DIONYSUS   Yes.

CIEL AS TIRESIAS   And the men of Thebes?

DIONYSUS   And Pentheus?

CIEL AS TIRESIAS   The spy who came to the mountain to peer at our revels.

DIONYSUS   He got his reward.

CIEL AS TIRESIAS   He threatened me with bonds, though my body is bound to god.

DIONYSUS   And you killed him.

CIEL AS TIRESIAS   Yes!

DIONYSUS   Good. Good. Well done.

CIEL AS TIRESIAS   He was a man, a man and nothing more. Yet he presumed to wage war with a god.

DIONYSUS   A man and nothing more.

I "wrote" this scene when I became Tiresias. It's a collage of lines from the text. It replaced a bit of dialogue called "the single Agave," the original justification of which is obscure. My scene afforded me the opportunity to re-emerge as Tiresias and to say my favorite line, previously not included in our text: "You walk among the ruins you have made." These were not very noble acting motivations.

Originally, the scene was quiet and businesslike. As I searched my reactions to the situation, night after night, my emotions gathered intensity until I became almost speechless, especially when doing the scene with Joan/Dionysus—confronting the spectre of female apotheosis. Recently (June 1969) I came to a solution that partially satisfies me: Tiresias, cringing and cavorting, shaken but essentially concerned with avoiding both personal responsibility and the god's reprisals. When I scream "Yes!" and violently grab my genitals, I still try to realize one precise moment of pain. The gesture, one of personal degradation and sexual guilt, is perhaps inappropriate for Tiresias. Or maybe it perfectly telescopes the agelessness and sexlessness I sought for in the role.

Ciel

AGAVE   You, citizens of this towered city, men of Thebes. Behold the trophy of your women's hunting. This is the quarry of my chase, taken not with nets or spears of bronze but by the white and delicate hands of women. What are they worth, all your boastings now? And all that uselessness your armor is? When I, with my bare hands, captured this quarry and tore his bleeding body limb from limb. But where is my father, Cadmus? He should come. And my son. Where is Pentheus? Fetch him. I'll have him set his ladder up against the wall and there upon the beam nail my trophy for all to see.

Cadmus pulls himself from the body pile, dresses, and arranges the other bodies in a neat way.

Father. Now, Father, yours can be the proudest boast of living men, for you are now the father of the bravest daughters in the world. All your daughters are brave, but I above the rest. I left my shuttle at the loom. I raised my sights to higher things, to hunting wild animals with my bare hands. Look! Here is the quarry of my chase, a trophy for our house. Take it, Father, take it. Glory in my kill, and invite your friends to share the feast of triumph, for you are blest, Father, by this great deed I have done.

CADMUS   Enough. No more. When you realize the horror you have done, you will suffer terribly.

AGAVE   Why do you reproach me?

CADMUS   This is a grief so great it knows no size. This is the awful murder your hands have done. This is the noble victim you have slaughtered to the gods. And to a feast like this you now invite all Thebes and me?

AGAVE   What's wrong with you?

CADMUS   What was the name of your husband?

AGAVE   Echion. A man born of the dragon's tooth.

CADMUS   And what was the name of the child you bore that man?

AGAVE   Pentheus. William. Pentheus.

CADMUS   And what is this?

AGAVE   What?

CADMUS   Look at it! Look!

AGAVE   No.

CADMUS   Yes! Look! Look!

AGAVE   It's Pentheus.

A version by Finley and Margaret of this discovery.

FINLEY AS CADMUS   And what is this?

MARGARET AS AGAVE   It's a mountain lion. The hunters told me.

FINLEY AS CADMUS   Look at it. Look!

MARGARET AS AGAVE   No.

FINLEY AS CADMUS   Who is this?

MARGARET AS AGAVE   That's Richard Dia.

FINLEY AS CADMUS   And this one?

MARGARET AS AGAVE   Jason Bosseau.

FINLEY AS CADMUS   And this one?

MARGARET AS AGAVE   That's Pat McDermott.

FINLEY AS CADMUS   And him? Who is he?

MARGARET AS AGAVE   I don't know.

FINLEY AS CADMUS   Who? Who?

He forces her down on the body.

MARGARET AS AGAVE   That's Bill Shephard!
Pentheus! Bill Shephard!

The standard text.

CADMUS   Pentheus. And mourned by me
before you ever knew.

AGAVE   Who killed him? Why am I holding
him?

CADMUS   You killed him. You and your sisters
killed Pentheus.

AGAVE   Where was he killed? Here at home?
Where?

CADMUS   He was killed on Cithaeron.

AGAVE   Why did he go to Cithaeron?

CADMUS   He went to your revels to mock your
god.

AGAVE   What were we doing on Cithaeron?

CADMUS   You were mad. I was mad. The
whole city was possessed.

AGAVE   Dionysus. Dionysus has destroyed us
all!

CADMUS   It was you! You! You outraged him. You denied that he was truly a god.

AGAVE   Father, where is my poor boy's body now?

CADMUS   There. I gathered the pieces with great difficulty.

AGAVE   Is it whole? Has it been laid out well?

CADMUS   He has no head.

AGAVE   But why should Pentheus suffer for my crime?

CADMUS   He, like you, blasphemed the god.

CORYPHAEUS   Let this scene teach those who see these things: Dionysus is the child of Zeus.

As I stood before a man in the audience, naked and covered with blood, addressing him as Agave, he grabbed me. His action implied that he found my body very real but not so the blood (although his jacket and beautiful white sweater were liberally smeared with the stuff). As the moment came for me to return to a central scene, I was unwilling simply to walk away from him, feeling that if I did I would reduce him to a prop and negate the interactions I had with him during the evening. I decided to take him home to daddy (Cadmus), but as I led him to the center, he broke away, dipped his hands into the bloodbath, and then began swiping at me. He was going to kill me with my own pretension. I felt constrained to continue with my lines and eventually he went away and sat down.

Ciel

Tiresias begins an antiphonal dirge. In one version, the dirge is sung until every one of the performers leaves the theatre. In another version, the dirge is transformed into a marching song. In both versions, the dirge is the basic sonic ground from which the final scene arises. Everyone sings the dirge except Dionysus.

TIRESIAS   Lead me guides where my sisters wait.

ALL   Lead me guides where my sisters wait.

TIRESIAS   Poor sisters of my exile let me go.

ALL   Poor sisters of my exile let me go.

TIRESIAS   Where I shall never see Cithaeron again.

ALL   Where I shall never see Cithaeron again.

TIRESIAS   Where that cursed hill may not see me.

ALL   Where that cursed hill may not see me.

TIRESIAS   Where I shall find no trace of thyrsus.

ALL   Where I shall find no trace of thyrsus.

TIRESIAS   I leave that to other Bacchae.

ALL   I leave that to other Bacchae.

The men rise from the body pile. Someone gets two buckets of water, some sponges, and brushes. People begin to wash the mats, scrubbing away the blood. The singing continues, over and over. Everyone dresses. In the version in which the performers march from the theatre, a trunk is carried on containing clothes and shoes for the outdoors. Otherwise, the performers are barefoot. They leave the theatre one by one after being cursed. They go upstairs and shower. Dionysus is the last to leave.

In October 1968 Jan Kott saw the play for the first time. As the performers marched out of the theatre into Wooster Street, I went over to Jan to see what his reactions were. We talked and, as we did so, Vicki and two of her assistants, Cara Crosby and Judy Allen, started to mop and scrub up the blood from the mats. Jan watched them and then said, "But, Richard, here is the true end to your play. Always the people come and clean away the blood." He was right and from then on we incorporated the clean-up in the performance.

Schechner

There are many versions of Dionysus's curse. In all of them, he speaks from a tower with a bull-horn. Many curses are lost because they depend on the events of a particular night's interaction. The curses which follow are presented roughly in the order in which they arose during the year's performances.

First, Finley's pre-Presidential election of 1968 curse. During the scene between Cadmus and Agave, Finley wipes the blood from his hands, combs his hair, and dresses in a blue suit and tie. He carries a red, white, and blue bag filled with *Dionysus in 69* buttons.

FINLEY AS DIONYSUS   I am William Finley, a god by any other name. A god that smokes seven brands of cigarettes, a god that eats food, men, and women. A god with a Social Security number. But an unemployed god. Dionysus, son of William and Dorothy, and still not recognized as a true god by everyone in this garage. When you could have known me, you

did not. And even now you're not sure. Dig it. I came to New York, the city where I was born, and I came to this garage and told you who I was. But instead of saying, "That's nice. He's Dionysus. I dig that," you made fun of me. You threw me in the pit. You didn't turn me on. You didn't freak me out. You didn't love me. Therefore, I will reveal to you the results of mistrust and rejection. The royal house is overthrown. Schechner will go to South America and never see what happens to this play. "So what?" you say. Well, the city streets are full of dogshit and fear. "So what?" you say. Well, look at each other now. Look long and hard because outside this place you'll be afraid to look at each other. Now, before I split, let me reveal the sufferings in store for those of little faith. Bill Shephard. Yes, you, Shephard. This man told me he had nothing for me. He came to us in rage. He put me in the pit and he did what he should least of all have done. He told the truth. He had nothing for me. He didn't satisfy me. Now he has only a false death, some stage blood, and the promise that he has to do the same damned thing tomorrow night. All he has is a little truth. What the fuck is truth anyway? Upon you, Agave, Ciel and Joan, I pronounce this doom. In some ways you took peace and solitude away from Bill Shephard. You tried to mortify him and you hardly touched me at all. You both shall leave this garage in expiation of the murder you have done. You shall wear out your wretched lives never knowing which of you played Agave. Next, I shall reveal the trials which await Cadmus. You, Richard Dia, shall change your name to Richard 37X. It is your fate to lead a great black army of black panthers. With a host so large its numbers cannot be counted, you shall burn many cities to the ground—Detroit, Cleveland, San Francisco, New Orleans, Chicago, Newark. Finally, your army will come to New York and plunder the Harlem shrine of Apollo. There, your homecoming will be perilous and hard. Yet in the end the great god Ares will turn you into a honky and bring you to live among the blest.

The nine remaining mourners
were not aware of the death
it is hard to see anything
I am the rushing sound in your ears.
My scenes just push the plot along
But S. told you to write you
the garage using my
Nothing like quoting yourself
out of context Dionysus
Smile life
I am the orgasm you never got together.

Finally Grot pays a call and sits near the bloodbath like
Joe Bonanno on the Papal throne. Shephard falls twenty feet
and fractures a bone. "That was authentic," says the Grot.
He toyed me for his use
Molested my own reproduction
feeding on my risks
purity from dummygods
Right; and he sticks me to it
I am going to burn the rubble.

I noticed that after a while every thing disintegrates.
Yellow Eyes was losing the cement that was under his feet.
Waving at empty Wooster below. Floating up the street on
waves of his own making. "William Finley Dionysus"

I will keep in touch, one way or the other.
sap runs and drips on the mat
squatting asmat
traveling to the gold dot at
trance circle where we united
inside, the head surpassed
Whomp-Whomp-a-DOO-Whomp

Finley

CADMUS   We implore you, we've done no
wrong.

FINLEY AS DIONYSUS   Too late. When there
was time, you didn't know me.

CADMUS   We've learned. You sentence is too
harsh.

FINLEY AS DIONYSUS   I am a god. I was
blasphemed by you.

CADMUS   Gods should be exempt from human
passions.

FINLEY AS DIONYSUS   Long ago, Euripides
wrote these things.

AGAVE   It's fated, Father, we must go.

FINLEY AS DIONYSUS   Why are you hassling
the inevitable? Split.

AGAVE   Terribly has Dionysus brought disaster
down upon this garage.

FINLEY AS DIONYSUS   I was terribly
blasphemed. My name dishonored in New
York.

He speaks to the audience.

As for the rest of you, I condemn you to remember what's happened here tonight. To remember William Finley. Remember him when you are awake. Dream of him when you are asleep. Most of all, remember him when you go into your voting booths this fall. Yes, I am running for President. Who else have you got? Remember me and write in my name. William Finley. W-I-L-L-I-A-M F-I-N-L-E-Y. A vote for Finley in 68 brings Dionysus in 69.

He climbs down the tower as the performers sing the melody of The Stars and Stripes Forever. They march and salute each other, raise the large garage door as if they were raising the flag. Dionysus raises a smaller overhead door, revealing a large picture of himself. He comes to where the performers are marching in step. They hoist him on their shoulders. He continues.

William Finley has many shapes. William Finley has many faces. William Finley brings many things to surprising conclusions. Some of the things you thought would happen here tonight did not happen here tonight. And for that you should be thankful. For I have found a way. A way no man expected. A way to end this play. Forward!

He throws the buttons to the audience. The performers march into Wooster Street, carrying Dionysus. They turn toward Broome Street and make a left on Broome. Dionysus campaigns. No performer returns to the theatre until at least a half hour has gone by. A few spectators usually follow the performers up the street.

My fellow Americans, citizens of Wooster Street! Awake and arouse yourselves! Follow me into the streets. You have nothing to lose but your minds. Follow me! My dance is swift. My wrath is militant. I ask you to mobilize yourselves! Get down! Delight in real contact with one another. Grab a thyrsus! Pack a .45! Arm yourself! Napalm the decay! Burn the slums! Shit bricks on The Man! Power to the Bacchae! If someone gives you lip on the subway, shoot him down! Not to kill, but to wound. In pain, the infidel will become a fellow reveler of me. Feel the pain! I ask only that you follow me. Only that you indulge your fantasies of violence and sensuality. Only now can it come true. Fuck fantasy! Make it real! Make it now! Okay your cocks. Explode your feelings. Freedom! Stroke your pussy hairs! Ball in the streets! Freedom! Delight in the raw flesh!

Freedom! Take Humphrey's clothes off! Give Mayor Lindsay a total caress! Blow kisses on Lyndon! Lay tongues on your leaders! Then tear them to pieces! Firebomb a cop! Roast a pig! Drop the jelly of joy on them! I am sick of reason and laws. I am tired of squashy liberals and concrete conservatives. Tired of Pentheuses and paper honkies. They must be eliminated! Torn limb from limb! I love the smell of riots, the orgasms of death and blood! We will tolerate no more false revolutions, no more false rituals and phony bloodbaths! We want the real thing!

After the election, Finley's curse changed.

FINLEY AS DIONYSUS   Good evening. This is William Finley. A god by any other name. A god that smokes seven brands of cigarettes, a god that eats food, men, and women, a god with a Social Security number, but an unemployed god. Dig it. I came here tonight by the Seventh Avenue subway to tell you who I was. You mocked me, you wouldn't participate in my ordeals. You wouldn't even clap for my rites. Therefore, before I split, I will reveal the trials that await those of little faith. First on the list is Dia, Richard Dia. Dia, you came to us in a void. You still feel nothing. As a result of your actions here tonight, of clearing spaces and having people hauled around the room, I got thrown in the pit. You didn't turn me on. And now you have nothing but stage blood and the promise that you'll have to do the same damned thing tomorrow night. On you, Agave, I pronounce this doom. In many ways you mocked Dia. Therefore, you have to leave this garage and live out the rest of your wretched lives never knowing which of you played Agave.

When Remi plays Agave.

On you, Agave, Remi, I pronounce this doom. You will have to discover each night that you have killed your own baby. The baby you have not yet given birth to.

Then Cadmus.

And you, Cadmus, Bill Shephard, you will go to the island of Scorpios. There you will become the bodyguard of Jaqueline Kennedy Onassis and there you will be contracted by the Greek Mafia to make a hit on Richard Nixon, who has decided that Spiro Agnew deserves the job.

Nixon is tired of the Presidency and is going to be the first President to commit suicide by assassination.

CADMUS   Finley, your punishment is too harsh. We've learned.

FINLEY AS DIONYSUS   I'm sorry, Bill, but I was a god and you blasphemed me.

CADMUS   But gods should be exempt from human passions.

FINLEY AS DIONYSUS   Gods aren't exempt from anything. They just have more power. As for the rest of you, I condemn you to forget what's happened here tonight. We are going to visit other cities. We are going to bring doom and blood and death all across the United States. Good evening, motherfuckers!

Jason's curse. Jason puts on an old, brown leather coat. As he watches the killing and the lament, he smokes his corncob pipe.

JASON AS DIONYSUS   Good evening. Once again this is Jason Bromius Bosseau, a god who knows forty-two of these United States, a god born and raised in Kansas, a god who lived for four miserable years in Southern California and three miserable years in an East Village tenement. Let us review what happened here tonight. I came here to tell you who I am, a god. Instead of saying that's nice—in fact, that is beautiful, this man is a god, I dig that, I love that, I would dance for this man, I would live for this man, I would march for this man, I would go to war for this man, I would kill for this man, I would die for this man. Instead of saying that, you mocked me, you threw me into the pit, most of you didn't dance for me, none of you really killed for me, and in general you dishonored me. So I'm going to throw you all out of here.

I am not interested in acting. I am involved in the life process of becoming whole. I do many technical exercises which organically suit that process. They act as a catalyst for my ability to let essence flow, to let my soul speak through my mind and body. The impulse becomes the action. The body is free to fly. The mind is liberated from tensions of the body, and flows with sounds, feelings, vibrations, everything. Everything becomes/is the flow. Mind/body are one. Thoughts/feelings/sounds/movements/vibrations are one. The flow pounds in my being, pulsates, jerks,

explodes, retreats, bounces, settles, redefines itself, re-integrates itself, and feeds everything from the depths of my gut to the outermost limitlessness of the universe.

Jason

But before you split, I'm going to leave each and every one of you with a curse on your head. First you, Richard Dia, Pentheus. You came to us in rage and you connected with your anger, but what you didn't do is connect with your love for me. As a result, the death you suffer you suffer justly. Your curse is that you must continue performing this play again and again and again until you finally realize that I am not acting, that I am a god, and that nothing less than your total submission to me and my demands can ever save you from a false death. And upon you, Remi, Agave, this doom. You must leave this garage in expiation of the murder you have done, for you are unclean, and it would be a sacrilege for you to remain here in my holy temple. It is your fate to go back to Houston, where you will live out the rest of your wretched life not knowing why you ever gave yourself to me. Upon you, Cadmus, William Shephard, I pronounce this doom. You will leave this city at 1 P.M. tomorrow on an Eastern Airlines flight for Washington, D.C. There you will go directly to the Pentagon. You will meet my friends who rule this great country. You see, I'm no longer living in the slums, I'm living in great mansions all over this beautiful land. It is your fate, Shephard, to become a United States Army general, and you will lead thousands and millions of troops through this country and make it pure again. In my name, your armies will plunder many cities. You will have your men stick bayonets in the bellies of each citizen who does not believe in America. You will end, once and for all, the problem of alienation in this land. Everyone is going to believe again!

CADMUS   Jason, your sentence is too harsh.

JASON AS DIONYSUS   I'm sorry, but it's too late. When there was time you didn't know me.

CADMUS   Gods should be exempt from human passion.

JASON AS DIONYSUS   Gods aren't exempt from anything. They simply have the power to do what they want. Now shut up and sweat and work. As for the rest of you, I condemn you to remember what happened here tonight. To remember me, Jason Bosseau, and what happens when I appear.

The middle section of another version of Jason's curse goes like this.

Richard Dia. Dia, you came to me in rage, you stopped my dancing, you threw me in that filthy pit. Then, obsessed by me, you went down there and I gave you your chance. But you did nothing for me. You didn't even touch me. So you must leave here with your false death. You will do the same thing tomorrow night. Upon you, Agave, Joan, and Ciel, this doom. You must leave this garage in expiation of the murder you have done, for you are unclean. You offend me. You offend my holiness. So split. And no real children. You will have to do the birth ritual night after night and you won't have any real children until you make your peace with me. Upon you, Shephard, Cadmus, I pronounce this doom. You will go with a huge army to Southern California, to Los Angeles County, and you will burn it to the ground. Then you will go to Orange County and burn it to the ground. Then to San Diego and do the same thing. Then you will get thousands of bulldozers and push all that plastic shit into the Pacific Ocean. You'll have all the money you need. And on your way back to New York you'll stop in Kansas and burn all of it to the ground too. In the end, the great god Ares will bring you to live among the blest.

As Jason curses each performer, they leave one by one through the side door. They go upstairs to the dressing room and shower. Toward the end of his curse, Jason throws *Dionysus in 69* buttons to the spectators. Then he too goes upstairs.

Joan's curse.

JOAN AS DIONYSUS   Good evening once again. This is Joan MacIntosh, a god who is a woman, a god who is much more than a woman. I came here tonight to reveal myself to you, to let you know me. I came here to liberate you, to turn you on. But instead of welcoming me, instead of believing me and worshipping me and loving me, you threw me into the pit. You didn't believe, you didn't love, you didn't turn me on. In fact, you turned me off. Therefore I shall tell you what lies in store for those of such little faith. First you, Bill Shephard. You came

I pronounce this doom

to me in innocence. You tried to destroy me with your physical strength and your curiosity. You didn't respect my female body. You never even touched me. Therefore I condemn you to leave this garage and sign up with Women's Liberation. I condemn you to see to it that a woman is made President of the United States within the next fifty years.

An alternative condemnation for Shephard.

I condemn you to perform this play over and over and over again until you learn to submit to me.

When Margaret plays Agave.

Upon you, Agave, Margaret, I pronounce this doom. You will leave this garage in expiation of the murder you have done, for you are unclean. You killed your son. Therefore you will stop performing, go back to Harlem, and be an unwed mother. You will have a child every nine months and name them all after me.

When Remi plays Agave.

Upon you, Agave, Remi, this doom. You will leave this garage in expiation of the murder you have done, for you are unclean. You will stop performing, and go back to Bobbs-Merrill. You will become the head of the International Children's Books Department. You will establish yourself in Biafra and teach those children how to read. You will teach them to love America.

After each is cursed, he leaves.

You, Cadmus, Finley. You will change your name to General Curtis LeMay. You will gain two hundred pounds, dye your hair black, shave off your mustache, and destroy your glasses. You will lead an army group into Vietnam and kill all the Americans and Vietnamese. On your way back home you will destroy all the major cities in the world. You will bomb your world back to the Stone Age, where it belongs. Out of the debris you will erect many shrines in my name, celebrating me.

CADMUS   Joan, your sentence is too harsh.

JOAN AS DIONYSUS   I'm sorry. Long ago Euripides wrote these things. It's too late. When there was time you didn't know me.

CADMUS   Gods should be exempt from human passions.

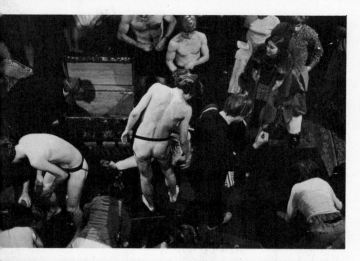

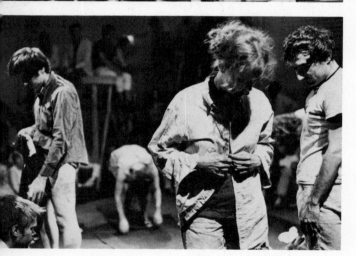

JOAN AS DIONYSUS   Gods can do whatever they please. They alone have the power. Now shut up, get back to work, and then split. As for the rest of you, I condemn you to forget what happened here tonight. I condemn you to leave this garage and support my revolution. You will follow me, and worship me, and love me! And you will never know when your leaders have betrayed you!

During the last part of her curse, Joan climbs down from the tower, bringing the bull-horn with her. She leaves the theatre on her last word. The theatre is empty, except for the audience.

When Dionysus throws his buttons down to the spectators, many scramble for them as if a button were a gold coin, so strong is the habit and hold of acquisitiveness. I sit smug and detached, and watch a double scene of genuine horror and poignancy. Here, Dionysus turned tyrant and fascist. There, spectators jostling each other for a cheap (but free) souvenir. Their behavior means they have not understood the play. Instead, they participate in it with the same unthinking power with which they validate their congressmen, bosses, priests, and presidents. The people deceive and betray themselves even as they listen to a warning against deception and betrayal.

Schechner

McDermott's curse takes two forms. The short curse continues until the performers have cleaned up and gone upstairs. The long curse goes on until all the spectators leave the theatre. This may be a half hour or longer. Like a prizefighter after a tough workout, McDermott has wrapped around his neck the towel he used to wipe the blood from his hands. On one occasion, he was carried out into Wooster Street, as in the first Finley ending.

MC DERMOTT AS DIONYSUS   Good evening. Hello, hello. I'd like to make a statement. Originally, I came here to announce that I'm a god. I was a god incognito. But I'm in a new position now. And now I want to announce that I'll be running as the fourth candidate, or the fifth candidate, or the fourth and fifth candidates, in the race for Mayor of the City of New York. I've made this decision only after careful consideration. After careful consideration, I've decided that, though the will of the people is crystal clear, only a god can make it work. What that means is this: we've got to get things moving, there isn't much time. Only a god can make it work. Only a god knows the will of the people well enough to make it work. We'll get to my platform in a moment. But first I'd like to thank all those who've helped me achieve this victory this evening. We've been through some desperate moments, and I don't know what I would have done without all my loyal supporters. It's a great victory we've won. And now it's time to forgive and forget. Forgive and forget. It's a time for bringing together all the elements in our society, and I know how. It's a time for peace and harmony, you got it? I said peace and harmony. I want to see some peace and some harmony. I'm anxious to tell you about my platform, but first I have to talk to my advisers. Stand up, Cadmus. Cadmus, you know that the people are very concerned about law and order. Well, I've got the answer. We all know why kids get into trouble. They get into trouble because they're on the streets. Now let's look at that. What do we do? This is what we do. Manufacture a pedometer shoe, a pedometer shoe, get it? Everyone will wear this thing, and it will count everyone's steps. And we will levy a street tax, get it? Yea, like the going rate will be a penny a step. So you see what that means? A bugaloo down Broadway will cost you about forty dollars, a walk in the park will cost you five or ten dollars. I want you to work on that.

CADMUS   I didn't know gods were like you.

MC DERMOTT AS DIONYSUS   Now you know. A god in my position is like me. You understand? Do you know what it's like to be a god in my position? No, of course you don't. Well, take it on faith. Stand up, Pentheus. Pentheus, you know that it is the will of the people to get some peace and harmony, right? Okay. Why do kids get into trouble? Because they're unhappy. Why are they unhappy? Because nothing is happening. They go out on the street looking for action. So I want you to get everything in motion. If everything's already moving, nobody's going to go out on the street looking for action. You see what I mean? Keep 'em moving and they're happy. Give everybody the sense of motion. It's the will of the people. I want cars to move and houses to move and office buildings to move. It will never be necessary to leave your auto, your house, your office. Everyone will stay in his place, yet

everything will move. It's the perfect solution. Everybody moves, but everybody stays. Perfect order. Work on that. Stand up, Agave. Agave, how would you like to come to Gracie Mansion with me? How would you like to be my social secretary? I want you to consider this carefully, because you have to be the people's instrument. You have to put on a great show. When people come to the mansion to picket and demonstrate, we'll entertain them out of sight. Drinks, girls, the works. People will demonstrate just to be bought off. Now I've got the lyrics for a good song. Here they are: "Call me god, call me god, Patrick McZeus, that's me." Find me a catchy tune for that. And get a new song for this clean-up job. We'll be mopping up many floors and streets before the campaign is over. We've got to have a soul sound, a sound that makes the brushes scrub. A sound to forgive and forget by. Got it? Work on that.

By this time, most of the performers and many of the audience have left. The stage lights are down and the house lights up. The spot remains on Dionysus.

Now here's my platform. I've discovered that inflation is the one problem that concerns all the people. End inflation, that's the will of the people. Inflation happens because money is based on gold. Gold is an unrealistic base for the currency of this nation. I'm going to put the currency on a solid base. I'm going to put our currency where it's really at. Power. Power is where it's at. I'm going to base money on power. Already you see the value of my system. It makes the most powerful the richest, without any intermediary materials like gold, without any hypocritical economic theories. Now what is power? Dig this. Power is power. Do you get it? Let it sink in. Meditate on this. Power is power. Do you see what that means? Power Power.

Tragedy can't be sustained. Steadily, the unstable compound seeks to resolve itself in thesis. Dionysus is good, or he is bad. Our play means this, or that. The moment-to-moment work of the performers is at last integrated by them into their experience. As we went on, it was harder and harder to re-actualize the events, to force ourselves away from certainty and into immediacy. Contradictions of spirit were verbalized and, as the text became more elaborate and complete, the action was unified. Things got clearer

and we took elegance in place of rough necessity. Almost without expecting it, our work was artful. And an old problem had a new face.

Schechner

I want Power Power. Power means power. I mean juice, baby. Electrical power is power. Currency is currency. Power is power. It goes through wires, it's in the tube, in the radio, it comes in little batteries that you can put in your pocket, it makes things move, it is the source of the sense of motion, it makes light, it makes the ticker tick. Power is power. Now we're going to control all the power. Everyone will have a tube in his home. On this tube we will give him all the information he wants. Everyone will be totally in motion and totally informed. Dig it. Power Power! Power Power! Power Power! Power Power!

Shouting his slogan, Dionysus leaves. Or, if McDermott is to wait out the audience, his speech goes on and on.

Now more details about my program. The penal system. I will develop a penal system that works perfectly but does not hurt anybody. Modern technology will do it for me. The deep-freezer, you understand? A misdemeanor will cost you a couple of days in the deep-freezer. A felony will cost you a couple of years. A capital crime and we put you in the deep-freezer forever. But you won't feel a thing. It's perfectly humane. There's no pain.

By now, usually, only about ten or fifteen people remain. Sometimes they heckle Dionysus. Sometimes they cheer him. Sometimes they just sit and listen, straggling out one or two at a time.

Communication. There will be no personal communication. All communication will be via power. Bullhorns, tubes, radios, telephones. No personal communication. Personal communication upsets people. Dictaphones, cablegrams, message units, yes. Personal communication, no. Now if you've come on a bus, or in a car with friends, or if your parents are waiting for you, they'll wait. Everything will wait on the will and word of god. If you've heard me today, and if I've touched your heart, I want you to